THE EUROMARKETS AND INTERNATIONAL FINANCIAL POLICIES

The Euromarkets and International Financial Policies

David F. Lomax
and
P. T. G. Gutmann

Foreword by Samuel Brittan

First published 1981 by
THE MACMILLAN PRESS LTD
London and Basingstoke
Companies and representatives
throughout the world

ISBN 0 333 23998 9

Printed in Hong Kong

Contents

List of Tables

Foreword

Samuel Brittan

There are two common reactions to the mention of 'eurocurrencies'. One is to treat them as developments of vast importance, which there is no hope of understanding. The other, on the part of professional financiers, is the pricking of the nostrils at the scent of profitable business.

The urgent need is for a book which takes a more detached look at euromarkets than the professional operator normally can, and which will also introduce some factual clarity in place of the dazed awe with which they are normally regarded.

This book meets both these needs. The basic facts, definitions and overall history are summarised admirably in the first chapter. This is followed by a detailed account of the diverse ways in which the markets have developed in different centres. A glance at the chapter headings is sufficient to show that the word 'euro' is too restrictive an adjective for what is now a worldwide development.

In the final chapter the authors give their own personal assessment of the effects that these markets are likely to have on economic policy. Here, as elsewhere in the book, David Lomax and Peter Gutmann show a characteristic combination of down-to-earth commonsense and refusal to accept conventional pieties.

Eurocurrency holdings are simply bank balances held outside the country responsible for the currency in question, for example dollar deposits held with a London bank. Eurobonds are just bonds underwritten by an international syndicate and sold principally in countries other than the country of the currency in which the issue is denominated. A euro-deutschemark bond might be raised for a company in Asia, but it would be denominated in deutschemarks and subscribers would come from all the main world financial centres.

There are some who have used these markets as a scapegoat for all the world's economic ills. Others have seen them as a perfectly effective channel for moving funds from, say, oil-producing countries in surplus to countries with deficits on their current accounts. Neither view is, as the authors show, convincing. The forces making for weakness in a currency, or chronic inflation, or unemployment, may be transmitted by the euromarkets, but their origins are usually domestic.

On the other hand, the flow of funds transmitted by these markets can only be the crudest of approximation to those called for at any particular time. The case for markets is not that they bring about a mythical optimum, but that they enable people to make the best of limited knowledge. All markets need rules and one worry has been that the euromarket rules have never been closely defined. The persistent enquirer is told that world central banks have informal 'lender of last resort' obligations to ensure that a default on a large loan to a developing country does not start a chain reaction of bank liquidations. But the commitment is to prevent a contraction of deposits, and not to the continued profitability or even existence of individual banks. A bank chairman who pushed hypothetical questions on this matter too far was told; 'Don't worry; we will be discussing the problems with your successor.'

This is no doubt entertaining to the *cognoscenti*. But a more formal statement of central bank intentions would relieve a lot of needless anxiety which still exists about the possibility of a banking crisis triggering off 'another 1931'. It would also discourage domestic politicians and interest groups from blaming euromarkets for their own failures of performance.

Occasionally, the euromarkets are presented as huge and uncontrollable factories for manufacturing money on a vast scale, thereby making national monetary policies ineffective. David Lomax and Peter Gutmann show that the creation of money both in ordinary domestic banks and in the euromarkets is limited by reserve ratios and other prudential restraints – the main difference being that the restraints are more explicit and more likely to be legally binding in the more traditional domestic sector. But it is still true that if the central banks control the creation of reserve assets, money cannot spawn of its own accord.

The euromarkets can be regarded in the same light as domestic technical developments (for example credit cards) which enable people to economise on their money balances. It does not matter if we widen the definition of money to include eurobalances or say simply that the velocity of circulation of money has increased. The conclusion still is that domestic monetary policies have to be tighter than they otherwise need be.

It is, as the authors show, a myth to suppose that there is any technical reason why countries should pursue identical economic policies – or even different policies co-ordinated on an international plane. On the contrary, the enormous increase in borrowing and lending made possible by these markets, together with the move to flexible exchange rates, allows countries to have different inflation rates or to run current account deficits and surpluses and live harmoniously together.

International co-operation is still required; but it is in more subtle matters, such as avoiding contradictory interventions in the foreign exchange markets, providing intelligence about the degree of exposure of different borrowers, and avoiding policies actually likely to cause depression, runaway inflation or both. This book is itself a contribution to making explicit the rules of the game and thereby increasing the potential for good of the world's financial markets, of which the euromarkets form part.

Preface

Writing a book is, like socialism, concerned with nothing if not the setting of priorities; selections must be made from a wide array of material and a limited number of themes chosen to be covered within the allotted length. This consideration was of particular importance as regards this book because the subject matter is vast. There is little purpose in merely duplicating lines of analysis which have already been well covered. What then is the specific *raison d'être* of this volume?

We set out to write this book believing that the existing general body of knowledge about the euromarkets and recent economic history tended to fall into certain limited categories. First, there are many market participants around the world who know in considerable detail the practices and regulations of their own markets. Second, the overall macro-economics of the decade of the 1970s has been well-studied. Third, the macro-figures of the global money flows in the euromarkets, bond and banking, have been well-documented. And fourth, the global international monetary history and policy of this period, such as the breakdown of the Bretton Woods system, the efforts of the Committee of Twenty and the revision of the Articles of the International Monetary Fund, have all been the subject of many well-known studies. However, we felt that the subject matter lying between the macro and micro areas of analysis merited further investigation which could well lead to important conclusions for future assessments of the overall situation.

Thus we have examined the specific factors which determine the international financial policies of the major countries and how these have changed in recent years. We have also examined the economic history of the period, how this has impinged upon the main countries and their economic and policy responses to this. The third strand of our analysis is how these two factors have affected the continuing structural development of the world's main financial markets. General conclusions are drawn at the end.

This approach required delving in some detail into the financial policies of various countries: at the same time one needed to take account of the main overall economic forces acting on countries. Analysing recent events has certainly been a useful learning process for the authors themselves, as regards an understanding of recent economic history and the functioning of the international financial system, and one would hope that it would be of similar benefit to others. Limitations of space prevent taking the analysis far wider than the subject matter just mentioned, but this study does lead into major questions affecting the markets, such as whether the markets have been a cause of major monetary expansion in the world and hence of inflation, whether the system is self-equilibrating, or at least not destabilising, and whether it is financially sound or not.

In preparing this book we have received help and support from members of the International Section of the National Westminster Bank's Market Intelligence Department. Various parts have been shown to colleagues within and outside the National Westminster Bank, and we should like to express our gratitude for the comments that were made. In the National Westminster Bank Head Office these include Roy Haines, Bob Stevenson and David Kern, and in offices around the world Messrs Coombs (Tokyo), Hurst (Hong Kong), Holden (Singapore), Fyfe (County Bank Dubai) and Bennett (Bahrain). Parts of the book have been shown also to many colleagues in other banks and financial institutions, and we are most grateful for the comments received. Those to whom texts were shown include Miss G. Kurtz (Deutsche Bank), Messrs J. Atkin (Citibank), D. Ashby and L. Brainard (Bankers Trust), J. Frentzel-Wagner (Westdeutsche Landesbank Girozentrale), M. Lutfalla (Credit du Nord), H. Bernard (formerly of Credit Lyonnais), N. Kagami (Nomura Research), H. Mast (Credit Suisse), F. Aschinger (Swiss Bank Corporation), R. Piloy (Société Générale, Brussels), M. Cockaerts, W. Janssens and J. Verhaeghe (Kredietbank), F. Limburg and A. D. de Jong (Amro Bank), Dr M. van den Adel (Centrale Rabobank), I. Christiansen (Den Danske Bank), B. Brovedani (Banca Nazionale del Lavoro), G. Tichy (Universität Graz), L. A. L. Guinea (Banco de Bilbao), A. Manock (Bank of New South Wales), F. Rogers (Bank of Nova Scotia), Dr B. V. Gestrin (Canadian Imperial Bank of Commerce) and R. Thomsitt (Standard Chartered Bank).

We are extremely grateful for these comments, which both removed glaring errors and at the same time gave us confidence that the analysis might perhaps be on some of the right lines. Nevertheless any responsibility for errors of fact or of analysis in this book lies, of course, with the authors.

London,   DFL

August 1979   PTGG

Acknowledgements

The authors and publisher wish to thank the following who have kindly given permission for the use of copyright material: the editor of *Euromoney* for permission to reproduce Table 1.11; National Westminster Bank Limited for tables from financial papers; OECD, Paris, for statistical data from official sources; the World Bank, Washington, D.C., for tables from published data.

List of Abbreviations

ACU	Asia Currency Unit (Singapore)
ADB	Asian Development Bank
BIS	Bank for International Settlements
BLEU	Belgium and Luxembourg Economic Union
DCE	Domestic Credit Expansion
ECSC	European Coal and Steel Community
ECU	European Currency Unit
EEC	European Economic Community
EIB	European Investment Bank
EMS	European Monetary System
EUA	European Unit of Account
IBRD	International Bank for Reconstruction and Development (World Bank)
IFS	International Financial Statistics
IMF	International Monetary Fund
LDCs	Less Developed Countries
MAS	Monetary Authority of Singapore
OBU	Offshore Banking Unit (Bahrain)
OECD	Organisation for Economic Co-operation and Development
OPEC	Organisation of the Petroleum Exporting Countries
OSA	Overseas Sterling Area
SAMA	Saudi Arabian Monetary Agency
SDR	Special Drawing Right

Notes to the Text

(i)   The $ sign is used throughout to refer to the US currency unless otherwise indicated (e.g. NZ$).

(ii)   References to currencies' trade-weighted movements are based on the National Westminster Bank's trade-weighted calculations started by Dr Lomax when he was manager of the bank's Economic Analysis Section and continued by that section since his promotion from that post. The calculations cover some thirty countries and are based on the trade flows among them.

1 Developments in the Overall Euromarkets

The main theme of this book is the inter-relationship among economic developments in recent years, the changing financial policies of countries and the structural developments in the euromarkets. But before analysing those factors it may be helpful to set out some of the overall changes which have taken place in the markets as a whole. This chapter is concerned with setting out a factual summary of some of the key developments over this period; the underlying reasons, and the developments in more detail, will be examined later.

An important element of the international financial background to these changes is presented in Table 1.1 which sets out the broad structure of the world balance of payments on current account over the period since 1971 and how this has changed year by year.

TABLE 1.1: World Current Account, 1971–8 (*$ billion*)

Country grouping	1971	1972	1973	1974	1975	1976	1977	1978
OECD	9.9	7.8	9.9	−27.5	− 0.3	−19.1	−26.3	6.4
OPEC	0.3	1.3	7.7	59.5	27.1	36.6	29.1	5.9
Non-oil developing	−9.8	−5.2	−6.2	−23.3	−37.5	−25.5	−23.0	−35.0

Source: OECD, *Economic Outlook* (June 1979).
Note: Figures do not balance because of statistical errors and because data on other countries (e.g. USSR, Eastern Europe and China) are not included.

The international markets are not required to finance all current account imbalances. Capital flows in other forms, such as aid programmes or direct investment, can account for a substantial part of the gap between a country's current account deficit and its overall balance. Moreover, by no means is all the financing in the international markets

1

linked formally to dealing with countries' current account deficits. Although capital flows ultimately have to add up in some form or another to balancing out current account deficits, in practical terms much of this financing is done to corporations and the main motivation for this is the structure of the corporation's financial situation at that particular time and how the international financial markets fit in with the requirements for finance of a particular nature. Thus, for example, lending in dollars to finance North Sea oil development is geared largely to the needs of the operating companies, although of course the resulting figures also appear in the UK's own balance of payments. Table 1.1 illustrates the enormous swings in current account performances in recent years, with OPEC accumulating a massive surplus in 1974 which has since been sharply diminished; correspondingly the non-oil developing countries had a large deficit after 1973 which has since fallen, though not as significantly. The performance of the OECD countries as a whole has varied over this period, with the US exerting a massive influence on the final figure. This table brings out not only the scale of the net imbalances to be financed, but also the volatility in the sense that deficit and surplus areas have changed both in size and in direction over this period.

TABLE 1.2: Position of Major Currencies in Relation to US Dollar, 1972–8

End year	1972	1973	1974	1975	1976	1977	1978
Canadian dollar	101	101	101	99	99	92	85
Japanese yen	102	110	102	101	105	128	159
French franc	100	109	115	115	103	109	123
German mark	101	119	134	123	137	153	177
Italian lira	100	96	90	85	67	67	70
Swiss franc	102	118	152	147	157	193	237
British pound	90	89	90	78	63	74	78

Source: National Westminster Bank calculations.
Note: 18 December 1971 = 100.

The sharp movements in the international balance of payments have naturally led to corresponding pressure upon exchange rates. Table 1.2 illustrates the movements in the major exchange rates since 1971 in terms respectively of the position against the dollar and of each currency's trade-weighted movement against all other currencies in the 'basket'. There have been both sharp trend movements, notably the enormous decline of the dollar in relation to the Swiss franc, deutschemark and yen, and also significant fluctuations within this period. These movements in exchange rates have led to accusations that the world monetary system as at present constituted is 'unstable'. Whether or not this is so will be a theme examined in this book.

Undoubtedly, the movement in exchange rates has been far greater than in the Bretton Woods period up to 1971. To some extent these changes reflect divergent experiences of inflation, but this raises the separate question of whether or not exchange rate movements cause inflation as well as being symptoms of it. On a purchasing power parity basis the relative valuation of currencies has undoubtedly changed. On any purchasing power comparison the dollar is, at the time of writing, undervalued and is certainly undervalued in relation to its position five or six years ago. Comparisons have also been made of the competitive element in a nation's economy and how international competitiveness has been changed by these exchange rate movements. Even taking into account inflation and productivity growth it has been found that the position of industries in the international competitive market has changed sharply over this period, because exchange rate movements have been larger than justified by any kind of inflation or productivity criteria. However, this argument begs the question whether exchange rates should be determined, or should be thought to be determined, wholly on those particular grounds. An international monetarist would regard the main determinant to be the monetary policy of the countries concerned. From the point of view of the concerns in this book, the sharp movements in exchange rates illustrate that the international financial markets have had the potential of being very treacherous places in which to operate, unless companies and countries were well advised and were able to hedge their risks accordingly.

It is not surprising that many major banks suffered large foreign exchange losses when they applied to their dealing in this era of floating rates the risk–reward ratio to which they had been accustomed under the Bretton Woods system. Under that system the risk of the exchange rate moving outside the parity band in the opposite direction to that expected was very limited, while the reward for guessing correctly when the exchange rate would move out of the band in the forecast direction was substantial. Under the present system the risk of an exchange rate moving in the opposite way to that expected can never be ignored, particularly because the day-to-day and month-to-month fluctuations have been relatively large, and the rewards for getting the exchange rate movement right are often not as substantial as those which resulted, for example, from guessing the correct weekend upon which an exchange rate would move by 5 or 10 per cent or even more under the old system. These recent years have been a period of reserve diversification as new reserve currencies have emerged. Table 1.3 indicates the distribution of reserve asset holdings in currencies of the central monetary institutions, as supplied in International Monetary Fund (IMF) statistics. These indicate the rise of the deutschemark to the second most important reserve currency and the relative decline of sterling. There is also some use of other currencies. The dollar, despite its decline, remains by far the most important reserve asset currency and its status, in this respect at least, has changed very little since 1971.

TABLE 1.3: Official Holdings of Foreign Exchange by Type of Claim, 1971–7
(*SDRs billion*)

Official holdings of	1971	1972	1973	1974	1975	1976	1977
US dollars	46.6	56.7	55.4	62.8	68.9	79.2	103.8
British pounds	7.3	8.1	6.5	8.3	6.4	3.2	3.3
German marks	1.0	1.4	2.2	2.4	2.5	4.3	5.7
French francs	0.8	1.0	1.2	1.1	1.1	0.9	0.8
Other currencies	1.0	0.9	1.6	1.5	2.7	3.8	4.6
Eurodollars	10.4	18.0	21.1	32.3	38.5	45.6	58.0
Other eurocurrencies	1.1	3.2	5.3	5.8	7.2	7.6	12.3
Residual	6.8	6.9	8.7	12.9	10.2	16.1	12.6
Total	75.0	96.2	102.0	127.1	137.5	160.7	201.1

Source: IMF, *Annual Report 1978*.
Note: Figures are 'end year'.

The above developments have been accompanied by very rapid growth in international financial markets – the eurocurrency market and the international bond market. Table 1.4 sets out the statistics of the annual growth in total eurocurrency deposits. This includes not only the European sector (which accounts for some 70 per cent of the total) but also positions in the Far East, the Caribbean and other centres. The term 'euro', which is usually retained for deposits even though they are located outside Europe, is used to refer to any deposit of a currency outside that currency's own natural domicile. Thus, for example, sterling deposited in Paris is eurosterling, whereas sterling deposited in London, even by a non-resident of the UK, is not.

In the early years of the market – some two decades ago – virtually all the deposits in the market were dollars. Table 1.5 shows that the dollar

TABLE 1.4: Growth of Eurocurrency Market, 1971–8 (*$ billion*)

	1971	1972	1973	1974	1975	1976	1977	1978
Gross size	140 (est)	192 (est)	295	361	442	548	658	903
Net size[a]	90 (est)	120 (est)	170	220	260	330	405	540

Source: Bank for International Settlements, *Quarterly Press Release on International Banking Developments* (June 1979).
Note: [a] Net of double counting due to interbank positions. Figures are 'end year'.

TABLE 1.5: Currency Composition of the European Sector of the Euromarket, 1973–8 (*$ billion*)

	1973	1974	1975	1976	1977	1978
Dollars	132	156	190	224	262	340
Deutschemarks	31	35	42	49	68	97
Swiss francs	15	14	15	18	23	28
Sterling	3	2	2	2	4	7
Guilders	1	2	2	4	4	7
French francs	2	2	3	3	3	6
Other	3	5	4	6	9	17
Total	187	216	258	306	373	502

Source: Bank for International Settlements, *Quarterly Press Release on International Banking Developments* (June 1979).
Note: Figures are 'end year'.

remains the predominant currency in this market although the deutschemark has shown significant growth in recent years, as have to a lesser extent some more minor currencies.

A point of some dispute is whether this market represents only a transfer of liquidity or a genuine increase of the world's money supply. A significant proportion of these funds is lent interbank, and the net amount lent outside the banking system is considerably smaller than the global figure. The total size of this market is comparable with the American domestic money supply, which implies a significant addition to world money, if one regards the total market figure as being money. But on any definition of money interbank transactions would be netted out, and the effect of this market on world monetary growth would relate to the much smaller net contribution to M3, that is to the funds taken in from whatever source and lent to the non-banking sector. Thus the monetary expansion from this market would depend on the expected importance of M3 in monetary theory, and the amount of M3 created from the yearly activity in this market.

The euro and foreign bond markets have expanded at a similarly rapid pace in recent years, as illustrated by Table 1.6 which shows the growth of these markets over time and by currency. In this case the relative growth of the non-dollar markets has been much more rapid than in the case of the currency markets, and in recent years they have collectively out-shadowed the dollar market. Although the statistics for both markets tend to be collected and discussed together as international bonds, in fact much of this market is foreign bonds, notably in deutschemarks, Swiss francs and yen. This factor reflects the improved balance of payments performance in recent years of Germany, Switzerland and Japan, and also their low rates of inflation, which have made their currencies desirable investment assets.

The distribution by category of borrowing country of syndicated eurocurrency credits is given in Table 1.7. A large number of countries

TABLE 1.6: Currency Breakdown of New International Bond Issues, 1971–8
(*$ billion*)

	1971	1972	1973	1974	1975	1976	1977	1978
Eurobonds								
(by currency)								
US$	2.2	3.9	2.4	1.0	3.7	9.1	11.6	7.3
Deutschemark	0.8	1.1	1.0	0.3	2.3	2.7	4.1	5.3
Guilder	0.3	0.4	0.2	0.4	0.7	0.5	0.5	0.4
Can$	—	—	—	0.1	0.6	1.4	0.7	—
Other	0.3	0.9	0.6	0.3	1.3	0.6	0.9	1.1
Total	3.6	6.3	4.2	2.1	8.6	14.3	17.8	14.1
Foreign bonds								
by currency								
US$	1.1	1.4	1.0	3.3	6.5	10.6	7.4	5.8
Deutschemark	0.3	0.5	0.4	0.2	1.1	1.3	2.2	3.8
Swiss franc	0.7	0.8	1.5	0.9	3.3	5.4	5.0	5.7
Guilder	—	—	—	—	0.2	0.6	0.2	0.4
Yen	0.1	0.3	0.3	—	—	0.2	1.3	3.8
Other	0.4	0.4	0.4	0.3	0.2	0.1	0.1	0.7
Total	2.6	3.4	3.6	4.7	11.3	18.2	16.2	20.2

Source: Morgan Guaranty, *World Financial Markets* (June 1979).

TABLE 1.7: Publicised Eurocurrency Bank Credits, 1971–8 ($ *billion*)

	1971	1972	1973	1974	1975	1976	1977	1978	Total 1971–8
United Kingdom	0.5	0.7	3.2	5.7	0.2	1.7	2.0	3.9	17.9
Italy	0.3	0.9	4.8	2.3	0.1	0.4	1.0	2.5	12.3
France	—	0.2	0.1	3.2	0.7	0.6	2.3	2.0	9.1
Spain	0.3	0.1	0.5	1.2	1.1	2.0	2.0	2.4	9.5
United States	0.4	0.9	1.6	2.2	0.8	0.7	0.8	1.3	8.7
All industrial countries	2.6	4.1	13.8	20.7	7.2	11.3	16.8	29.0	105.5
Algeria	0.1	0.2	1.3	—	0.5	0.6	0.7	2.6	6.0
Iran	0.2	0.3	0.7	0.1	0.3	1.4	1.2	1.1	5.3
Indonesia	—	0.1	0.2	0.7	1.3	0.5	0.8	1.1	4.7
Venezuela	0.1	0.2	0.1	0.1	—	1.2	1.7	2.1	5.5
All OPEC	0.4	0.9	2.8	1.1	2.9	4.0	7.5	10.4	30.0
Brazil	0.3	0.6	0.7	1.7	2.2	3.2	2.8	5.6	17.1
Mexico	0.3	0.2	1.6	0.1	2.3	2.0	2.7	7.2	16.4
South Korea	—	0.1	0.2	0.1	0.3	0.7	1.3	2.7	5.4
Philippines	—	0.1	0.2	0.8	0.4	1.0	0.7	2.1	5.3
Peru	—	0.1	0.4	0.4	0.3	0.4	0.2	—	1.8
Taiwan	—	—	—	0.3	0.1	0.2	0.5	0.3	1.4
All non-OPEC LDCs	0.9	1.5	4.5	6.3	8.2	11.0	13.5	26.9	72.8
Communist (mostly Comecon)	0.1	0.3	0.8	1.2	2.6	2.5	3.4	3.8	14.7
International organisations	—	—	—	—	0.1	0.1	0.2	0.2	0.6
Total	4.0	6.8	21.9	29.3	21.0	28.9	41.4	70.3	223.6

Source: Morgan Guaranty, *World Financial Markets* (June 1979).

now raise finance in this market; for example thirteen industrialised and thirty-eight developing countries did so in the fourth quarter of 1978, but only the main ones are shown in the table.

Unlike most industrial countries which have fairly healthy economies and relatively low debts, developing countries experience some resistance to borrowing in the international bond market. A two-tier euromarket has thus evolved: one in bonds for prime borrowers and a second in medium-term credits for less credit-worthy borrowers. As Table 1.8 shows, however, developing countries have been able in recent years to tap the bond market on an increasing scale.

TABLE 1.8: International Bond Issues by Categories of Borrowing Countries
(*$ billion*)

	1974	1975	1976	1977	1978
Industrial countries	5.4	15.2	24.2	23.9	25.0
Developing countries	0.3	0.6	1.6	3.4	4.2
Developing as % of industrial	5.6	4.0	6.6	14.2	16.8

Source: Morgan Guaranty, *World Financial Markets* (June 1979).

Table 1.9 looks at borrowers in the international bond market in more detail. The industrialised countries' continuing dominance in this market reflects not only their high credit rating, but also the fact that a hard currency circuit has developed with borrowers in hard currency countries, such as much of Northern Continental Europe, the Middle East and Japan, being willing to borrow in Swiss francs, deutschemarks and yen on a substantial scale, despite what would appear to other countries to be significant foreign exchange risks of accumulating such debt in hard currency. Moreover, many of the major international borrowers, such as the World Bank or European Investment Bank (EIB), have borrowed substantially in these hard currencies, on the basis that their spread of assets is so diverse that some upward exchange risk on their borrowing is acceptable as long as it is limited in scale. The eurobond market tends to move in a volatile way in that periods of high interest rates or accelerating inflation can cause the market to dry up. Thus there have been two periods of buoyant international bond activity over these years: the first in the very early 1970s, the second developing since 1975.

Loans are raised by a wide variety of borrowers (see Table 1.10). The distribution amongst the various categories is quite different in the bond market from that in the credit market. In particular, fund raising by international organisations through bond issues is sizeable while their eurocurrency issues are negligible; private enterprises also feature much more prominently in this sector than in the credit market.

The market has naturally favoured banks which have access to placing power, either in the international flow of funds, particularly in the trust business in Switzerland, or in domestic markets. Thus the Swiss, German and American commercial banks, supported heavily by the American investment banks, have tended to be the dominant managers in the eurobond markets. But the Belgian banks have also been very important because of the placing power within Belgium itself,

TABLE 1.9: New International Bond Issues by Country (*$ billion*)

	1971	1972	1973	1974	1975	1976	1977	1978
Industrial countries								
Australia	0.1	0.2	—	0.1	0.7	1.1	1.1	1.2
Austria	—	0.1	0.1	0.5	0.9	0.7	1.4	1.0
Canada	0.8	1.5	1.2	2.1	4.5	9.3	5.3	4.8
France	0.3	0.3	0.1	0.4	1.8	2.7	1.9	1.3
Japan	0.1	0.1	0.1	0.2	1.7	2.1	2.0	3.5
Netherlands	0.3	0.2	0.2	0.5	0.7	0.5	0.7	0.3
Norway	0.1	0.1	0.1	0.1	0.9	1.4	1.9	2.8
Sweden	0.1	0.2	0.2	0.1	1.0	1.1	1.6	0.9
UK	0.7	0.9	1.2	0.2	0.3	1.0	1.9	1.4
US	1.3	2.2	1.4	0.2	0.3	0.5	1.4	3.0
Total	4.9	7.4	5.8	5.4	15.2	24.2	23.9	24.9
Developing countries								
Brazil	—	0.1	0.1	—	—	0.3	0.7	0.8
Mexico	—	0.2	0.2	0.1	0.3	0.4	1.3	0.6
Philippines	—	—	—	—	—	0.4	0.1	0.2
Total	0.1	0.5	0.6	0.2	0.5	1.5	2.8	2.7
OPEC								
Algeria	—	—	0.1	0.1	—	0.1	0.2	0.7
Venezuela	—	—	—	—	—	—	0.4	0.6
Total	—	0.1	0.1	0.1	0.1	0.1	0.8	1.5
Developing countries								
Total	0.1	0.6	0.7	0.3	0.6	1.6	3.4	4.2
Communist countries								
Hungary	—	0.1	—	—	0.1	—	0.2	—
Total	—	0.1	—	—	0.2	0.1	0.2	—
International organisations	1.2	1.7	1.3	1.2	3.9	6.6	6.5	5.0
Total	6.3	9.7	7.8	6.9	19.9	32.5	34.0	34.2

Source: Morgan Guaranty, *World Financial Markets* (June 1979).

and these banks have been significant innovators in the use of new currency units. Table 1.11 indicates the banks which have led in placing power over the years and how this has changed; the same banks have tended to keep near the top in this particular league, but there have been

TABLE 1.10: Distribution of Euromarket Borrowers, 1978

	Eurocredits (%)	International bonds (%)
Central government	29.3	22.4
Local government	2.3	2.7
Public (non-financial) enterprises	28.9	11.0
Private (non-financial) enterprises	18.7	18.6
Deposit money banks	2.7	14.9
Central monetary institutions	4.1	0.2
Other public financial institutions	12.6	8.5
Other private financial institutions	1.1	5.0
International organisations	0.3	16.9
Total	100.0	100.0

Source: World Bank, *Borrowing in International Capital Markets* (March 1979).

significant changes in relative standing among the important top positions.

A further feature of the internationalising of finance over this period has been a significant expansion of bank networks around the world, with many banks being keen to provide, for example, a 24-hour dealing service and a comprehensive banking presence in all the major financial markets around the world. The general improvement in telecommunications, together with the possibility of analysing and presenting data in a more desirable form due to advances in computer technology, has meant that banks can both co-ordinate and control business around the world in a way which would have been impossible even a decade ago. Banks can, for example, analyse their foreign exchange position daily in all their offices. Table 1.12 indicates the increased scale of bank representation in some of the major financial centres from 1971 to 1978.

The first wave of this increased representation will almost certainly have been completed now, because most banks are represented in the markets they consider most essential; expanding outside these areas could well lead rapidly to their facing the law of diminishing returns. The main area of competition and expansion has been in the wholesale markets; to expand internationally in retail banking is impracticable, except on a limited and selective scale.

Finally Table 1.13 shows the changes in the location of eurobanking business over this period, giving the amount and proportion of eurodeposits held in the main financial centres. It will be seen that the

TABLE 1.11: Leading International Bond Underwriters, 1971–7

	1971		1972		1973		1974		1975		1976		1977	
	A	B	A	B	A	B	A	B	A	B	A	B	A	B
Deutsche Bank	37	886	53	1612	30	1134	12	408	54	2126	102	5146	110	7733
Credit Suisse White Weld	33	824	46	1121	28	915	20	507	53	1884	119	5967	109	7495
Union Bank of Switzerland (Securities)	18	443	40	1190	20	803	11	324	57	2042	116	5890	94	6531
Swiss Bank Corporation	7	200	24	559	18	561	11	332	47	1668	112	5518	103	5723
Westdeutsche Landesbank Girozentrale	16	339	23	626	22	801	15	351	42	1447	81	3323	94	5380
Dresdner Bank	20	445	28	832	11	343	14	422	36	1306	59	2287	63	4566
Amsterdam–Rotterdam Bank	23	460	32	693	20	646	23	629	34	1044	52	3086	54	3774
S. G. Warburg & Co.	22	516	38	910	26	831	10	300	30	1127	53	2634	62	3650
Commerzbank	10	263	12	347	10	334	4	112	39	1231	54	2742	56	3508
Kredietbank SA Luxembourgeoise	24	475	36	851	30	896	27	523	84	2686	75	2981	63	3332
Banque Nationale de Paris	6	112	14	299	10	232	7	165	27	907	42	2128	42	2900
Banque de Paris et des Pays-Bas	28	561	38	984	16	576	14	321	34	1236	52	2580	49	2841
Société Générale de Banque	11	250	6	253	9	400	18	468	45	1370	46	1970	39	2497
Algemene Bank Nederland	21	412	33	662	18	476	18	493	33	868	31	1396	38	2416
Crédit Lyonnais	11	233	11	257	13	647	13	226	29	869	35	1433	41	2257
Société Générale	9	182	10	223	12	484	9	200	32	1096	34	1946	31	2210
Morgan Stanley International	23	691	23	659	9	317	6	181	24	814	41	1631	34	1955
Salomon Brothers International	—	—	—	—	—	—	—	—	—	—	16	740	26	1818
Orion Bank	3	82	9	262	8	228	7	147	17	391	33	1115	34	1703
Banca Commerciale Italiana	12	288	25	829	19	748	6	232	9	433	18	1174	20	1697

Sources: Euromoney (October 1977) and Credit Suisse White Weld.
Notes: A – Number of issues managed.
      B – All international bond issues in US$ billion equivalent.

TABLE 1.12: Expansion of Bank Representation in
Major Centres, 1971–8 (No. of banks represented
by branch/subsidiary)

	1971	*1978*
Amsterdam	15	25
Brussels	26	42
Frankfurt	20	30
Hong Kong	26	102
Jeddah	4	6
London	217	268
Los Angeles	6	27
New York	55	89
Paris	38	66
Rio de Janeiro	9	20
Rotterdam	7	12
Singapore	23	73
Tokyo	19	52

Source: Banker Research Unit, *Who is Where in World Banking*.

biggest centre by a significant extent is still London, but growth has been more rapid elsewhere, notably in Luxembourg, the Cayman Islands and the Bahamas, Bahrain, Singapore and Hong Kong. In some cases such as Luxembourg these developments are linked with the increasing use of non-dollar currencies; in others such as the Cayman Islands and the Bahamas, geographical factors in relation to New York have enabled countries to be used as 'booking' locations for dollar transactions; in other cases again, such as Bahrain, Singapore and Hong Kong, growth stems from countries pursuing suitable monetary and fiscal policies, supplemented by geographical factors which give them an appropriate relationship to sources of funds and/or outlets. These factors are discussed in more detail in the appropriate chapters. These figures indicate the changing nature of the location of euromarket business, and give some support to the view that London has various natural advantages (notably as regards time zones) which it has been able to maintain and build on by the appropriate policies, although of course in a global environment no one centre can hope to dominate the market.

These statistics and other facts in this chapter are intended to enable the reader to have a fairly ready access to the main perspectives in the international financial markets and provide a framework within which

TABLE 1.13: Location of Eurocurrency Business, 1971–8

	$ billion 1971	Percentage of total	$ billion							Percentage of total
			1972	1973	1974	1975	1976	1977 (Sept.)	1978 (June)	
Belgium	6.2	4.3	7.8	10.8	13.4	16.6	19.8	23.1	29.4	4.0
France	14.4	10.0	19.6	28.0	33.5	39.0	49.7	54.1	60.7	8.2
Germany	3.1	2.1	4.0	6.7	8.2	9.8	14.4	13.0	15.8	2.1
Italy	13.2	9.1	20.1	25.5	15.3	16.4	16.7	18.5	20.4	2.8
Luxembourg	5.4	3.7	8.5	14.2	20.1	26.6	33.5	39.8	48.6	6.6
Netherlands	5.2	3.5	6.7	10.2	13.7	17.3	21.4	23.4	30.2	4.1
Switzerland	6.5	4.4	8.5	9.2	12.1	13.8	17.2	17.3	21.9	3.0
UK	61.9	42.5	81.7	125.6	153.4	172.2	201.4	219.8	248.1	33.7
Other	1.7	1.2	2.4	3.9	1.8	24.9	24.4	24.4	45.4	6.2
Total Europe	117.6	80.8	159.3	234.1	271.5	336.6	398.5	433.4	520.5	70.7
Canada	8.0	5.5	9.7	14.5	17.0	17.0	21.3	24.4	28.5	3.9
Japan	9.4	6.5	13.0	20.0	31.0	32.2	34.9	33.6	40.4	5.5
Bahamas and Caymans[a]	8.2	5.6	13.1	23.8	31.7	45.2	66.7	78.4	84.7	11.5
Bahrain	—	—	—	—	—	1.7	6.2	13.2	20.0	2.7
Hong Kong	0.5	0.3	1.0	1.8	3.1	4.2	5.9	7.3	8.1	1.1
Panama	0.6	0.4	1.1	2.6	5.2	7.1	7.9	7.2	10.7	1.5
Singapore	1.1	0.8	3.0	6.3	10.4	12.6	17.4	19.3	23.0	3.0
Total	145.4	100.0	200.2	303.1	369.9	456.6	558.8	616.8	735.9	100.0

Source: Morgan Guaranty, *World Financial Markets* (March 1978 and January 1979).
Note: [a] Branches of US banks only.
   Dates are 'end year' except where specified.

the more detailed examination of various issues in the rest of this book takes place.

REFERENCES

These are the main general sources of information for the book. Sources specific to individual countries are given at the end of the relevant chapters.

Bank for International Settlements: press releases from the Monetary and Economic Department on 'International Banking Developments'.

Euromoney: various articles and statistical presentations.

Financial Times: supplements on euromarkets and individual countries.

Inter-Bank Research Organisation: *Banking Systems Abroad* (April 1978).

International Monetary Fund: *Annual Report*; *Monthly International Financial Statistics*; *Annual Report on Exchange Restrictions*.

Organisation for Economic Co-operation and Development: *Financial Market Trends*; *Economic Outlook*; individual country reports.

World Bank (IBRD): *Borrowing in International Capital Markets* – a quarterly report on foreign and international bond issues and publicised eurocurrency credits.

World Financial Markets, published by Morgan Guaranty Trust Company of New York.

2 The United States

INTRODUCTION

Since 1971 the position and standing of the US in the world financial economy has changed enormously and at the time of writing (1979) further significant changes are underway. Many themes interrelate over this period. These are the continuing developments from the vast investment by American multinational companies around the world, the internationalisation of the major American banks and the role of the dollar as a reserve currency, the main intervention currency, and the 'world' currency in the euromarkets. The capital account of the balance of payments has shown significant changes with the abolition of controls on financial investment from the US, the much increased borrowing in the American domestic market by certain traditional foreign borrowers, such as Canada, and massively increased foreign central bank holdings of American government securities stemming from the recent imbalances in countries' external accounts. Internal debate on the correct formulation of financial policy has been resolved in favour of broadly monetarist ideas, but these have been supplemented twice in this period by controls over wages and prices. The Americans may be attempting to transfer various international financial transactions from foreign countries back to the US – in particular, back to New York. The underlying momentum for the changes in these various fields stems from the evolution of American economic history itself over this period, as this has set the conditions for the operation of the financial markets and has allowed or impeded, as the case may be, the continuance or formation of new financial policies. In particular there has been a structural deterioration in the American economy with declining investment and productivity growth and growing dependence on imports, not least for energy.

UNDERLYING INTERNATIONAL FINANCIAL POLICY

Up to the late 1960s American international financial policy was still conditioned largely by the structure established immediately after the Second World War. Although an initiator and signatory of the Bretton Woods Agreement which established the IBRD – International Bank for Reconstruction and Development (the World Bank) – and the IMF, the US was the only country which could never be disciplined externally by either of those organisations. Its liberal internal policies, buttressed by the strong constitutionality of its political system, was matched by a liberal attitude towards external economic activity, including world trade and payments. Exchange control was at a minimum, and American companies were free to invest abroad with only limited restraint. The year 1971 was perhaps the end of the big wave of American internationalism after the Second World War linked with the Marshall plan, the direct investment abroad by American companies, which contributed so heavily to the recovery of other parts of the world (notably Western Europe), and the movement abroad during the 1960s of American financial institutions following their customers.

The American balance of payments had come under pressure on various occasions. On 15 August 1971 the US authorities were forced to close the 'gold window', that is to refuse to supply foreign central banks with gold in exchange for dollars. This movement marked the end of the immediate post-war era. The official dual international reserve system, based on gold and the dollar, had come to an end. Until that point – and indeed until late 1978 – American internal economic policy had largely been unaffected by external financial pressures. The major departures from this liberal scenario were the controls over capital outflows implemented by the Kennedy administration in 1963 (these will be discussed later) – but even these were removed during the period we shall be analysing – and the policy measures of the Carter administration towards the end of 1978.

ECONOMIC EVENTS

The end of the Bretton Woods era in August 1971 was marked by the decision of the US not to honour its par value commitments under its IMF agreements by refusing to make over gold to other central banks at the par prices. This was followed by a period of uncontrolled floating, ending with the Smithsonian settlement in December 1971, which established new central values for exchange rates and incorporated a devaluation of the dollar, which in turn aided American international trade. During 1972 and 1973 the American economy showed rapid growth of over 5.5 per cent per annum, accompanied by an increase in inflation from 3.3 per cent in 1972 to 6.2 per cent in 1973. The exchange rate remained relatively stable on a trade-weighted basis during 1972 but fell 6 per cent in 1973 because of a formal devaluation in February and subsequent depreciation. Partially as a result of the increase in American competitiveness but also as a consequence of heavy agricultural sales, the American current account moved from a deficit of $5.8bn in 1972 to a surplus of $6.9bn in 1973. That year, a period of accelerating inflation in the industrialised world because of the synchronised expansion in most major countries, saw major increases in oil prices and the precipitation of a world recession. This recession, although often blamed upon OPEC, whose price increases coincided with the change in overall economic conditions, was also caused by two other major factors. The first was the overall inflationary situation in the industrialised countries, which had to be controlled, and which in itself would have demanded a tightening of monetary and fiscal policy. Second, many major industrial disequilibria had been built up over the post-war period, such as in shipbuilding and shipping, and the resolution of these structural problems was almost certain to precipitate a period of slower growth. Growth in the US was negative in 1974 (minus 1.3 per cent) and inflation increased to 11 per cent as the price effects from oil and the past inflation filtered through the system. Nevertheless the current account remained in surplus by $1.2bn, and the dollar remained stable. The recession continued with a fall in GNP of 1 per cent in 1975 accompanied by inflation down only a small amount to 9.2 per cent. The current account recorded a surplus of $17.7bn associated with appreciation of the dollar on an effective trade-weighted basis back to its Smithsonian level.

By 1976 the Ford administration, partly with the election in mind, had seen the opportunity of relaxing monetary and fiscal policy, and growth approached 6 per cent. Inflation was reduced even further to 5.8 per cent, and the current account remained in surplus by $4.3bn. The dollar showed further appreciation. This broad pattern continued in 1977 with growth of 5 per cent and inflation of 6.5 per cent, but the current account was deteriorating under the stimulus of the fast recovery. The US was out of synchronisation with most of the rest of the industrialised world and the aggressive export promotion policies of other countries. Thus the deficit reached $15.3bn in 1977, and $16.0bn in 1978. The dollar remained relatively strong during 1977, but by the end of the year was moving downwards rapidly and the American administration came under severe criticism from other countries for their neglect of the dollar's exchange rate. In 1978, when the American economy was enjoying a record recovery entering its fourth year, fears were aroused about the inflationary potential in the system, and increased concern was expressed about the dollar. Throughout 1978 the US administration was forced to take steps to defend the dollar, culminating in a series of measures in November intended to reduce inflation and strengthen the dollar in the world's financial markets. Indeed in 1978 the administration had to adopt domestic policy measures which were quite clearly the consequence of external pressure – the first time the Americans had had to do that.

TABLE 2.1: Main Economic Indicators of the US, 1972–8

	1972	1973	1974	1975	1976	1977	1978
Change in GNP (%)	+5.8	+5.4	−1.3	−1.0	+5.8	+4.9	+4.0
Inflation (%)	3.3	6.2	11.0	9.2	5.8	6.5	7.7
Current account ($m)	−5824	+6892	+1168	+17738	+4300	−15292	−15963
Effective exchange rate[a]	100	94	94	99	100	97	94

[a] National Westminster Bank calculations.
Figures are 'end year' (18 December 1971 = 100).

Thus the economic story over this period can be divided into three main stages. It started with an initial boom in which the American economy performed very well but was subject to increasing inflationary difficulties. Second, came the post-OPEC recession, in which the economy adjusted to the new pressures, and the dollar and the external balance of payments problems were handled well. From the point of view of the market the US was probably better able to face OPEC pressures than most other countries; so the Americans were able to react to this situation by liberalising some of their exchange controls and by helping support world trade and payments. In the third phase this headlong American expansion brought its own consequences in the form of a massive deterioration in the balance of payments and a sharp fall in the dollar. This forced the Americans towards the end of 1978 to rein back their domestic economy when they would have preferred not to, and to take firm action against domestic inflation as a means of supporting the dollar. The Americans thus reached a situation by the end of 1978, similar to that which the British faced in the 1950s and 1960s, of having to conduct their domestic monetary policy with one eye on the external reaction and consequences. At the time of writing (1979) this phase has by no means reached its denouement.

MONETARY POLICY AND THE INTERNATIONAL MARKETS

Economic policy in the US has recently become much more monetarist with the authorities publishing target ranges for various definitions of the money supply. This approach was first adopted in January 1974 and monetary targets have been announced for every year since then. The main technique of the authorities has been to operate on the level of bank owned reserves; through the purchase and sale of securities in the open market in order to create the interest rate conditions thought consistent with the desired monetary growth. Interest rates that were used for this purpose include the discount rate, but the pivot of the system has been the Federal funds rate which is moved by intervention to a level thought to be appropriate to the desired monetary base. Intervention takes place heavily through open-market operations including re-purchase agreements with the licensed securities dealers.

One important element of the international dimension of the dollar as it relates to monetary policy and the capital markets is the substantial financing of the American budget deficit which has been possible through overseas central bank purchases of dollar assets. This has reduced the amount required to be financed in the domestic capital markets while at the same time helping to correct the American balance of payments. Problems have arisen, however, when the acquisition of these assets by foreign central banks has been 'reluctant' rather than 'voluntary'; this has reflected the need to make purchases in order to support the dollar and stop their own currencies appreciating too rapidly. There has, however, in the US been no attempt to make any formal use of capital inflows and outflows as a policy instrument for controlling the domestic monetary base (in strict contrast, for example, to the policy pursued in Switzerland). The authorities have been unable to control positively any elements of the capital market as a means of influencing monetary growth, given the liberalism of American policy, with rationing applied in virtually no capital or credit markets. One problem associated with this has been that because the US has been running a current account deficit and also financing capital outflows, the growth of the domestic money supply may have given a poor indication of total domestic credit expansion, and hence of the pressure of demand in the economy and, more important, on the exchange rate. The

Americans have not used a monetary indicator corrected for the balance of payments performance (they have no equivalent to the DCE analysis used in the UK), so their figures of money supply growth will have understated the pressure of demand in the system.

There has been very little positive feedback, either way, between demand in the capital markets, domestic and foreign, and domestic monetary expansion. Nevertheless American policy has influenced the international markets, mainly because the eurodollar market is the off-shore market of the American economy itself. Conditions in the domestic money markets have influenced very strongly those in such international markets. The essential link has been interest rate policy. Interest rates in the eurodollar and domestic dollar markets tend to move closely together unless exchange controls or reserve requirement controls are applied in such a way as to separate the domestic and international markets. This may happen at certain times if Regulation Q is applied to hold down interest rates in the US, in which case bank interest rates may be higher in the euromarket than in the domestic market. But even under those circumstances eurodollar rates are likely to correspond to and move with the main internal short-term market rates (notably the commercial paper rate). Table 2.2 indicates the close relationship between domestic and international interest rates.

TABLE 2.2: US Interest Rates and Eurodollar Rates, 1972–8 (%)

	1972	1973	1974	1975	1976	1977	1978
3-month CDs in US	5.63	9.25	9.25	5.50	4.70	6.80	10.90
Federal funds rate[a]	5.33	9.95	8.53	5.20	4.65	6.55	9.91
3-month eurodollars	5.88	10.13	10.19	5.81	5.00	7.19	11.69
3-month prime indus-trial paper in the US	5.65	9.47	9.60	5.91	4.75	6.84	10.57

Source: Morgan Guaranty, *World Financial Markets* (March 1978 and June 1979).
Note: [a] Monthly average for December.
Dates are 'end year'.

Because the off-shore market is in a sense 'marginal' to the domestic dollar market, conditions tend to be more volatile. This arises in particular because American banks may draw funds from the off-shore market, or be net lenders to it, depending on the movement of loan demand in the domestic and international markets and the underlying credit conditions. Table 2.3 indicates the liabilities of the American

TABLE 2.3: Gross Liabilities of American Banks to their Foreign Branches
(*$ million*)

1972	1973	1974	1975	1976	1977	1978
824	1766	3177	1429	3149	3426	4692

Source: *Federal Reserve Bulletin* (August issues for years 1972–8).
Note: Figures are mid-year and relate to large weekly reporting commercial banks.

banks in relation to the euromarket and how these have changed over the period under review.

Apart from the influence exerted by differences in basic economic conditions, domestically and internationally, the reserve requirements on deposits taken by the US from abroad will also affect the US banks' disposition of funds. The movement for recent years of Regulation M, which determines the reserve requirement on these deposits, is shown in Table 2.4, indicating that at certain times the authorities have wished to impose penal restraints upon the banks' borrowing abroad and at other times have been more relaxed.

TABLE 2.4: Changes in Regulation M, 1971–8

*Reserve requirements on net balances due from US banks to
their foreign branches*

Rate effective from:	7 January 1971	20 %
	21 June 1973	8 %
	22 May 1975	4 %[a]
	24 August 1978	0

Source: *Federal Reserve Bulletin* (September 1976, September 1977, September 1978).
Note: [a] From 1 December 1977 until 23 August 1978 reserve requirements on deposits that foreign banks lend to US residents stood at 1 %.

Regulation D, which applies to the reserve requirement on deposits placed by foreign central banks in the American domestic banking market, has also varied over this period; at present this reserve requirement is also nil. Thus the American authorities use the international short-term money market in as much as they can to help further domestic policies or attempt to isolate the domestic market from conditions in the euromarket, as and when necessary. The political consequences for US domestic policy of the situation in the euromarket are much less important; hence the condition of that market is of less concern to the authorities than is that of domestic market.

This is an important factor for the users of the international market, including major companies and major countries, whether as lenders or borrowers. Many countries have large interest payments to make in dollar terms, on a roll-over basis linked to eurodollar rates, and indeed in 1977 it was said that Brazil, for example, was more exposed to a rise in interest rates than an increase in oil prices – net annual interest payments being greater than the cost than of net oil imports. Thus the international markets have an acute interest in the condition of American domestic economic policy and in the fate of the dollar. Over the period in question these movements have had very diverse effects upon different categories of participant in the market. The fall in the dollar in recent years has benefited borrowers substantially, and correspondingly has had adverse effects upon depositors. This has had a particularly strong effect on OPEC countries, which nevertheless have accumulated significantly larger reserves over this period, and have managed to retain some very substantial benefits from the oil price rises. The borrowers, who include many developing countries, have benefited in capital terms from the weakness of the dollar, but in recent years have had to make much higher interest payments because of the increase in dollar interest rates. While the overall situation will almost certainly have benefited borrowers, including developing countries, changes in interest rates have a sharp short-term effect upon their balance of payments and in some years the effect may well be substantially adverse.

Whatever the advantages to the international economy of a stronger dollar buttressed by much higher domestic interest rates, such a development would place a greater burden upon debtor countries. It is remarkable, however, that most debtor countries appear to have taken a sophisticated view about developments in the market, and accept that if they are to retain their independence they have to accept the good with the bad and take their own decisions so as to protect their interests as far as possible. In discussions in World Bank and IMF circles in late 1978 no instances came to light of developing countries complaining about the rise in American interest rates which had taken place and was likely to persist. However, any further significant rise in American interest rates or major strengthening of the dollar may lead to a slightly more vocal lobby over this matter.

Developments in the dollar eurobond market are largely independent of the domestic capital market, except that certain investors and borrowers have the opportunity of alternating and in some cases arbitraging between them. But the eurobond market will clearly be affected by the future of the dollar. If the dollar becomes an inflationary currency, subject to high and fluctuating interest rates, this will make it unsuitable for long-term international investment. Investors would fear capital losses, given the possibilites of further interest rate increases and currency weakness. In these circumstances the dollar would have followed sterling's path in yet another way. It remains to be seen whether the policy measures of the Carter administration will remove inflation from the system and strengthen the dollar, or whether the dollar will be faced in 1980 with an exceptionally advanced case of stagflation with high interest rates and high inflation. In the latter case the dollar would weaken further as an international long-term investment medium.

CAPITAL CONTROLS

At the beginning of our period of study capital flows were constrained by measures imposed during periods of dollar weakness in the 1960s. In 1963 the Kennedy administration acted to prevent purchases by US residents of foreign debt and equity securities by instituting an interest equalisation tax (IET). This was administered by the US Treasury and adjusted roughly in accordance with changes in the gap between US and foreign interest rates and bond yields. In 1965 the Johnson administration urged US non-financial corporations with foreign operations to abide by a set of 'voluntary' guidelines regarding their direct investment outlays abroad, and the Federal Reserve Board simultaneously issued a programme of voluntary foreign credit restraints (VFCR) on foreign lending by banks and other financial institutions, with ceilings on the growth of such lendings. In 1968 the voluntary direct investment controls were replaced by a mandatory foreign direct investment programme (FDIP) administered by the Office of Foreign Direct Investment (OFDI) within the US Department of Commerce. Direct investment was defined to include net transfer (outflows), through limits in the form of maximum 'allowables' calculated as a proportion of actual levels in certain base periods. In addition the amount of earnings remittances by foreign subsidiaries to their US parents had to meet certain minimum standards. The severity of the controls was related to three different groups of countries: Schedule A – less developed countries – where the restrictions were relatively mild; Schedule B – the UK, Japan, Australia, New Zealand, Ireland, Spain and a number of oil producing countries; and Schedule C – the most severely restricted area – comprised of South Africa and the remainder of the industrialised nations of Western Europe. US direct investment in Canada, as well as purchases of Canadian securities and lending to that country, were by and large exempted from these programmes because of the traditional extremely close financial relationship between the two countries.

The effect of these proposals was not in any serious way to hinder direct investment abroad by American companies, or the healthy growth of the American presence in international banking, finance and industry. The main effect was almost entirely on the way in which this was financed. It led of course to significant pressure for enhanced growth in the eurodollar and eurobond markets.

YANKEE BOND MARKET

All these programmes were abolished by President Nixon in January 1974, a time at which the administration could note the improvement in the American balance of payments and the current strength of the dollar in the exchange markets. There was also an official desire to permit countries suffering large oil-induced trade deficits to seek compensating financing in the US capital market. In retrospect it seems clear that many of the expectations about what would happen following the lifting of controls were exaggerated. The possibility was envisaged that much financing could come back to New York at the expense of the euromarkets – long and short term. There were fears that the policy might by itself seriously weaken the dollar. New York might regain its financial prominence at the expense of London, and of US bank branches there and elsewhere. Soon after the relaxation several European and Japanese borrowers announced plans for major bond offerings in New York, seemingly confirming the validity of these expectations.

In the event however, the capital raised from the American long-term market through 'Yankee bonds' was relatively small. Total money raised in this market increased from $1bn in 1973 to a peak of $10.6bn in 1976 and then fell back to $7.4bn in 1977 and $5.8bn in 1978. However, the greater part of these funds were raised by countries and institutions which had not previously been debarred by the IET from this market: in particular in recent years up to October 1978 Canada raised no less than $ 18.8bn, which reflected her own sharply increased borrowing needs in

TABLE 2.5: Foreign Bonds Issued in New York, 1973–8 (*$ billion*)

Type of borrower	1973	1974	1975	1976	1977	1978
Canadian	0.9	1.9	3.1	6.1	3.0	3.1
International organisations	0.0	0.6	1.9	2.3	1.9	0.5
Other borrowers[a]	0.1	0.7	1.5	2.2	2.5	2.2
Total foreign bonds in US	1.0	3.3	6.5	10.6	7.4	5.8
Total eurobonds	4.2	2.1	8.6	14.3	17.8	14.1
Total international bonds	7.8	6.9	19.9	32.5	34.0	34.3

Source: Morgan Guaranty, *World Financial Markets* (December 1977 and June 1979).
Note: [a] Previously barred by IET.

view of the deterioration in her balance of payments in recent years. International agencies raised $7.2bn. The proportion raised over these years by organisations and countries which had been debarred previously by the IET was only 24 per cent. Moreover, the total funds raised in the Yankee bond market were eclipsed by the massive growth of the eurobond market and by the use of other international bond markets. In 1974 the Yankee bond market accounted for approximately half the total of international bonds raised: in 1975 and 1976 the proportion was approximately a third, by 1978 it was not even a fifth. Thus in absolute and relative terms the Yankee bond market fulfilled few of the hopes at the time of its redevelopment after the Nixon measures.

Nevertheless the American credit market was still the widest and deepest in the world, in terms of both the amounts that could be raised and the maturity range of debt that could be issued. More than $399bn was raised in 1977, of which $69bn was for the US government, $59bn for the financial sector, and $172bn for the private non-financial sector. Many countries and organisations have accordingly taken the opportunity of issuing bonds there as a means both of raising necessary funds and of establishing their credit rating, which may be used either later in that market or as a help towards capital raising in other markets.

In recent years most of the major countries which have had to undertake significant balance of payments borrowing have tapped this market – in some cases to a substantial extent. The major and regular borrowers include Canada, the UK, France, Australia and Norway. Other sovereign risk borrowers include Sweden, Denmark, Belgium, Finland, Iceland, New Zealand, Venezuela, Mexico and Brazil. In some cases this borrowing represented a substantial proportion of the country's requirements for a particular year, such as the $350m taken by the UK in 1978, the $343m for Sweden in 1977, the $315m for Norway in 1977 and the $225m by Australia in the same year.

By far the greater part of the borrowing in this market is by governments and public sector organisations, with the main exception of Canada whose borrowers include some private sector companies, as well as the central government, provincial governments, local governments and public corporations (including hydroelectric institutes). Canadian borrowers also include relatively small organisations such as minor muncipalities and companies. In most other cases corporate borrowers are relatively few and are mainly blue-chip companies. They include British Petroleum, ICI and the Imperial Group from the UK, the Scandinavian Airways System (SAS) and the Ito–Yokado company of Japan. The main exception to this rule is a small Dutch computer leasing company Algemeine Computer Vermietengsgesel, which raised $2.9m in 1977. To illustrate the nature of the market, this was by private placing rather than public offering.

The main international borrowing organisations have used this market as a matter of course when the time was right and some, notably the IBRD, have borrowed very substantial sums indeed – more than $2bn over the period we are considering. Other such borrowers include the Inter-American Development Bank, the Asian Development Bank, the EIB, the EEC and the ECSC. Unless this market becomes closed because of future exchange control changes it is likely to retain its attractiveness for such international borrowers. Its advantages include the large size of loan, with $100m being quite frequent and the largest borrowings over $300m, and the length of maturities. The longest maturities of thirty years are roughly double those in the European markets, and maturities of fifteen and twenty years are relatively common. The costs of an issue, about 1 per cent, are roughly half those in the dollar eurobond market, a third those in the eurobond deutschemark market, and only a quarter those of the foreign Swiss franc market. The interest yield is roughtly $\frac{1}{2}$ per cent higher than for prime domestic borrowers, with approximately 0.3 per cent more for a private placement. Unrated borrowers pay, of course, significantly more – perhaps 3 per cent or so more than a prime domestic borrower.

Disadvantages and specific costs include the need to adopt American accounting practices, the disclosure requirements of the Securities and Exchange Commission, associated fees and printing costs and the need in some cases for a credit rating. Distribution may in some cases be external as a result of these bonds being tax-exempt for non-US residents. In as much as distribution takes place within the US,

American insurance companies are not allowed to invest more than 1 per cent of their investments in foreign obligations (but up to 10 per cent in Canadian obligations), so this is an ultimate constraint although there is at present significant spare capacity. Although the private placement market may be more convenient from some points of view, such a distribution to not more than thirty-five 'large and knowledgeable' investors makes the security then unmarketable. Although this market is only one of the many components of the international capital market, it has too much capacity to be ignored by future substantial borrowers. At the same time it retains the prestige of being the most difficult market to which to obtain access, so borrowing there confers considerable and useful status on the borrower.

THE CAPITAL ACCOUNT

US financial policy has shown some anomalies; for example the balance of payments pattern, including capital movements, has become inconsistent with other features of the economic situation. In recent years the US has clearly become a mature reserve currency country, in that the financial position of the dollar around the world has become disproportionate in relation to the intrinsic economic strength of the country itself. Net dollar holdings in the eurocurrency market total over $400bn, a figure comparable in scale with the domestic American money supply. Additionally, the dollar accounts for some 80 per cent of central banks' foreign exchange holdings. Overseas central bank holdings of dollars have increased very rapidly in recent years as a consequence of support operations for the dollar, and a significant proportion of these have been invested in marketable or non-marketable US Treasury instruments (see Table 2.7).

In recent years the American economy has had substantial current account deficits, implying that the domestic economy is facing more difficulty in financing the standard of living now enjoyed within the country. The dollar has been weak, compelling foreign central banks to purchase large amounts of dollars and invest them in American domestic money market instruments, in order to prevent their own currencies appreciating too rapidly. Yet at the same time the long-term capital account of the balance of payments has been that of a country running solid current surpluses. Apart from the relatively small capital export through Yankee bonds, there has been direct investment abroad, and the American government itself has been the cause of a significant

TABLE 2.6: US Balance of Payments: Selected Statistics, 1972–8 (*$ billion*)

	1972	1973	1974	1975	1976	1977	1978 (*provisional*)
Current account	−6.0	6.9	1.7	18.4	4.3	−15.3	−16.0
Balance of merchandise trade	−6.4	0.9	−5.3	9.0	−9.4	−31.1	−34.1
Net direct investment flow (net outflow = minus)	−6.8	−8.6	−4.3	−11.6	−7.3	−8.9	−9.8
US private net increase (−) in holdings of foreign securities	−0.6	−0.7	−1.9	−6.2	−8.9	−5.4	−3.4
Increase (+) in private foreign investment in US securities	4.4	3.8	1.1	5.1	4.0	3.4	5.1
Increase (−) in US official reserve (net)	0.3	0.2	−1.4	−0.6	−2.5	−0.2	0.9
Increase (+) in foreign official assets in the United States (net)	10.3	5.1	10.3	5.3	13.1	35.5	31.2

Source: US Department of Commerce, *Survey of Current Business.*

TABLE 2.7: Foreign Official Assets in the US ($ billion)

	1972	1973	1974	1975	1976	1977	1978
Foreign holdings of marketable US Treasury bills and notes	5.9	6.2	5.7	7.7	15.8	38.6	44.9
Foreign official assets held at Federal Reserve Banks							
1. Deposits		0.3	0.4	0.4	0.4	0.4	0.4
2. US Treasury securities (marketable and non-marketable)		52.1	55.6	60.0	66.5	92.0	117.1
3. Government gold		17.1	16.8	16.7	16.4	16.0	15.5
Foreign exchange reserves held in dollars[a]	65.7	75.7	92.3	92.7	101.8	140.5	n.a.

Source: Federal Reserve Bulletin (May 1979). Foreign exchange reserves held in dollars: IMF Survey (22 May 1978).

Note: [a] Data relate to 76 reporting countries.
Figures are 'end year'.

capital outflow both short and long term. The Americans have thus had to rely upon public and private sector capital inflows, largely of a short term financial nature, to put right their balance of payments at the very time when the financial markets were not attractive enough to encourage a private capital inflow. This has at times placed the entire burden upon foreign central banks who need an outlet for the dollars they obtain when keeping their own exchange rates down. This is not a balance of payments structure which is stable on a long-term basis, and it may well be the case that the measures (late in 1978) by the American authorities to strengthen the dollar will be followed in due course by other policy measures on the structure of the balance of payments.

INTERNATIONAL BANKING MARKETS

One of the striking features of the international financial markets is the close integration between the activities and offices of the American banks around the world, the structure of the eurodollar market and its integration with the domestic dollar markets. It has been said that two of the main impetuses for this American financial expansion have been the desire of banks and financial institutions to follow their customers – this applies in the bond market as well as in the provision of normal banking services – and the limitations on the domestic expansion of American banks. In particular the restriction of operations to one state has meant that the obvious outlet for any drive for expansion and growth was abroad. Be that as it may, the American presence around the world in banking is phenomenal and the vast bulk of eurodollar deposits are held with those banks.

There is much controversy whether the eurodollar market acts as a money multiplier or is merely a transmission mechanism, and whether its effects are inflationary or not. This book is concerned with structure and therefore will not consider this question at length, but we tend to accept the view that the international markets are an extension of the domestic markets of the main banks concerned. It is a means whereby they can economise on capital and on reserve assets and thus do more banking business in relation to their reserve and capital constraints. Arbitrage between the eurodollar market and the domestic market is substantial, whatever the restrictions and regulations happen to be.

In 1969 when Regulations Q ceilings limited the interest rates that American banks could pay in the internal market, the American banks were forced to borrow heavily in the eurodollar market in order to maintain their balance sheets; as a result euromarket rates rose to extremely high levels. During the 1970s, even in periods of tight money such as during 1974, this situation has not existed, and interest rates in the two markets have remained more in line. The main effect on relative interest rates is the reserve requirement, if any, imposed by the Federal Reserve on deposits taken from the euromarket and placed back with American parent banks in New York and elsewhere. If Regulation M is lower than the domestic reserve requirement there is an incentive to borrow in the euromarket at equivalent rates of interest: if Regulation M is non-existent or is higher, then the balance between the two sources may be altered. In general, however, euromarket rates have to be competitive with the equivalent domestic rates, which are largely regarded as those of commercial paper, as there are many channels of arbitrage between the two markets.

This large financial presence abroad, and integration of the markets, has led both to invisible earnings being a very substantial source of income to the American economy generally (from manufacturing and other services as well as banking) and to profits of international activity being a large component of the total profits of the major American banks.

Not only are profits from international banking very substantial for the major banks, but they have also been increasing much more rapidly than have profits on domestic business. The American banks have played a major part in most of the modern developments of the market,

TABLE 2.8: International Earnings Growth of Major US Banks, 1971–8
(*$ million*)

	1971	1972	1973	1974	1975	1976	1977	1978	Annual average % growth 1971–8
International earnings	231	318	451	612	818	834	913	1043	24
Domestic earnings	773	741	817	866	769	805	884	1239	7
International earnings as percentage of total earnings	23	30	36	41	52	51	51	46	

Source: Salomon Brothers, Bank Stock Department, *Statistics on US Multinational Banking* (20 July 1979).

including the enormous increase in syndicated lending in recent years. Associated with the very large invisible earnings for the American economy has been the massive presence of American multinationals abroad, whose physical assets totalled $137bn at the end of 1976.

The basic activity of the international markets themselves is described in a separate chapter, but it may be relevant here to mention some of the key features of these markets as they affect the American financial institutions. The dollar was the first major currency for eurobond and eurocurrency transactions, and the American banks have always had a very strong position in this field. In particular, the investment banks have played a very active part as issuers and dealers in eurodollar bonds. The American banks have been relieved internationally from the responsibilities and requirements of the Glass–Steagall Act, which forbids banks in America from taking part in both deposit and investment banking. Thus some of the major deposit banks in the US have been able to take a more direct part in issuing and dealing in bonds in the international market than would be possible in America itself. In particular, Morgan Guaranty has operated the eurobond clearing system (Cedel), which is described in more detail in Chapter 8.

Not only has the American financial presence abroad coloured the international markets, it has also greatly influenced the internal markets of many countries, including in particular those which have allowed foreign banks to play a major part in their domestic currency business.

This applies significantly to the UK and Germany. In recent years the Americans have also allowed foreign banks to play a greater part in the American market. Foreign bank assets in the US amounted to some $116bn in 1978. This process has already led to the transmission of innovation and new banking practices around the world and to sharply increased competitive pressure for many banks in their own domestic markets. It is likely to continue, bringing about even greater integration of banking practice and competition to the extent to which the banks are willing and/or able to compete, and the degree of protection given to them by their own monetary authorities, whether in the guise of monetary controls or direct protection of the banks' business. We are seeing the transfer of business from a retail to a wholesale basis through the forum of international banking. It is a classic example of the long-term supply and demand curves being effective: services which can be provided on a low-cost, wholesale basis are being forced away from high-cost, retail networks by the demands of customers to have services at the cheapest available price. This competitive pressure works its way in the end even into highly restricted environments, and international banks are one of the means by which this fundamental structural change in banking is taking place.

THE EXCHANGE MARKETS

The liberalism of American policy as regards the exchange rate is one of the important components of the world's free foreign exchange markets. The dollar is the dominant currency for intervention purposes. The main effect on market structures of economic developments in the early 1970s was the transition from a fixed exchange rate system in which banks suffered relatively limited risks, to a floating rate system in which the risks were substantially greater because under free floating the exchange profit of one bank is more likely to find its counterpart in the loss of another. Central bank losses are not as large or consistent as under a fixed rate system. Many banks adapted slowly to the learning process and suffered substantial losses. The market became thinner and more volatile after the Herstatt affair, when that German bank went bankrupt as a consequence of its over-exposure in the foreign exchange market. The result was much greater caution on the part of major banks, a limitation on the number of banks with which they were willing to deal and much increased surveillance individually and jointly by central banks in the major countries.

INTERNATIONAL MONETARY REFORM

The main feature of the American attitude to international monetary reform, as regards the markets, is their policy towards gold. The Americans were strong advocates of removing gold from its legal position in the international monetary system and were behind measures to change the Articles of the IMF as appropriate. The Committee of Twenty, set up within the IMF after the formal breakdown of Bretton Woods, with the aim of negotiating a new international financial order, failed technically to achieve its objective, and it was disbanded without loss of face when the OPEC price rises took place. At the IMF meeting in August 1975, however, it was proposed that the SDR should formally replace gold as the numeraire for official parities, and that steps be taken to dispose of IMF gold holdings. The Americans were well satisfied with this proposal, as they regarded gold as a rival to the dollar and have long been keen to have it removed from the international financial system.

Accordingly, American gold sales – linked with this policy – have become a significant feature of the gold market. These auctions began in 1975, but from June of that year gold sales were suspended for almost three years. During this time US Treasury spokesmen regularly issued statements to the effect that gold policy had not changed. Sales were resumed in May 1978. At the same time IMF auctions of gold were taking place linked with their plan to hand back 1/6 of their gold to the countries which had donated it, and to sell a further 1/6 over a period with the funds being made available to certain developing countries. The American gold sales have increased in scale as they have wished to further their policy of financing their balance of payments deficit and strengthening the dollar. They are now running at a level approaching $1bn a year, which is a significant contribution to the annual supply in the gold market and to the financing of both the US government and balance of payments deficits. The prohibition on American domestic ownership of gold was removed by the Nixon administration in 1974. Since then domestic demand has increased very substantially indeed.

OFF-SHORE BANKING

Apart from the very substantial presence of American banks in major centres such as London and locations in the Middle and Far East, banking operations have also been established much nearer home. The growth of the off-shore banking centres near North America is given in

TABLE 2.9: US Gold Auction Results

Date	Quantity bid (thousand troy ounces)	Sub-scription ratio	Amount sold (thousand troy ounces)	Average (I) of common (II) price ($)	Value of gold sold ($m)
1975					
6 Jan.	954.8	0.48	754.0	165.67(I)	124
30 June	3987.8	7.98	499.5	165.05(II)	82
1978					
23 May	1364.4	4.55	300.0	180.38(I)	54
20 June	1036.0	3.45	300.0	186.91(I)	56
18 July	1385.6	4.62	300.0	185.16(I)	56
15 Aug.	564.4	1.88	300.0	213.53(I)	64
19 Sept.	772.2	2.57	300.0	212.76(I)	64
17 Oct.	832.2	2.77	300.0	228.39(I)	69
21 Nov.	911.6	1.21	750.0	199.05(I)	149
19 Dec.	2717.2	1.81	1500.0	214.30(I)	322

Source: US Treasury.

TABLE 2.10: IMF Gold Auction Results

Year	Amount sold (*thousand troy ounces*)	Value of gold sold ($m)
1976	3900	477.4
1977	6030	890.6
1978	5915	1131.1

Source: Data derived from tables in IMF *Annual Report* (1978) and issues of *IMF Survey* (June–December 1978).

TABLE 2.11: Growth of Main Caribbean Off-shore Centres. (*External liabilities of banks of major reporting countries and off-shore branches of US banks, $ billion*)

	1971	1972	1973	1974	1975	1976	1977
Bahamas and Caymans[a]	8.5	12.6	23.8	31.7	45.2	66.7	79.1
Netherlands Antilles	0.1	0.1	0.1	0.1	0.1	0.3	0.6
Panama	0.6	1.1	2.6	5.3	7.1	8.4	10.6

Source: Estimates based on Bank for International Settlements and US Federal Reserve data.
Note: [a] US branches only.

Table 2.11, indicating the rapid growth in business particularly in the Bahamas (Nassau), the Cayman Islands and other Caribbean centres. The attraction of these low tax areas is that they can be used by American banks to reduce their global average tax rate to the maximum allowed as an offset (currently 46 per cent) against American taxation. By and large these have developed as off-shore booking centres for North American activity; the management located in these centres is minor and the dealing is done by telex from New York and elsewhere. These centres offer little genuine local financial services. As a result of the enormous increase in the efficiency of modern communications, financial markets are exceptionally mobile. There seems no reason why these centres which have a developed legal framework and which are used by some of the most substantial banks in the world should not continue to develop. However, if changes in US legislation permit 'off-shore' banking in New York, they could be badly hit.

As means of creating jobs and of transferring this business back in a less artificial way to the mainland, proposals have been put forward for domestic international banking facilities (IBFs) in New York and possibly elsewhere. The New York state legislature has passed the necessary legislation to lessen the taxation on this activity, and other states which have to pass such tax concessionary legislation may well do so – although in many states tax is not the main issue. The main requirement now is for the Federal Reserve to relax its regulations in order to enable off-shore transactions to take place on the American mainland without penalty of reserve costs. (If reserve requirements were applied this would make such business unattractive in comparison with the international booking centres or other main financial centres around the world.) At the time of writing (1979) it remains to be seen whether the Federal Reserve will make the necessary concessions, which would involve further complications as regards monetary statistics and monetary control. Undoubtedly the effects would be felt first by the purely off-shore centres, but other main financial centres could well suffer extra competition in due course, although time zone considerations would protect many centres from competition from New York.

CONCLUSION

Recent years have clearly seen the end of the American financial hegemony which began after the Second World War, and the American administration now has much less room for manoeuvre in many policy areas. The pattern of market growth and the structure of the American balance of payments are to some extent inconsistent with the present economic situation of the US. Perhaps the decisive factor has been that in trying to obtain such a massive benefit for themselves, in terms of both higher real income and the accumulation of financial assets, the OPEC countries ended by achieving their own objectives to a lesser extent than envisaged, and brought down the dollar in the process. The various economic responses to the high price of oil softened the harsh effects of the OPEC measures, but the result was, perhaps inevitably, ultimate damage to the standing of the dollar in world markets. This is not to be regarded as any conspiracy on the part of the West, including the Americans, but merely the way in which economic forces ultimately had their effect.

The institutional structure of the eurobond and eurocurrency markets is now well established and the dollar is at present the dominant currency within them. Holdings of dollars around the world are likely to dominate the markets for some years to come. But in the future a greater marginal growth of business, in both the public and private sectors, is likely to take place in other currencies. Portfolio capital investment may well take place out of New York, but probably on a relatively small scale in relation to global capital markets. One may well see credit controls and possibly exchange controls being applied in the near future if the American authorities feel compelled to take further action to protect either the balance of payments or the value of the dollar. Apart from that the basic attitude of the Americans towards markets, both internal and external, may well continue much as before. The American authorities will have to look more closely at domestic problems and be more on the defensive in the international arena. Should the world-wide exchange markets be disappointed with the position of the dollar as a financial asset, in terms of both interest rates and inflation prospects, and exert more pressure on the American administration for conservative domestic policies than the domestic political situation will be able to bear, then the Americans will face a very sharp conflict between internal and external objectives. In that situation one would expect the external pressures to have to give way to a great extent, and one could envisage a sharp change in the American attitudes towards external financial markets. This could be a parallel to the changes which took place in the UK in the 1950s and 1960s because of corresponding problems, implying fundamentally the separation of the off-shore and on-shore markets through a widespread network of exchange controls.

This would be a massive change in American policy, which would in turn be exceptionally difficult to effect because of the very large number of American banks around the world, and of the scale of international dollar holdings. The best outcome would be for the American economy to show the strength and resilience which would not force this choice upon the administration.

REFERENCES

Robert Z. Aliber, 'The integration of the off-shore and domestic banking system', unpublished paper (University of Chicago).
K. Areskoug, 'The liberalisation of US capital outflows: international financial consequences', *The Bulletin* (NY University Graduate School of Business Administration, 1976–8).
C. H. Columbus and R. E. Howard, *The Expanding Yankee Bond Market*.
Federal Reserve Bank of New York, *Monetary Aggregates and Monetary Policy* (October 1974).
Federal Reserve Bank of New York, 'The strategy of monetary control', *Federal Reserve Bulletin* (May 1976).
Federal Reserve Bank of New York, 'Recent developments in US international transactions', *Federal Reserve Bulletin* (April 1978).
M. S. Mendelsohn, 'Yankee bonds in perspective', *The Banker* (October 1977); and 'Why is it cheaper to borrow in New York?', *The Banker* (Oct. 1978).
OECD, *Monetary Policy in the US* (1974).

3 Germany

INTRODUCTION

There has been substantial development in Germany's attitude to and standing in international financial markets in recent years. This has resulted from several factors. First, the country's great economic success over the entire post-war period and the strength of its balance of payments have led to a need to facilitate capital exports as a means of balancing the balance of payments and thus reducing excess upward pressure on the exchange rate. Second, the appreciation of the exchange rate has led to reduced profitability for manufacturing in Germany itself and hence much greater direct investment abroad by German companies. Third, the economic strength of Germany has facilitated growing strength among the German banks, whose position in the table of the world's leading banks ranked by assets has increased steadily over the years. These banks have been keen to increase their business opportunities, and the institutional structure of the German capital market has made it easier for them to arrange foreign placings in the long-term markets. They have also been willing to facilitate the increasing international use of the deutschemark in bank credits. The minimum reserve requirements in Germany and other banking regulations have encouraged the establishment of a very substantial euro-deutschemark market, which is largely based in Luxembourg. This is virtually an integral part of the German banking system; Luxembourg is mainly used just for booking transactions with management decisions taken in Frankfurt, Düsseldorf or elsewhere. Germany's great success against inflation, making it a persistent upward revaluation prospect in Europe, has naturally encouraged others including central monetary institutions to try to acquire deutschemark assets. Thus the German currency has become a more substantial international reserve asset in recent years; for example, it is now more widely used than sterling (see Table 1.3, p. 4).

Because of its economic strength Germany can hardly avoid being drawn prominently into the major economic controversies of the day. She was instrumental in setting up the European 'snake' (to a large extent a German currency zone) and, more recently, the EMS and in policing financial stability within Europe. She has been a persistent critic of American policy in recent years, and an advocate of greater conservatism in that country's economic policies.

ECONOMIC EVENTS

From the Smithsonian settlement until 1973 Germany was concerned with coping with domestic inflationary pressures and resisting upward pressures on the deutschemárk. The balance of payments was in current account surplus over that period and growth relatively rapid. Domestic monetary policy was being used to cut back internal monetary pressures, but inflation approached the very high rate – by German standards – of 7 per cent in 1973. In spring 1973 the government and the Bundesbank therefore launched a major deflationary programme. Stiff fiscal measures were introduced and monetary policy was tightened sharply as soon as the floating of exchange rates allowed for an effective national monetary policy. In the second phase, after the OPEC price rises, the rate of inflation did not increase as it did in virtually every other major country, and Germany's current account was maintained in surplus – partly because of the temporary persistence of demand for investment goods.

A restrictive monetary stance was maintained throughout 1974 with long-term rates in particular remaining high. Yields on government bonds exceeded 10 per cent from March despite a pause in new issues. In the case of short-term rates, which had been pushed to very high levels by a series of five increases in the central bank discount and Lombard rates between November 1972 and June 1973, and accompanying action in respect of reserve requirement ratios, there was only a moderate reduction during 1974. During the spring of 1974 further measures in the form of a 75 per cent utilisation ceiling on rediscount quotas were introduced to prevent monetary growth from accelerating, but it was not until December 1974 that the Bundesbank published for the first time a growth target for the central bank money stock. The target for January to December 1975 was set at 8 per cent. Attempts to curb inflation were facilitated in the early months of 1975 when pay settlements were generally at half the level of the previous year (at around 6 per cent), while the appreciation of the deutschemark helped keep down wholesale prices. At the end of 1975, when unemployment started to rise sharply, pressure mounted for the introduction of a measure of reflation to combat the economic recession. The Government introduced a package designed to boost the economy moderately, and a robust recovery was registered in 1976. Since then growth has been at a steady 3 per cent per annum, and inflation declined to below 3 per cent in 1978.

TABLE 3.1: Main Economic Indicators, Germany, 1972–8

	1972	1973	1974	1975	1976	1977	1978
Change in GNP (%)	+3.4	+5.1	+0.7	−2.5	+5.7	+2.7	+3.4
Inflation (%)	5.5	6.9	7.0	6.0	4.5	3.8	2.6
Current account ($m)	+768	+4307	+9807	+3982	+3847	+3697	+8100
Effective exchange rate^a	101	111	118	115	131	141	150

^{a} National Westminster Bank calculations.
Figures are 'end year' (18 December 1971 = 100).

MONETARY POLICY

In recent years Germany's monetary policy has been torn between two basically irreconcilable objectives: regulation of the exchange rate or domestic monetary control. The Germans have been acutely aware of this dilemma. If, on the one hand, they peg the exchange rate, then they lose control over domestic monetary policy and may have more rapid inflation than they consider acceptable. On the other hand, if they devote their efforts to controlling domestic inflation, they lose control of the exchange rate, which may appreciate to levels resulting in adverse effects on certain industries, and unwelcome structural effects within the economy. In the early 1970s the authorities moved uneasily between these two objectives, but on the whole there was a reluctance to allow the deutschemark to appreciate. After the OPEC price rises, policy was more decisive and Germany was one of the first countries to announce firm monetary targets and a firm system of controlling the money supply. This was introduced in 1975 and consists of a policy for controlling the monetary base in the economy (cash in circulation plus the reserve assets of the banking system). These monetary targets have been applied ever since, although in point of fact they have generally been exceeded. However, they have been accompanied by a substantial reduction in the velocity of circulation of money and the overall success of anti-inflationary policy has been maintained. The effects on Germany of unemployment from the restrictive policy measures of 1973 and 1974 and of the general slow-down of the economy during the recession and in the following years was mitigated by some half a million guest workers in Germany returning to their native countries. Thus unemployment, in Germany, although increasing to over 1 million in 1975–7 and averaging 4.6 per cent of the labour force during that period, was much less than it might have been.

The main instruments of monetary policy have been variable reserve requirements, changes in banks' rediscount quotas and changes in the Lombard and discount rates. In recent years the aim of the authorities has been to encourage industrial investment where possible and interest rates have been relatively low, a posture made easier by the general confidence in the deutschemark. Loan demand within Germany has been exceptionally low, but many companies have found it preferable to borrow euro-deutschemarks, which have been available on even more attractive terms.

TABLE 3.2: Domestic and Euromarket Deutschemark Interest Rates, 1972–8

	1972	1973	1974	1975	1976	1977	1978
Domestic lending rate[a]	8.5	14.0	11.0	7.0	6.5	6.0	5.5
Commercial bank deposit rate	7.3	11.5	8.0	4.2	4.2	3.4	3.5
Euro-deutschemark deposit rate	4.0	12.3	7.9	3.8	4.7	2.5	3.7

Source: Morgan Guaranty, *World Financial Markets* (July 1979).
Note: All rates are for 3-month money; all figures are 'end year'.
  [a] Approximate overdraft rate for first-class borrowers.

CAPITAL MOVEMENTS

As Germany has moved towards being a mature industrial economy, with very high income standards and an appreciating exchange rate benefiting from both the balance of payments strength and a declining rate of inflation, so the structure of the capital account of the balance of payments has changed. This is the result of developments associated with the private sector and the three major types of transaction in which it engages: direct investment, portfolio investment and advances and loans. Germany has traditionally had less direct investment abroad than other countries such as the UK with perhaps more cosmopolitan industrial companies. Nevertheless, gross outflows of direct investment have been appreciable, at over DM4bn in every year since and including

1972. Whereas these outflows have been on a rising trend, direct investment inward has been reduced significantly, and the effect of this has been a major change in the overall position. Thus from 1972 to 1974 direct investment provided a net inflow to Germany of DM3.7bn, while in the following three years a net outflow of no less than DM7.2bn was recorded. The net outflow continued on a larger scale in 1978.

Recent years have also seen a reversal of the direction of portfolio investment. Although the figures tend to fluctuate more from year to year in accordance with the conditions in particular financial markets and with expectations about both exchange rates and interest rates, a clear pattern emerges if one looks at periods longer than one year. In total, over the three years 1975–7 portfolio investment showed a net outflow of DM3.4bn, compared with a net inflow of DM11.9bn in the preceding three-year period, and the outward trend continued in 1978.

The propensity to export rather than import long-term capital is also evident in the case of advances and loans. Gross outflows from this source have increased substantially, partly because of the German banks' support for German exports, many of which are capital goods financed on long-term credit. The German success in the OPEC markets, with whom a surplus has now been achieved, is reflected partly by the increased financing of exports. Advances and loans into Germany have at times been sizeable (for example in 1978) but normally the net flow is outward, so that this sector also contributes substantially to the systematic capital outflow which Germany experiences in the private sector.

Official capital flows are significantly smaller in scale than private flows and their fluctuations are also less. In the period 1972–7 the average net flow was less than DM0.5bn.

This picture is likely to continue for the foreseeable future unless there should be a massive change in the fortunes of the deutschemark, which seems most unlikely. The appreciation of the deutschemark has led to very high labour costs in Germany by world standards, and the profitability of exporting basic goods has been severely diminished. Germany is no longer a natural manufacturing base for world markets, except in goods where quality considerations or product specifications tend to tie the purchaser to a German source. The economy, with its high rate of saving, is thus now a natural capital exporter and German manufacturing companies can be expected to make their presence felt in markets around the world, with local manufacturing bases, rather on the lines that British companies have followed for a considerable time. In particular this has been an opportune period for investing in the US

TABLE 3.3: The German Balance of Payments: Long-term Capital Flows (*DM billion*)

| | | | | Private sector gross flows | | | | | | | |
| | | | | Outflows | | | | Inflows | | | |
	Total (net)	Official total (net)	Private total (net)	Direct investment	Portfolio	Advances and loans	Other	Direct investment	Portfolio	Advances and loans	Other
1972	+15.5	−1.5	+17.0	−5.0	+4.0	+2.1	−0.8	+6.2	+10.7	—	−0.1
1973	+13.0	−2.2	+15.2	−4.4	+0.4	+4.1	−0.8	+5.3	+6.5	+3.9	+0.1
1974	−5.8	−0.9	−4.9	−5.0	−1.1	−2.8	−0.6	+6.6	−2.5	+0.4	+0.1
1975	−16.8	+1.2	−18.0	−4.9	−2.6	−13.8	−0.5	+3.1	−1.6	+2.4	—
1976	−0.3	+2.4	−2.7	−6.2	−0.9	−10.0	−0.5	+3.9	+4.8	+6.3	−0.1
1977	−12.9	−1.7	−11.2	−6.4	−5.4	−9.9	−0.6	+3.3	+2.3	+5.5	−0.1
1978	−2.3	−3.1	+1.1	−7.2	−4.2	−8.8	−0.5	+3.3	+3.7	+15.1	−0.1

Source: Deutsche Bundesbank, *Statistical Supplement* (July 1979).
Note: + signifies an inflow; − an outflow.

given the relative weakness of the dollar, which on any kind of cost comparison has been overdone. Not only has investment been profitable, but the strength of the deutschemark has made it easier for German companies to buy American assets. During 1975–7 as much as a quarter of overall direct investment abroad from Germany was directed to the US.

Nevertheless, the proportion of total investment by the German business community which is spent abroad is still relatively small. From 1966 to 1968 direct investment abroad as recorded in the balance of payments (in other words not including investment financed by credits from abroad) averaged 2.5 per cent of German domestic investment; in the next three years the figure reached 3.4 per cent and in 1972–4, 4.2 per cent. In the latest three year period, 1975–7, such investments averaged 4.6 per cent of domestic capital expenditure. By international standards these are relatively low percentages and are significantly lower than in the case of UK for example. At present the stock of foreign investments in Germany seems still to be greater than German investment abroad, while the net income flow is still significantly outwards. During the period 1975–7 German receipts from direct investments abroad (including reinvested profits) averaged just under DM2bn, while the corresponding figure for payments was DM5.25bn. Germany is likely for the foreseeable future to run a deficit on direct investment income, but the size of this deficit may well decrease gradually as income from abroad increases both in absolute terms and in relation to the outflow from this type of investment.

TABLE 3.4: Germany's Direct Investment Income or Outflow, 1972–8
(*DM million*)

	1972	1973	1974	1975	1976	1977	1978
Receipts	1159	1348	1491	1711	1885	2071	1854
Outflows	4253	4497	6097	4412	4956	6716	4446
Balance	−3094	−3149	−4606	−2701	−3071	−4645	−2592

Source: Deutsche Bundesbank, *Statistical Supplement* (July 1979).

FOREIGN AND INTERNATIONAL BONDS

Deutschemark international bonds have become a major feature in the international long-term capital market as the weakness of the dollar has

TABLE 3.5: New International Bond Issues, 1971–8 (*$ billion*)

Euro plus foreign issues	1971	1972	1973	1974	1975	1976	1977	1978
US$	3.3	5.3	3.4	4.3	10.2	19.7	19.0	13.1
DM	1.1	1.6	1.4	0.5	3.4	4.0	6.3	9.1
Other	1.8	2.8	3.0	2.0	6.3	8.8	8.7	12.1
Total	6.2	9.7	7.8	6.8	19.9	32.5	34.0	34.3

Source: Morgan Guaranty, *World Financial Markets* (March 1978 and June 1979). See also Table 1.6, p. 6.

led to a reduction in its use for long-term loans. In 1978 non-dollar issues comprised for the first time over 60 per cent of international bond issues.

The present market structure goes back to the first foreign bonds issued in 1959, shortly after the German currency was made convertible, as a means of enabling borrowers from abroad to tap the German capital market. The original purpose was to provide a vehicle for the export of capital and to offset some of the capital inflow, but even from the beginning a significant proportion of the foreign bonds were sold to customers abroad who were keen to have an asset denominated in deutschemarks.

Although statistics are recorded separately for foreign bonds and eurobonds, the practical difference is very limited indeed, being simply that eurobonds are syndicated internationally while foreign bonds are syndicated among German banks only. There is no other difference; both types of bond are issued in bearer form (denominations may be as low as DM1000), the interest is free and clear of any withholding tax, and there are no restrictions concerning the sale to non-residents. Listing and secondary markets are maintained on and off the Stock Exchange, but although there is some Stock Exchange trading most of the volume is transacted between banks and dealers. Private placements have the character of a public issue without listing and underwriting.

The prior approval of the government is not required for the issue of these foreign and international bonds. The procedure is for the 'calendar' to be decided at the regular monthly meeting of the Foreign Bonds Sub-Committee of the Central Capital Market Committee. This sub-committee brings together the six main issuing banks with representatives of the Bundesbank to set a calendar of all new issues of foreign bonds for each month. This procedure ensures an orderly market and in particular helps ensure that capital demands through the different types of bonds are reasonably consistent. The Germans control relatively tightly the domestic financial assets which may be held by foreigners; so buying foreign and international bonds is one of the relatively few ways in which non-residents may buy deutschemark financial assets. It is estimated that at the end of 1977, 85 per cent of outstanding international deutschemark bonds were held by foreigners.

Given this high foreign ownership of deutschemark bonds, and the fact that the Bundesbank requires international borrowers to convert the proceeds out of deutschemarks immediately after the issue has been completed, the economic effect of this market upon the German economy itself is relatively limited. It has a small effect upon the flow of funds across the exchanges on a net basis, and hence on the demand for net domestic savings. The deutschemark is essentially used as a unit of account in denominating a contract between foreign borrowers and foreign lenders.

The market is likely to continue to develop steadily. It is well-established, an efficient secondary market has been built up around it, and the deutschemark seems likely to retain the confidence of international investors, given the strength of the German balance of payments and the notable success of anti-inflationary policies. Although borrowing deutschemarks must be unattractive to borrowers in weak currency countries, there has been no shortage of borrowers willing to take on the exchange risk, including private sector as well as government organisations. Exchange risk considerations are not dominant for large world-wide organisations such as the World Bank which have very heavy international borrowing programmes; similarly government and private companies which are based in hard currency areas such as Japan, Scandinavia, or elsewhere in continental Europe may feel well able to bear the exchange risk, given the nature of their own earnings and financial structures. Perhaps in some cases developing countries may have been ill-advised to have taken deutschemark borrowing, particularly when their main trading partners were weak currency countries, or when their main exports, such as commodities, were priced in dollars. However, provided that only a limited proportion of their borrowing was in hard currencies such a spread, whose outcome of course would not be known beforehand, need not have been too inadvisable.

FOREIGN INVOLVEMENT IN THE DOMESTIC CAPITAL MARKETS

Germany has quite a different pattern of capital control from that which operates in the two main earlier reserve currency countries, the US and the UK, and this has had a considerable effect upon the pattern of growth of the capital markets. The two basic laws and regulations affecting foreign investment in the financial markets in Germany are the Law on Foreign Economic Relations (*Aussenwirtschaftsgesetz*) and the Ordinance on Foreign Economic Relations (*Aussenwirtschafts-Verordnung*). Paragraphs 22 and 23 of the former set out the powers of the German government regarding capital exports and imports, and the Ordinance sets out the detailed regulations. The sale to non-residents of Treasury bills, domestic bearer or registered bonds, or any other domestic fixed rate securities denominated in deutschemarks with a remaining life of four years or less, is subject to approval by the Bundesbank. At present, this consent is being withheld.

A potential means of control of external capital flows under the Law on Foreign Economic Relations is the *bardepot*, which is a reserve requirement to be paid by German residents of up to 100 per cent on loans or other forms of credit from non-residents. Although not in force since 1974, this cash deposit system could be restored to deter the import of capital.

Investment by foreigners in West Germany is also affected by the minimum reserves required by the Bundesbank. These minimum reserve ratios vary according to different kinds of liabilities (sight, time and savings deposits), the scale of the liabilities, and sometimes also whether they come from residents or non-residents. Moreover, minimum reserves may be applied not only to the average level but also to the growth of these liabilities and in the latter case may be extremely high. The possibility of differentiating between the reserve requirements applicable to non-residents and residents gives the authorities the opportunity to influence capital inflows; for instance the placing of deposits up to four years with a bank in Germany may be made less attractive to the foreigner because the interest rate which the bank can afford to pay is reduced by the high reserve requirement which may be imposed.

As an operational device the reserve requirement on non-resident deposits or other assets with German banks in Germany is to some extent not successful. The obvious effect is to reduce the interest rate which banks can afford to pay. However, German bank balance sheets in Luxembourg or elsewhere outside Germany are not subject to these reserve requirements. Thus the effect is that any foreigner wishing to hold deutschemark deposits does so in the euromarket and mainly in Luxembourg, and the interest rate obtainable there will reflect a wide variety of facts, including that the German banks there do not have to bear the same reserve costs as in Germany.

WITHHOLDING TAX AND INVESTMENT INSTRUMENTS

Although German regulations permit non-residents to hold certain assets – domestic fixed-rate securities denominated in deutschemarks with a remaining life of more than four years – a consideration to be kept in mind is the tax position and in particular that regarding withholding tax. On 25 March 1965 a 25 per cent withholding tax was introduced to be deductible on interest payments to non-residents. In certain cases, according to the tax treaty between the country of the foreign holder and West Germany, some or all of this withholding tax may be recovered. However, for the 'pure' international investor this tax position is a significant deterrent to investment in the German financial market. At the end of 1977 foreign investment in German domestic bonds was estimated at DM19.8bn, only 4.7 per cent of all such bonds outstanding.

According to the German tax regulations no withholding tax is levied on interest payments to non-residents for promissory notes (*Schuldscheindarlehen*) and global certificates (*Globalurkunde*). Of these by far the most important are promissory notes which are used extensively in international financing. An investor in deutschemark securities, faced with an absence of a double taxation agreement, has basically a choice between international (foreign and euro) deutschemark bonds and promissory notes. Promissory notes at a fixed interest rate are issued, as a medium or long-term loan (maturities vary from one to fifteen years) by a wide variety of borrowers, including the Federal and State governments, specialist banks and industrial companies. They resemble a syndicated issue with institutional investors in the private market and take the form of a document, issued and signed by the borrower, confirming receipt of a certain amount on specified terms and conditions. A minimum of DM1m is generally raised in this way, rising to as much as DM100m or more. The borrower usually seeks the funds from institutional investors such as insurance companies, pension funds, building societies and banks. The notes may be placed directly with the lender, or indirectly through a broker or bank, in which case they may be syndicated or refinanced by the ultimate holder. Transfer of promissory notes is effected by the assignment of the claim, in some cases with certain restrictions as to the number of times this may be done. They are not traded on a bond exchange, but there is a market among banks and institutional investors. It is an extremely flexible financial instrument which has achieved very wide usage because of its legal simplicity and its favoured tax status in the international markets.

THE EUROCURRENCY MARKET

On the eurocurrency market the deutschemark has now comfortably achieved the position of being the most important currency after the dollar. Deutschemark deposits, mainly in Luxembourg, are about a fifth of the total eurocurrency market as reported by the Bank for International Settlements (BIS), and this compares with the dollar figure of about two-thirds. The share has not increased drastically over the most recent period, but its growth has kept pace with dollar activity.

TABLE 3.6: Foreign Currency Position in the European Sector of the Euromarket (*$ billion*)

	1974	1975	1976	1977	1978
Dollars	156.2	190.2	224.0	268.4	339.5
Deutschemarks	35.0	41.6	48.7	70.4	97.4
Swiss francs	14.4	15.4	17.9	23.6	27.9
Other	9.6	10.9	14.7	22.4	37.2
Total	215.2	258.1	305.3	384.8	502.0

Source: Bank for International Settlements, *Quarterly Press Release on International Banking Developments* (June 1979).
Note: Figures are 'end year'.

A recent development in the attitude of the German authorities towards the eurocurrency market is the mounting pressure they are beginning to exert for co-ordinated international action to control the huge expansion of international credit it generates. They wish to know, and if necessary to limit, the size of the international risks of the banks; but they also believe that regulation of the market must be an essential ingredient of any genuine strategy to stabilise the dollar. The attraction of such control, which is clearly a long-term aim, is that it would reduce the magnitude of operations by the Bundesbank (and other central banks with strong currencies) to support the dollar, and increase correspondingly the control of such central banks over their domestic money supply. Some DM12bn net was spent in 1978 by the Bundesbank in dollar support operations, resulting in a much faster expansion of the German money supply than the authorities would have liked.

THE DEUTSCHEMARK AS A RESERVE CURRENCY

Table 1.3 (see p. 4) showed the change over the past few years in the general composition of foreign exchange reserve holdings. Table 3.7 concentrates specifically on the deutschemark and its share of the total.

TABLE 3.7: Deutschemark Component of Foreign Exchange Reserves, 1970–7
(*$ million equivalent*)

	1970	1971	1972	1973	1974	1975	1976	1977
Deutschemark	738	1975	3800	6339	6776	6839	8590	11995
Total reserves	35595	66685	83012	95188	114586	114107	126642	173112
DM as percentage of total	2.1	3.0	4.6	6.7	5.9	6.0	6.8	6.9

Source: IMF Survey (22 May 1978).
Note: Data relate to seventy-six reporting countries. Figures are 'end year'.

Table 3.8 gives the foreign exchange portfolio composition of different sorts of countries in 1970 and 1977 indicating the growing role of the deutschemark.

The big growth in the deutschemark's importance as a reserve asset took place between 1970 and 1973, with its share rising from 2.1 to 6.7 per cent over that period. At the end of 1977 the ratio was only slightly greater at 6.9 per cent. Nevertheless, the absolute value of deutschemark reserve holdings increased over sixteen-fold over the whole period, to the equivalent of $12.0bn. In comparing the different groups of countries, we see that those with their largest proportion of deutschemarks in their reserve assets at the end of 1977 were basket peggers and sterling peggers. On average, countries in the European 'snake', those pegged to the dollar or floaters had much smaller proportions of deutschemarks in their reserves – in each case less than 10 per cent.

During 1978 significant flows of central bank money into deutschemark bonds and deposits were reported by bankers in Germany and Luxembourg. The methods of acquiring such assets include direct participation in the euro-deutschemark market, and with interest much

TABLE 3.8: Foreign Exchange Portfolio Composition of Official Holdings
(*$ million*)

Exchange arrangements (number of countries)	Dollars	Sterling	DM	Other
	31 December 1970			
Floaters (11)	11672	264	409	593
(percentage of total)	90.2	2.0	3.2	4.6
Snake (6)	10471	10	38	904
(percentage of total)	91.7	0.1	0.3	7.9
US dollar peggers (27)	3519	385	38	282
(percentage of total)	83.3	9.1	0.9	6.7
Sterling peggers (4)	116	487	2	68
(percentage of total)	17.2	72.4	0.2	10.1
Basket peggers (21)	2479	2055	174	743
(percentage of total)	45.5	37.7	3.2	13.6
	31 December 1977			
Floaters (11)	58539	746	3422	6481
(percentage of total)	84.6	1.1	4.9	9.4
Snake (6)	41057	12	563	1747
(percentage of total)	94.7	0.0	1.3	4.0
US dollar peggers (27)	20355	309	2022	1998
(percentage of total)	82.5	1.2	8.2	8.1
Sterling peggers (4)	1114	393	547	445
(percentage of total)	44.6	15.7	21.9	17.8
Basket peggers (21)	16452	1043	5066	7043
(percentage of total)	55.6	3.5	17.1	23.8

Source: *IMF Survey* (22 May 1978).

less selective than it used to be buying has taken place across the quality and maturity range. Even some Group of Ten countries have been subscribing on occasion to deutschemark issues, breaking their undertaking not to invest currency reserves in the euromarket. Central banks have taken on increasing amounts of promissory notes issued by German borrowers. The borrowers on deutschemark bonds are mainly governments or state agencies, who must be tempted to keep the deutschemarks obtained. They are required by the Bundesbank to convert the proceeds of deutschemark bonds into dollars or some other currency immediately after the issue has been completed, but it is always possible to reconvert back into deutschemarks if these are held in some financial centre over which the Bundesbank has little knowledge and less influence.

Central bank participation on the deutschemark deposit market in

Luxembourg is reported as having been considerable during 1978, with one of the German banks believed to have at one time over DM3bn ($1.5bn) of such deposits. Another bank is reported to have deutschemark deposits from about forty central banks. The Bundesbank's powers to stop the increasing use of the deutschemark as a reserve asset are fairly limited, particularly because of their lack of control over developments in the euromarket, including both the deposit market and the longer-term capital market.

EXCHANGE RATE PROTECTION

The main defences against exchange rate speculation which would exacerbate upward pressure on the deutschemark have been mentioned in the course of this chapter. Four separate major techniques of control may be identified. (i) Laws prohibiting access of non-residents to certain domestic markets, including the money markets have been widely used and are currently in force. (ii) The *bardepot* has also been used. This is a high reserve requirement on non-resident holdings of deutschemarks; the intention is to make it prohibitive for residents to import capital. (iii) The reserve requirement on banks' foreign liabilities to non-residents has also been varied from the domestic reserve requirement at times. (iv) The authorities have also controlled borrowing abroad by residents in order to ensure that they do not transfer their liabilities abroad, and thus exert upward pressure on the deutschemark.

It remains true that these measures have had only limited success and the deutschemark has appreciated to levels which are uncomfortable for the German authorities from other points of view. The difficulty of controlling in detail the currency purchases of the company sector has meant that leading and lagging can exert very substantial pressure on the exchange rate, and there is little indeed that the authorities can do to prevent it. Closer economic integration within Europe has so far had little effect upon the exchange control regulations applied to non-residents in the various countries. These measures were made more intense about 1972 and 1973, but were then relaxed following the currency uncertainty after the OPEC price rises.

BANKING

There have been substantial tightening of the surveillance of the German banking system and changes in the regulatory arrangements regarding banks since the Herstatt affair. The failure of that bank stemmed from substantial over-trading in the foreign exchange markets, and indeed German banks had been noted, if not notorious, for the scale of the positions which they had taken in the foreign exchange markets, particularly towards the end of the era of fixed exchange rates and for a short time afterwards. Other foreign currency losses took place at that time, although few of a sufficient scale to threaten the structure of the banks themselves. The rules regarding the scale of position that may be taken have been tightened considerably since October 1974. On 1 May 1976 amendments to the Federal Banking Act came into effect, increasing the powers of the Federal Banking Office in Berlin, and imposing stricter rules for licensing and reporting. The regulations include the provision that large credits are to be limited to 75 per cent of the lending bank's own capital.

Growth in the euromarkets, particularly that transacted by Luxembourg subsidiaries, combined with their strong position in the capital markets has given German banks the opportunity of consolidating their position among the leading banks in the world. Table 3.9 shows how the position has changed between 1972 and 1978. Given that most of their assets and liabilities are denominated in deutschemarks, an appreciating currency, it is not surprising that the German banks have moved up the league table of bank size in recent years and there is little in the current situation which makes it likely that this will alter significantly in the foreseeable future. This growth is reflected in the considerable expansion which has taken place outside the domestic financial scene. At present 35 banks are represented by 300 branches in the major commercial centres of the world. At the end of 1977 the volume of international banking business transacted by German banks totalled some DM220bn.

TABLE 3.9: Major German Banks: World Ranking by Assets

	1972	1978
Deutsche Bank	10	4
Dresdner Bank	21	9
Westdeutsche Landesbank Girozentrale	23	16
Commerzbank	38	20
Bayerische Vereinsbank	46	23

Source: The Banker: The Top 300 in World Banking: Annual Review (June 1979).

CONCLUSION

In conclusion, Germany is a classic case of a country whose currency is acquiring international and reserve currency status. In this phase a series of inter-related factors operate so as to bring the currency into international use and to strengthen the country's financial institutions in international competition. Because German exports require export credit, and hence create deutschemark debts for the purchasing countries, these countries exert pressure to be allowed to hold offsetting deutschemark assets, and thus to build up the use of the deutschemark as a reserve currency. Germany's balance of payments strength and relatively low inflation make the deutschemark attractive in the international banking and capital markets, and give advantages to banks for which it is the natural currency. The relative appreciation of the currency which occurs under such circumstances enhances the relative value of the capital of German financial institutions and hence increases their capacity for operating in world markets. Given Germany's liberal political and economic system and her close integration, financially and economically, in the Western economic system and in particular in the EEC, it would be very difficult to stop the further internationalisation of the deutschemark – even if that were the objective. The German authorities and financial institutions have so far developed German international financial policy in an adaptive, constructive and co-operative manner, and there seems no reason why this should not continue.

REFERENCES

Banker Research Unit, *Banking and Sources of Finance in the European Community.*
Deutsche Bundesbank, monthly reports.
Uwe Flach, *Investment Opportunities in the Deutschemark* (Investment and Property Studies Ltd., 1978). Conference, 19–20 June 1978.

4 Switzerland

INTRODUCTION

Switzerland has been somewhat unique in its response to the recent world recession, but the response is consistent with the rather exceptional structure of its economy and balance of payments. During the boom years of the early 1970s Switzerland registered steady real growth at about 3 per cent per annum, but inflation was increasing at a relatively rapid rate for that country, averaging over 7 per cent a year. The balance of payments was in current account surplus but at a low level. The exchange rate suffered some upward pressure, in line with the general upward pressure on European currencies.

TABLE 4.1: Main Economic Indicators, Switzerland, 1972–8

	1972	1973	1974	1975	1976	1977	1978
Change in GNP (%)	+3.2	+3.0	+1.5	−7.4	−1.3	+2.8	+1.0
Inflation (%)	6.7	8.7	9.8	6.7	1.7	1.3	1.1
Current account ($m)	+220	+279	+171	+2587	+3497	+3441	+5150
Effective exchange rate[a]	102	109	133	137	152	174	196

[a] National Westminster Bank calculations.
Figures are 'end year' (18 December 1971 = 100).

The inevitable sharp increase in the total cost of imports after the oil price rise thus hit the Swiss at a time when inflation was high by historical standards and the balance of payments not particularly strong. The effects of the OPEC action were likely both to increase the rate of inflation and weaken the balance of payments. This was indeed seen in 1974, although the balance of payments deterioration was not appreciable, partly because the rate of growth of the economy was also cut back to just 1.5 per cent. At this point the Swiss authorities decided that the appropriate policy objective was to eliminate inflation, and to this end they engineered a severe recession in the economy, with GDP falling by as much as 7.4 per cent in 1975. A further fall took place in 1976 and only slight growth in 1977. Inflation remained fairly rapid in 1975, but since then has fallen very sharply indeed and was negligible in 1978. Correspondingly, the balance of payments has improved very substantially, with annual current account surpluses averaging over $3bn in the period 1975–8. The strength of the balance on current account combined with low inflation has caused very substantial upward pressure on the exchange rate. This seems likely to continue, producing a further reduction in Switzerland's export competitiveness.

TABLE 4.2: Switzerland's Balance of Payments (*$ million*)

	1974	1975	1976	1977	1978
Exports, *fob*	11945	13609	15458	17990	23900
Imports, *fob*	13690	13177	14657	17736	23300
Trade balance	−1745	432	801	254	600
Services and private transfers, net	2055	2288	2852	3400	4550
Official transfers, net	−139	−133	−156	−213	
Current balance	171	2587	3497	3441	5150
Non-monetary capital	2436	2601	−822	1217	n.a.
Banking funds	−2160	−3653	−73	−3989	n.a.
Capital movements, net	276	−1052	−895	−2772	1770
Balance on official settlements	447	1535	2602	669	6920

Source: OECD, *Economic Survey on Switzerland* (April 1979).

The emergence of a very large current account surplus has been partly due to a steep rise since 1974 in exports of consumer goods accompanied by buoyant capital goods sales aided by substantial exports of machinery to oil-producing countries. This strong export performance is the more remarkable in having been achieved in the face of relatively slow growth in important Swiss markets and the rapid appreciation of the Swiss franc. The traditionally strong invisible sector has also contributed to the large current account surplus.

The main item in invisible earnings is income from investments abroad which have been financed out of current account surpluses. Switzerland has been traditionally a capital exporting country. Its markets have been geared to enable Swiss national companies to export

TABLE 4.3: Structure of Switzerland's Invisible Transactions (*$ million*)

	1970	1973	1976	1979
Overall balance on invisibles	922	2413	3620	4398
of which major items:				
Travel	479	834	984	1141
Investment income	707	1497	2132	2510
Other services	449	916	1392	1528
Foreign border workers' earnings	−216	−584	−784	−795
Migrants' remittances	−314	−565	−412	−400
Official transfers	−42	−125	−156	−212

Source: OECD, *Economic Survey on Switzerland* (April 1979).

domestic savings and to enable foreign nationals and companies to borrow the savings generated within Switzerland. The sharp improvement in the balance of payments in 1975 enabled the Swiss to re-establish capital exporting, and financial market policies were modified to enable this to take place.

While a current account surplus, that is an excess of domestic savings over domestic investment, is the fundamental condition for net capital exports, the market structures and their development have also been conditioned by other features of the Swiss situation. These are the ways in which monetary policy is implemented. Because there is little in the way of domestic liquid assets, such as short-term government paper, the foreign exchange market and the foreign liquid holdings of the banks are used substantially for this purpose. Considerable emphasis is given to tight control over the money supply, which implies control in particular over the official reserves as well as over domestic credit and other sources of domestic monetary expansion.

There has been enormous foreign demand for Swiss franc assets, as hedges against inflation, and the Swiss have needed to control particular markets in special and different ways in order to ensure that their markets are not abused and undue pressure not exerted upon the exchange rate. Nevertheless, despite the wide ranging and rigorous controls which have from time to time been applied there has been persistent upward pressure on the exchange rate, which has threatened balanced development and created structural pressures on the Swiss economy. In some cases these upward pressures have been accepted, but in others action has been taken to ameliorate the situation – for example by offering exchange rate guarantees for certain exporters. It is the

TABLE 4.4: Changes in Swiss Monetary Variables (*SwFr million*)

	1973	1974	1975	1976	1977	1978
Changes in amounts outstanding from corresponding period of previous year						
Monetary base	639	2670	1807	1836	1558	3936
Foreign assets	1768	−635	2353	2648	3979	5687
Holdings of securities	0	92	−88	60	495	−211
Refinancing credits	−557	2316	−303	2316	−4418	−2017
Other	−572	897	−155	−3188	−1502	−477
Percentage changes from corresponding period of previous year						
Monetary base	2.5	10.1	6.2	5.9	4.8	11.5
Money supply (M1)	2.1	1.1	5.9	8.1	4.1	22.6
Money supply (M2)	5.9	7.8	0.7	1.7	5.7	7.0
Money supply (M3)	7.6	6.0	7.9	7.5	8.2	8.9
Bank credit to residents[a]	8.2	7.4	4.3	6.5	7.8	7.5

Source: Swiss National Bank, *Monthly Bulletin*.
Note: [a] Data relate to 71 banks with assets of over SwFr100m; figures are 'end year'.

conjuncture of these separate elements, allied particularly to the Swiss devotion to a liberal economic system and their unique constitutional structure, which sets the background parameters within which the development of their international financial policy and their international financial markets have taken place.

MONETARY POLICY

The underlying basis of monetary policy in Switzerland shows certain features distinct from those in most other industrialised countries. In the first place there is the need to operate extensively through the foreign exchanges. For this reason monetary policy links specifically with the international capital markets. In recent years the Swiss have decided to maintain strict control over the rate of monetary expansion, with firm guidelines for monetary growth, which means in turn firm guidelines for growth of the monetary base – the stock of central bank money. Thus in the context of the desire to control the monetary base and the need to operate through the foreign exchange market, it becomes vital to the Swiss to ensure an adequate capital outflow at times of strong short-term inflows, with the twin aims of relieving upward pressure on the exchange rate and minimising the effect on the monetary base of the current surplus or currency inflow. The structure of the international financial markets in Switzerland is thus intimately bound up, in a direct quantitative sense, with the Swiss approach to monetary policy.

A further unusual feature of Swiss monetary policy is that it is controlled in ways which may appear illiberal to people in other countries – for example the US. Demand on the domestic capital market, issues of foreign bonds on the capital market, the allocation of those bonds between domestic and foreign investors, and the growth of bank credit, are or have been for much of the time specified in direct quantitative terms. Allocation has been by rationing and not by price. For instance, the authorities have controlled the issue of foreign bonds by means of a ceiling on the total figure, quarter by quarter, so as to preserve monetary balance and also to avoid excessive claims on the capital markets when there are substantial domestic requirements. They have also announced ratios as to the minimum which must be sold to domestic investors. On the other hand the Swiss authorities have had limited control over the banking system in terms of legislative authority. The necessary measures have been implemented for much of this period by so called 'gentlemen's agreements' with the banks, rather than through direct legislation. These agreements between the Swiss National Bank and major Swiss commercial banks provided for the implementation of necessary corrective measures, such as adjustments of interest rates, maintenance of minimum reserves against foreign deposits, limitations on lending and the placing by banks of special deposits with the Swiss National Bank. While the 'gentlemen's agreements' have proved useful they have not been completely effective, and one of the key elements in the changing monetary situation over recent years has been the search for, and the achievement of, greater legislative power on the part of the central bank in order to cope with the increasingly serious upheavals in the world monetary system.

In the early 1970s the authorities were concerned with moderating upward pressure on the exchange rate and also dampening down the domestic boom. Up to late 1973 a series of monetary measures were adopted with these objectives in mind, based on the 'gentlemen's agreements'.

The emphasis of monetary policy was changed following the increase in the price of oil in the autumn of 1973, that led to considerable uncertainty in financial markets about the effect on exchange rates and national economies. The Swiss reacted with a package of anti-inflationary measures, intended to forestall any concern over the Swiss economy and currency, placing a premium on curbing inflation.

TABLE 4.5: Swiss Monetary Measures, 1972–mid-73

		Reserve requirements	*Bank credit*	*Legal powers*
5 April	1972	Based on a 'gentleman's agreement' of 16 August 1971. Minimum reserve requirements of 20% against sight deposits and 2½% against savings deposits were imposed on the growth of banks' domestic liabilities. This sterilised some SwFr1bn.		
21 July	1972	Reserve requirements on the growth in banks' domestic and foreign liabilities were increased, sterilising some SwFr1bn.		
24 July	1972		Based on a 'gentleman's agreement' of 6 September 1969. Credit institutions were requested not to allow a higher growth of domestic credit than would have been permitted under the agreement which expired on 31 July 1972.	
4 December	1972			Package of emergency measures included provision to increase powers available to authorities to combat inflation

16 January	1973	In light of powers granted on 4 December 1972, National Bank introduced a ceiling limiting expansion of bank credit up to 31 July 1973 to 6 % over permitted level on 31 July 1972.
1 March	1973	External pressures on exchange rate led National Bank to strengthen minimum reserve requirements against banks' foreign liabilities.
24 July	1973	Rate of credit growth in year to 31 July 1974 set at 6 % over the level allowed on 31 July 1972.

TABLE 4.6: Swiss Monetary Measures, mid-1973–74

	Reserve requirements	*Bank credit*
1 November 1973	Minimum reserve requirements on banks' foreign liabilities were increased to an average 72.5 %. A reserve requirement of 10 % was imposed on the growth in resident held time deposits.	
10 December 1973	Some modification of the requirements introduced on 1 November 1973 was implemented.	
31 January 1974	Minimum reserve requirements reduced to 60 % on both foreign and domestic liabilities.	
26 April 1974	Minimum reserve requirements reduced to 45 %.	National Bank raised permitted rate of growth in domestic bank credit from 6 to 7 % in year to 31 July 1974 (based on level of 31 July 1972).
23 June 1974	Minimum reserve requirements on domestic liabilities reduced to 33 %.	
25 October 1974	Minimum reserve requirements on domestic liabilities reduced to 20 %.	
25 November 1974	Minimum reserve requirements on growth of domestic liabilities reduced to zero.	

On 3 October 1974 the National Bank clarified its policy towards both the domestic monetary markets and the external markets by announcing that its twin objectives were to keep the 'primary liquidity' of the Swiss banks near the existing level of about SwFr5bn, and at the same time to whatever extent possible to keep the interest rate on 3-month euro-Swiss francs below that on comparable eurodollars. In other words Swiss monetary policy was intended to be relaxed in the external markets so as not to attract funds into Swiss francs, but not to be so lax domestically as to increase the inflationary potential. This policy was pursued further on 25 November when it was announced that as from 1 December there would be no minimum reserve requirements on the commercial banks'

growth in domestic liabilities. The difficulty of maintaining a single monetary policy with twin external and internal objectives was indicated early next year when on 7 February 1975 the National Bank was forced to increase the reserve requirements on the growth of liabilities to non-residents from 20 per cent to no less than 50 per cent (as from 28 February).

A departure in policy occurred in January 1975 when the Federal Council, in agreement with the National Bank, issued the liquidity and credit guide lines for 1975. The money supply (M1) was to be increased by 6 per cent (about SwFr3bn) and the monetary base by about SwFr1.5bn. This was the first adoption of formal monetary targets by the Swiss authorities. The ceiling on the growth of bank credit remained at 7 per cent but in various ways was to be operated somewhat more liberally than hitherto.

Noteworthy features of monetary policy over this period were the extreme severity of policy after the OPEC price rise, which caused a deep recession in Switzerland but also restored the balance of payments quickly and stamped out inflation. This meant that the authorities were able to adopt a relaxed monetary policy domestically as from 1976, with the intention of trying to help domestic industry. In view of the success against inflation there was little fear that this might re-kindle in-flationary expectations. Indeed it is significant that in 1977 and 1978 monetary growth was well in excess of the targets, but there was little expectation of increased inflation. The appreciation of the exchange rate helped to keep prices down, but the increase in the money supply would have led – on most monetarist theories – to potential increases in demand and prices. The restoration of the current account of the Swiss balance of payments, and the determination to maintain monetary targets as far as this could be done, meant that the authorities had to develop and increase capital exports of a long-term nature in order to give monetary policy a chance of succeeding. It is clear from Table 4.1 (which shows the effective exchange rate continuing to rise steadily) and Table 4.4 (which shows sizeable increases in the various definitions of money supply) that 1978 was a particularly difficult year for the authorities.

There was a major shift in monetary policy in 1978, with the Swiss National Bank giving priority to preventing too large an appreciation in the Swiss franc as against the objective of moderate monetary supply growth, a change necessitated by the weakness of the dollar in the exchange markets and corresponding upward pressure on the world's strong currencies. As a result the money supply rose steeply, by 22.6 per

TABLE 4.7: Swiss Monetary Measures, 1975–6

	Reserve requirements	Bank credit	Monetary target
9 January 1975		Ceiling for growth remained at 7 % (on base of 31 July 1972).	Formal monetary target set for first time – 6 % rise targeted for Ml in 1975.
7 February 1975	Reserve requirements on the growth of liabilities to non-residents raised from 20 to 50 %.		
11 April 1975	Reserve requirements on foreign liabilities reduced by some SwFr300m.		
23 April 1975		Ceiling on growth of bank credit lifted in view of success in achieving other policy targets.	
28 May 1975	Further reduction (some SwFr400m) in reserve requirements against foreign liabilities.		
5 January 1976			Target for Ml in 1976 set at 6 %.
2 July 1976	Pressure in foreign exchanges caused an increase in reserve requirements against liabilities to non-residents to be implemented. These were released in September.		
26 November 1976			Target announced of 5 % for Ml in 1977.

cent for M1, although a target of 5 per cent had initially been set. Although there is no official money supply growth target for 1979, M1 actually fell in the first five months of the year to show a year-on-year rise of only 7 per cent. Monetary retrenchment was made possible by the strengthening of the dollar which enabled the National Bank to sell the

US currency, sharply reducing bank liquidity, and the slow rate of credit expansion because of the sluggish domestic economy.

LEGAL POWERS

Over much of the period we are studying the basis for the actions by the authorities in monetary policy was an Emergency Decree of 8 October 1971 on the Protection of the Currency. It conferred powers on the Federal government to take any special measures it might consider essential as regards monetary policy in the country's general interest, and notably in order to limit the undesirable inflow of foreign capital funds. It included the power to impose negative interest rates on foreign funds and to declare the 'gentlemen's agreements' which so far had been negotiated with the large banks to be binding on all credit institutions. This emergency decree was extended by referendum in June 1972 for two years and in June 1974 for three years more.

On 20 December 1972 a separate key source of power in this field was established, a Federal Decree on measures in the field of Credit and Banking, which increased the powers of the National Bank substantially. The Bank received powers to impose reserve requirements on external liabilities, differentiating between Swiss franc and foreign currency liabilities; it also provided for a Capital Issues Committee, which was established on 17 January 1973 and had the power to ration the demand for credit in the main capital markets. The first ceiling on bond issues was announced in January 1973. In December 1973 the continuation until December 1975 at the latest, of the anti-inflationary package in force since December 1972, was approved by national referendum. However, in 1975 the government had the humiliation of a referendum held on 2 March turning down certain constitutional amendments designed to increase the economic powers of the Federal government and the National Bank. On 28 July 1975 the Federal Council sought a five-year extension beyond the expiry on 31 December 1975 of the powers of December 1972, and these were indeed extended by referendum in December 1976 for two further years with effect from 1 January 1977.

Intervention in the foreign exchange market also presented legal problems for the National Bank. Intervention was originally under Emergency Decree, but in September 1975 the Federal Council announced its intention of replacing the Emergency Decree by an amendment to Article 14 of the National Bank Law, which would give the bank permanent powers. In March 1976 Parliament approved the amendment, and on 1 July it became statutory law.

Depending on one's point of view these illustrations indicate both the strengths and weaknesses of the Swiss situation. In some areas the Swiss authorities have had fewer powers than their counterparts in other countries, but the extreme conservatism of the Swiss, including that of their constitution, is one of the reasons why they have achieved their economic and financial success.

CAPITAL EXPORTS

A variety of policy considerations have underlain the Swiss authorities' attitude towards fund raising in the domestic capital market, the main one being the importance of long-term capital exports in the control of monetary policy. It should be emphasised that there is no such thing as a euro-Swiss franc bond issue. All raising of long-term capital in the Swiss franc market, domestic and international, takes place under the same legal jurisdiction and surveillance. The international bonds are 'foreign' bonds, not 'euro' bonds. The various considerations facing the authorities have been, first, to prevent as far as possible the Swiss franc becoming an international reserve asset for governments and central banks, which means trying to discourage central banks from obtaining possession of Swiss franc bonds and other assets. Second, in as much as control of the monetary base and of the balance of payments requires capital exports, it is helpful to enable non-residents to tap the net supply of domestic savings. Third, the authorities have various priorities regarding approaches to the capital market, and in particular do not like to see the public authorities squeezed out of the market when private demand is exceptionally high. Thus they have desired at times to ration private claims on this market. Fourth, they see no reason to discourage unnecessarily foreigners acquiring Swiss franc denominated assets, as far as this can be done without jeopardising the balance of payments or monetary control. Such business can also enhance Swiss earnings from financial intermediation. The authorities have not discouraged the issue of bonds which non-residents may purchase, provided the proceeds are immediately converted into non-Swiss currencies. Under such circumstances the Swiss franc is being used purely as a unit of account.

The existence of the cartel of Swiss banks which traditionally has shared the underwriting and provision of finance for major public issues has always granted a certain gentlemanly air to the capital markets in

Switzerland. The desire of the authorities to obtain quantitative control over the balance of payments, the exchange market and the monetary base, has led to the authorities (in conjunction with the private sector organisations) to control by rationing the amount of funds, and their type, that may be raised. It is not difficult to understand why investors have been desirous of holding Swiss franc assets: in recent years the gain from the appreciation of these assets has far outweighed any reduced interest income. It is perhaps more surprising that borrowers have been willing to take on Swiss franc debt, because in many cases they could not have any corresponding Swiss franc assets to offset the exchange risk. Nevertheless there has, in recent years been excess demand for capital in the Swiss market to the extent that the authorities have felt the need to apply a system of rationing. In global terms the Swiss franc market is relatively small, taking into account the small population of Switzerland, despite its high income per head and high level of domestic saving.

Swiss capital exports reached relatively high figures in the early 1970s as a means of offsetting the influx of funds into Switzerland in the currency instability following the breakdown of Bretton Woods. The total increased steadily to almost $3.0bn by 1973. However, the balance of payments strain of 1974 and the changed monetary conditions caused

TABLE 4.8: Swiss Franc Capital Exports

| | Swiss Fr million | | | | Total |
	Bonds	Notes	Bank credits[a]	Total	$m[b]
1968	1009	470	1223	2702	628
1969	956	2207	2334	5497	1272
1970	806	1769	2260	4835	1121
1971	1917	4841	3652	10410	2562
1972	2903	3321	3110	9339	2444
1973	2877	3408	3170	9455	2982
1974	1011	2769	1876	5656	1897
1975	2355	7162	2482	11999	4650
1976	3420	10483	5167	19070	7628
1977	3700	9300	5400	18400	7625
1978	4400	9000	8500	21900	12262

Source: Swiss National Bank.
Notes: [a] Bank credits are a minority in currencies other than the Swiss franc.
[b] Dollar totals at average exchange rates for each year.

a substantial reduction in the long- and medium-term capital outflow, but there was a recovery in 1975. Since then, the capital outflow has increased massively as the conditions obtaining in the early 1970s have returned.

The long-term capital outflow has taken three different forms: foreign bonds, notes (or private placements) and bank credits, corresponding to the three markets which are especially open to foreign investors and borrowers. Swiss franc foreign bonds are issued publicly through the bank cartel and are normally of relatively high denomination and substantial scale. The amount which may be issued in any quarter is specified in advance by the authorities and is usually fully taken up. The issuing costs are relatively high, at about 4 per cent, compared with the eurobond market's normal maximum of $2\frac{1}{2}$ per cent and a much smaller figure in other markets, such as New York. Private placements account for a much larger proportion of total capital exports, nearly three times as much as bonds in the last two years. The notes are non-negotiable, and may not normally be placed with central bank authorities, except that certain types may be placed with OPEC monetary authorities. These placements are made privately without publicity of any kind and one of the advantages is that whatever competition there might be between this demand for funds and Swiss domestic demand does not become public knowledge at the time.

Both these financial instruments are subject to strict regulations, which may be changed from time to time, as to the proportion of funds which may be held by non-residents, and the proportion of the proceeds of the issue that must be converted immediately into non-Swiss franc currencies. These ratios may change at short notice, and are intended to produce an orderly market and ensure that the capital flows fit in with overall economic requirements.

Swiss franc bank credits also account for a larger share of total capital exports than do bonds. They are granted like euro-credits at floating rates of interest, for periods of over one year to non-resident borrowers, and are open to participation by foreign banks. Early redemption is not normally allowed and foreign banks must undertake in writing to the Swiss National Bank that they will hold their participations to maturity. As in the case of bonds and notes, regulations in force since October 1978 require borrowers to convert half the proceeds immediately into dollars through the central bank.

The monetary history of the past half dozen years indicates regular and substantial changes in the regulations surrounding the detail of these capital flows. By now, however, the system has settled down and operates on a substantial scale. Providing there remains demand for these funds from borrowers willing to bear the exchange risk, then both the general net supply of savings in Switzerland and the overall willingness of investors to hold Swiss franc assets should ensure a continuation of these markets:

SWISS BANKING

Switzerland's importance, particularly in the past two decades, as an exporter of capital, and its reputation as a safe and stable repository for foreign funds, have heightened its traditional role as an international financial centre. Banking now contributes between 5 and 6 per cent of GNP, and 1.2 per cent of the population are employed in that sector; these figures are exceeded only in Luxembourg. The country has a heavy concentration of banks with one branch per 1311 inhabitants, over twice the density of the UK.

Domestic business is more or less equally divided among the main categories of banks – the twenty-eight cantonal banks, the five large national banks, the regional and savings banks and the private banks. International operations are dominated by the five national banks – in particular the 'big three' of Swiss banking: Swiss Bank Corporation, Union Bank of Switzerland and Swiss Credit Bank (the other two are the Swiss Volksbank and the Bank Leu, both of which are smaller than the largest cantonal bank).

Foreign banks have been attracted in large numbers to Switzerland by opportunities to participate in eurocurrency business. There are some ninety Swiss-registered foreign banks (banks in which over 50 per cent of the shares are held by foreigners), a further eighteen overseas banks with branches in Switzerland and numerous representative offices.

Through their membership of the Cartel of Swiss Banks, the 'big three' handle virtually all underwriting of domestic issues and are the principal underwriters in the euromarkets. The size of their off-balance sheet fiduciary funds adds considerably to their placing power. Fiduciary business involves a Swiss bank making investments and accepting deposits in its own name but, by contractual agreement, at the risk of the depositor. In addition there is a large volume of asset management undertaken by the Swiss banks. Official figures are not available but a director (Dr Nicholas Baer) of the Swiss bank Julius Baer has estimated that each of the 'big three' Swiss banks is managing funds of between SwFr50 and 60bn. Thus, while the major Swiss banks do not rank particularly highly in *The Banker's* annual compilation of the ranking of banks by assests – Swiss Bank Corporation was 27th in 1978, Union Bank 32nd and Swiss Credit Bank 48th – their relative strength is understated. If security business and portfolio management were taken into account the Swiss banks would rank much higher. Against this background the 'big three' banks play an increasing role in placing borrowings not only in Swiss franc issues but in the international markets as a whole. It is widely estimated that about a third of all eurobond issues are now placed through these banks. Table 1.11 (see p. 11) shows that amongst international bond underwriters in 1977 these banks occupied second, third and fourth places, Union Bank of Switzerland and Swiss Bank Corporation having increased their standing sharply since 1971.

DEFENCE OF THE EXCHANGE RATE

The Swiss franc has been under risk of revaluation for much of the past twenty years, and the Swiss have for long been concerned to control the appreciation of their currency by appropriate measures to prevent inflows of foreign currency and to promote capital exports. By and large, these measures have not had the expected effect, and the Swiss franc has risen to an extent which has caused severe problems to certain of their industries. After the breakdown of the Bretton Woods agreement the Swiss franc joined the Smithsonian settlement, but by 1973 the upward pressures had become so great that the franc had to float. Since then there has been further upward pressure, varying according to the circumstances at the time, but it was particularly great in the latter part of 1978 because of the lack of confidence in the dollar and the realisation of Switzerland's outstanding performance against inflation, not to mention its stable political and social arrangements.

Within the markets themselves the main defence mechanisms have been to limit the markets in which non-residents may acquire Swiss franc assets; that is, to impose specific bans upon non-residents entering certain markets, and to create sharp dis-incentives to their entering others through tax and other penalties. One of the key controls has been the charging of negative interest on deposits in Swiss francs, with these negative interest rates varying according to the circumstances at the time. At the same time the banks have been forced to hold different ratios of reserve assets against changes in non-resident (as against resident) deposits, and in many cases these reserve asset ratios have been effectively penal.

In view of the possibility of traders avoiding the letter of the law on negative interest changes by engaging in forward transactions, the authorities have also controlled the volume of forward business that may be undertaken by the banks. In many cases the volume is linked with the amount of forward business outstanding at some past date. The authorities have also intervened on their own account in the markets from time to time using various techniques such as swap transactions with the banks.

The regulations regarding the import and exchange of foreign bank notes have also been amended from time to time, although this has been as much to give support to the efforts of the Italian government to prevent speculation against the lira, as to form a defence of the Swiss currency itself. The rules regarding the purchase by non-residents of Swiss securities have also been tight at times, as have those regarding the holding of currencies resulting from dealing transactions, and the period of time in which they may be held in Swiss francs. In January 1979 the Swiss authorities felt that upward pressure on the franc had eased sufficiently for them to lift the ban imposed in February 1978 preventing non-residents from buying Swiss securities; at the same time they lifted the restriction on the import of foreign bank notes.

In some areas the rules have been as much related to domestic political problems as to the defence of the franc itself; the question of control of Swiss companies and in particular the purchase of Swiss real estate touch domestic political nerves to the extent that many other transactions in Swiss assets do not. Operations of non-residents in these markets have been tightly controlled with few periods of relaxation.

EXPORT HELP

The obverse of the defence of the franc against pressures for appreciation has been the mitigation of structural effects on different sectors of industry. These structural effects have, in particular, made it much more difficult for Swiss exporting industries to compete in world markets, and certainly made Switzerland less competitive as a tourist centre. Thus a system of exchange rate guarantees for exporters was established in 1975, on lines somewhat parallel to those implemented by many other OECD countries in the period of flexible exchange rates. In addition special government guarantees have been given to certain industries, such as the hotel industry, and a new scheme has recently been announced for more industries to be included; watches and some parts of engineering are in this group. Favourable rates for medium and long-term export financing and special terms for re-discounting export paper for consumer goods have also been extended since 1975. It is doubtful whether the totally free play of market forces necessarily produces the best of all possible worlds, and this action to mitigate the structural effect of the movement of the Swiss franc seems perfectly defensible. The adjustment process in Switzerland was made much easier for the resident population to the extent that much of their labour force previously comprised guest workers from abroad, notably from Italy and Yugoslavia, and many of these simply went home when economic conditions deteriorated in 1974. Thus unemployment in Switzerland has not become as serious as in many other countries.

THE SWISS FRANC AS A RESERVE CURRENCY

On 28 February 1972 banks were reminded that official policy continued to be to prevent the use of the Swiss franc as an international key currency and particularly as a reserve medium. They were thus asked to report every few months to the National Bank on the amount, maturity, and geographic origin of Swiss franc deposits held by foreign central banks and other official currency agencies. Earlier in 1972 central banks had already been requested to reduce their Swiss franc holdings to normal working balances.

Because of the steady growth of the euro-Swiss franc market over this period, and of Swiss franc foreign bonds in circulation, it became very difficult to prevent central banks acquiring Swiss franc assets. The pressure from OPEC, and the fact that the assets of some countries are held in commercial as well as official organisations, made the situation more difficult to control. Nevertheless, the latest figures (see Table 1.3, p. 4) indicate that world-wide central bank holdings of Swiss franc assets as reserves are relatively small. The Swiss are effective in keeping foreign central banks out of their domestic money markets, not least because there are very few suitable money market instruments in circulation which they might wish to acquire. Central bank reserve holdings thus have to go largely into the euro-Swiss franc deposit market, or into the longer-term capital markets.

EXCHANGE CONTROL

The main foreign exchange problem facing the Swiss authorities has been the steady upward pressure on the exchange rate which they have tried to counter by appropriate measures to prevent inflows of foreign currency and to promote capital exports. Almost throughout this period pressure has been upward. Major measures to restrain the Swiss franc's rise have been imposed in late 1973, early 1975, in summer 1976 and in both spring and autumn of 1978. By and large these measures have failed; the Swiss offer the world the 'product' of financial stability. The essential point is that unless the Swiss authorities intend to pursue a policy which produces inflation rates more in line with those of other countries, Switzerland must be a natural haven for financial assets and the exchange rate will appreciate. The Swiss franc has risen well beyond what is regarded as desirable by the Swiss authorities, which causes severe problems to certain of their industries, although in general the current account is still very strong.

The controls have two main objectives: to prevent inflows of foreign currency and to promote capital outflows. On the inflow side there have been a series of measures to discourage the holding of Swiss franc securities and deposits. As from July 1972 (with only a one month break in 1974) foreign and fiduciary accounts invested in Swiss francs earn no interest beyond their totals at the end of 1974, apart from small increases which are allowed per family. From 1 April 1978 the ceiling on which interest could be earned was reduced by 20 per cent. Negative interest has been charged on foreign Swiss bank accounts for much of the period, with the negative interest moving to penal rates at times of severe speculation against the Swiss franc. From March 1978 these rules also applied to foreign central bank deposits. The negative interest rate was 2 per cent per quarter from July 1972 to October 1973, when the rule was relaxed. It was then applied at 3 per cent per quarter from November 1974 to January 1975, and since then has been at the extremely high level of 10 per cent per quarter. As from July 1972 there has been a ban on any increases in Swiss franc fiduciary accounts.

Since February 1975 there have been limits on the sales of forward Swiss francs to foreigners, with the permitted volume being reduced below the level outstanding at a previous date, the end of October 1974. The permitted volume was initially set at 70 per cent of that level, and was then reduced at the end of October 1975 to 60 per cent and in June 1976 to 50 per cent. In September 1977 there was a further reduction on short-term contracts, which was then lifted in February 1978. Daily balancing of each bank's overall foreign currency position has also been required, incorporating at times daily balances in positions in each currency. The daily balancing of each bank's overall foreign currency position was introduced in July 1972 and has been retained throughout much of this period. From June 1976 the banks were involved in a 'gentleman's agreement' with the National Bank that their subsidiaries abroad should avoid transactions with speculative buyers. The banks concerned undertook not to make deposits from Switzerland in euro-Swiss francs or to make placements in Swiss francs for the account and in the name of their subsidiaries or branches.

Swiss companies are also in the exchange control code in that since July 1972 they had been required to obtain permission before borrowing money abroad above a certain minimum amount, with the intention of preventing them from deserting the Swiss capital market for currency reasons.

Controls over investment by foreigners in Swiss securities have been imposed from June 1972; they were relaxed in 1974 and then re-introduced in toughened form in February 1978 when any sale of Swiss securities required immediate conversion of the proceeds into foreign currency. (This latter rule was relaxed in October 1978 simply so as not to prevent all security switching.)

The rules on long-term capital exports have been covered largely in the section discussing the bond market. The most recent rules are that since October 1978 private placements for foreigners must have a fixed maturity (preventing early redemptions increasing the pressure on the franc). Since March 1975 the banks have had to report capital repayments by foreign borrowers.

A separate but related factor has been the desire to control the foreign exchange market, stemming partly from the problems caused by the Herstatt affair. Since January 1976 the banks have had to report their foreign currency positions, both spot and forward, monthly, and for big banks, weekly. Daily reporting of foreign exchange turnover in excess of SwFr15m per day was introduced in September 1976. On a voluntary basis since March 1975 the Swiss banks and multinational companies have reported individual spot and forward transactions of more than $5 million. Under a 'gentleman's agreement' of April 1976, lasting until March 1978, Swiss multinationals have been expected to indicate their forecast capital flows over the following month, and to report once a year on the amount of foreign currency that could be repatriated. This measure did not in the end work out successfully, but it was designed to give the authorities greater understanding of currency flows.

There have also been repeated changes in the regulations regarding other assets in Switzerland, such as real estate. Distinctions here were drawn between residents and non-residents, alien non-residents and non-residents of Swiss nationality, registration requirements in different cantons and also the timing of the changes in relation to the business cycle. Relaxations, when introduced, have applied primarily to tourist resorts where construction is a vital component of economic activity. Moreover, the Swiss did not wish to turn away suitable prospective residents so the rule has been applied with considerable discretion. The rules have been relaxed for 'hardship' cases. But it is possible that the word 'hardship' means in this context not quite what it would elsewhere.

At the end of this period the authorities have not finally solved the problem of maintaining an exchange rate low enough to help their various industries, while at the same time satisfying their financial objectives in an open world economy, but are applying great determination in keeping the rate at an adequately low level.

The Swiss franc has floated since 23 January 1973 when the National Bank suspended its intervention in the exchange markets. In an attempt to reduce the upward pressure on the Swiss Franc, the authorities attempted to negotiate the accession of Switzerland to the European 'snake' arrangement in March 1975; however negotiations were abandoned in November, largely it is believed because of French opposition. Since October 1978 the Swiss have attempted to peg their currency to the deutschemark. At that time the Swiss National Bank made a fundamental change in policy to drive the Swiss franc down to a more acceptable level in relation to the deutschemark.

CONCLUSION

During the period under review Switzerland has retained a steadfast attitude to domestic and international economic policy, and has retained its unique features: the massive trust funds under management, large capital exports, a current account surplus, a very conservative political system and economic policy and a very strong position in the international banking and capital markets. Within this framework, which is vital to Switzerland's unique position among countries, she has not solved the problem of achieving balance between exchange rate policy and other monetary objectives. It remains to be seen whether the new objective of in effect linking the Swiss franc with the deutschemark can be achieved, and if so what the implications will be for Swiss inflation and the other elements of her unique financial arrangements.

5 Japan

INTRODUCTION

Japan's relationship to the world economy has changed, both industrially and financially, substantially over the past decade. The Japanese economic presence has become massive in most markets, and because of her industrial influence an entire re-thinking of financial policies has been necessary.

Over the past decade Japan has had three fairly well-defined macroeconomic periods. First, in the early seventies Japan was growing very rapidly and accumulating increasing current account surpluses. The main financial effect was upward pressure on the yen, which by and large the Japanese resisted as they wished the exchange rate to remain relatively low and certainly under control. The second phase began with the oil price rises at the end of 1973, when Japan was forced to undertake substantial adjustment policies in terms of both domestic demand and economic structure. Many of the previous detailed policies were reversed and Japan embarked upon a massive export drive. The domestic economy remained stagnant for over two years.

The third phase began when the Japanese had succeeded in reaching their objectives in response to the OPEC challenge, and began to achieve a massive presence in world export markets and large current account surpluses. In this phase the Japanese had to contend not only with considerable upward pressure on the yen, but also a structural surplus and had to consider policies such as capital outflows to use the net savings being accumulated. The financial surplus of the private sector moved steadily upward from 2.7 per cent of GNP in 1973 to over 9 per cent in 1978. In this phase too the structural problems within the Japanese economy, and in particular such industries as textiles and shipbuilding, became acute. As the seventies draw to a close Japan's macroeconomic policy is by most normal standards achieving outstanding success, but the structural features of the economy which will require attention are ever more prominent.

76

TABLE 5.1: Main Economic Indicators, Japan, 1972–8

	1972	*1973*	*1974*	*1975*	*1976*	*1977*	*1978*
GNP increase (%)	+ 8.9	+ 10.0	− 0.5	+ 1.4	+ 6.4	+ 5.4	+ 5.6
Inflation (%)	4.6	11.8	24.3	11.9	9.3	8.1	3.8
Current account ($m)	+ 6624	− 136	− 4693	− 682	+ 3680	+ 10918	+ 16500
Effective exchange rate[a]	102	103	95	98	104	125	152
Private sector financial surplus (% of GNP)	4.7	2.7	2.8	7.0	8.1	8.5	9.6

[a] National Westminster Bank calculations.
Figures are 'end year' (18 December 1971 = 100).

POLICY FRAMEWORK

In Japan government policy influences most areas of the economy, including in particular the financial markets. The Japanese have based their success on the growth of manufacturing industry and have regarded the role of the financial markets as almost completely subordinate to that. The Japanese financial market is the most regulated and protected section of the Japanese economy. In most financial markets the government attempts to specify essentially both the price (or interest rate) and also the quantity (such as of money, or loans or securities) which should be traded. The regulation is so detailed as to be almost inconceivable in London or New York, but these are being increasingly eased in certain segments of the market – notably the call market and the secondary bond market – and this process could well continue as pressures for change build up.

The economy has traditionally been subjected to the use of interventionist techniques to encourage desired developments, including the curtailment of imports, and the promotion of exports. In applying such techniques in order to retain a high degree of control over the economy, the Japanese have inevitably become regarded as pursuing traditionally somewhat illiberal policies. As Japan has become more prominent in the world, other countries have exerted greater pressure on her to modify some of her practices.

Two themes in particular have been persistently present over the past decade. First, Japan has come under increasing pressure to be a good neighbour and to liberalise her trade, and in particular imports. This policy would have the effect of reducing her balance of payments surplus to a more appropriate level. Second, there has been pressure for a more liberal policy on inward investment into Japan on the basis of reciprocity with the practices of other industrialised countries. This has indeed taken place in recent years as Table 5.2 shows and the Japanese capital market now offers an attractive opportunity for international investors to diversify their currency portfolios.

THE BALANCE OF PAYMENTS

Table 5.2 illustrates the composition of the long-term capital account and shows that Japan had a significant net long-term capital outflow up to 1974 that peaked in 1973. Direct foreign capital investments in Japan have always been relatively modest. The main year to year variation occurred through changes in security investments and other activities in the stock and bond markets. In these markets there was a net investment in 1971 and in particular in 1975, but heavy disinvestment in 1973 and 1974. (These features are discussed in greater detail in this chapter.)

Japanese capital movements were larger but equally volatile. Direct investments have been a significant feature since 1973, running somewhere near $2bn, and there have also been very substantial capital outflows in the form of loans, over and above those specifically identified such as in support of Japanese exports. In addition there have been substantial security investments abroad on certain occasions, notably in 1973.

The structure of the long-term capital account changed in reaction to the OPEC price rises in 1973/74. In 1975 and 1976 the net outflow from Japan was relatively small, less than $1bn in each year. The main element in this change was the net inflow of foreign capital, in excess of $3bn in each year, the bulk of this coming from security investments and bonds. In those two years the Japanese maintained their substantial direct investments abroad and also made significant loans, although security investments dwindled to negligible amounts. Since then the balance of payments has been displaying more the pattern of the early 1970s and there have been very heavy outflows in the form of direct investment and also from capital raising operations on the Tokyo market.

EXCHANGE CONTROL

Japan's economic policy has reflected the three different phases of this period: the heavy surplus in the early 1970s, the difficulty after the OPEC

TABLE 5.2: Capital Account of Japan's Balance of Payments (*$ million*)

	1971	1972	1973	1974	1975	1976	1977	1978
Foreign capital	1149	533	−1282	182	3120	3575	2063	2540
Direct investments	210	169	−42	202	226	113	21	8
Security investments	940	696	−591	−865	1518	1595	1256	1654
Import credits	8	11	−12	−6	−26	−5	−13	−19
Loans	20	−197	−313	−232	166	326	−324	−7
Bonds	8	−105	−198	80	1235	1509	1099	887
Others	−37	−41	−126	1003	1	37	24	17
Japanese capital	−2231	−5020	−8468	−4063	−3392	−4559	−5247	−14843
Direct investments	−360	−723	−1904	−2012	−1763	−1991	−1645	−2370
Security investments	−195	−1188	−1787	−141	−24	−146	−1718	−5351
Export credits	−863	−324	−1048	−672	−29	−571	−1388	−64
Loans	−594	−1684	−3038	−1136	−1295	−1525	−472	−6294
Others	−219	−1101	−691	−102	−281	−326	−24	−764
Net	−1082	−4487	−9750	−3881	−272	−984	−3184	−12303

Source: Bank of Japan, *Balance of Payments Monthly.*
Note: Minus sign indicates capital outflow.

price rises, and then the much greater confidence from 1977 when it was clear that Japan had responded successfully to the earlier challenges. We are concerned mainly with the structural elements of Japan's policy, and in particular with the capital markets, but policy has also had to accommodate different phases of the business cycle. There have been very substantial changes in exchange control regulations on a variety of subjects, in response largely to such influences.

Cyclical factors affect the finance of exports and imports, the application of quotas to trade and the amount of credit that may be offered on trade in both directions. The access of foreigners to the domestic market to purchase stocks and bonds, and correspondingly the ability of domestic investors and institutions to place portfolio investment abroad both varied with the position of the balance of payments. At the personal level regulations about permission to spend sums abroad such as for travel or the purchase of real estate, and the ability to buy and hold gold have changed frequently. The ability of non-residents to have free yen accounts, the limits on them and the reserve requirements placed by the Bank of Japan on the Japanese banks' liabilities in the form of free yen accounts have also moved with the state of the balance of payments. Similarly, the requirements placed on foreign banks in Japan for impact loans (which will be discussed later) reflect balance of payments requirements, as do the rules regarding pre-payment for exports and the use of advance export receipts. Another regular theme of policy concerns the rules for the holding of foreign currency deposits by residents in banks at home or abroad. These rules, and limits on the use and maturity of foreign exchange contracts, have been regularly amended.

There have been regular yen defence programmes, particularly in the earlier years, with the aim of controlling upward speculation against the exchange rate. The rules regarding the disposal of the proceeds of yen-denominated bonds, financing investment abroad and export insurance have also been changed with the fortunes of the Japanese economy.

To itemise the changes which have taken place since 1971 in these elements of policy would take up far too much space, and most of them are only of limited historical interest. There are many subjects over which the Bank of Japan and the Ministry of Finance exercise a detailed exchange control, and have been willing to change their policy significantly according to the conjuncture of the time.

MAIN STRUCTURAL FEATURES

In order to understand clearly the structural changes in the financial markets in recent years it is important to realise that the Japanese have made one major policy decision of key importance over this time. During the period up to 1973 the Japanese made various yen defence arrangements to ensure that upward pressure on the exchange rate was under control. Similarly, after the oil price rise when Japan thought it desperately important to restructure the economy and regain her export trade to improve the balance of payments, it was also vital to keep down the value of the yen so as to ensure manufacturing competitiveness. But when Japan had achieved a strong current account position – reflecting in large measure the export strength of the manufacturing sector – concern over the exchange rate became somewhat more limited. Japan has accepted the position of being a strong currency country and the implication that the structure of world manufacturing trade will change so that other Southeast Asian countries will assume some of her markets. Japan has also accepted that it is not consistent to try to control inflation through a tight monetary policy, unless the exchange rate is allowed to appreciate at the same time. Thus, while it is undoubtedly true that the Japanese do not wish to see the yen go forever higher, they have to a large extent accepted the responsibilities and economic implications of being a hard currency country with a very mature industrial stock. They have taken steps accordingly to restructure direct investment and their financial markets to respond to this situation. The following analysis of the structure of the financial markets should be viewed against the substantial change in Japanese attitudes which took place once it had become clear that they had successfully faced the challenge put to them by OPEC.

SAMURAI BONDS

Table 5.3 shows the massive increase in recent years in Japanese foreign bond issues; their volume is now comparable with that of the dollar and other hard currencies, notably the deutschemark and the Swiss franc. These bonds are a major feature of the restructuring of the Japanese balance of payments. They have also become a very significant source of supply in the world's long-term capital markets.

In December 1970 the first foreign borrower, the ADB, used the Tokyo yen market to raise 6bn yen. Since then borrowers have included

TABLE 5.3: New Foreign Bond Issues, 1975–8 (*$ million*)

	1975	1976	1977	1978
US dollar	6462	10604	7428	5795
German mark	1089	1288	2181	3789
Swiss franc	3297	5359	4970	5698
Dutch guilder	182	597	211	385
Japanese yen	67	226	1271	3826
Other	248	116	144	671

Source: Morgan Guaranty, *World Financial Markets* (March 1978 and June 1979).

such international names as the World Bank, the EIB and the ADB on several other occasions plus sovereign risks and entities such as the Province of Quebec. Table 5.4 indicates the earlier issues up to December 1976. For reasons of space later borrowings are excluded.

TABLE 5.4: Yen-denominated Foreign Bonds

		Amount (yen bn)	Coupon rate (% per annum)	Period (years)
ADB	Dec. 1970	6	7.40	7
IBRD	June 1971	11	7.75	10
IBRD	Oct. 1971	12	7.50	10
ADB	Nov. 1971	10	7.40	7
IBRD	Feb. 1972	15	7.40	10
ADB	May 1972	10	7.30	10
Australia	July 1972	10	6.90	10
IBRD	Aug. 1972	20	7.00	15
Quebec	Sept. 1972	10	6.90	12
IBRD	Dec. 1972	20	7.00	15
IBRD	July 1973	20	7.50	15
Mexico	Aug. 1973	10	7.90	12
Brazil	Nov. 1973	10	8.25	12
Finland	July 1975	10	9.25	12
New Zealand	Nov. 1975	10	9.00	12
ADB	Mar. 1976	15	8.70	12
Mexico	June 1976	10	9.00	10
EIB	Aug. 1976	10	8.90	12
Brazil	Oct. 1976	10	9.00	10
Denmark	Nov. 1976	10	9.00	12
Singapore	Dec. 1976	10	8.90	12

Source: Yamuichi Securities Co. Ltd.

The wide variety of later borrowers included some of those in Table 5.4 returning to the Tokyo market, several on more than one occasion, plus Venezuela, the Philippines, Argentina, Malaysia, the Korean Development Bank, Spain, Norway, Sweden, the French Railways, other Canadian Provinces and the Inter-American Development Bank. In 1979 the issuing of Samurai bonds was extended to private foreign corporations. The first such issue – for the yen equivalent of $100m – was raised by Sears, Roebuck and Co. in February of that year.

The market is not attractive or available except to first-class international borrowers. The borrowers must be aware of the exchange risk they are taking, and it would be inadvisable for companies to borrow in this market unless they had substantial yen proceeds or assets. In many cases borrowers will not be particularly pleased with the exchange costs they have borne so far; however, provided that not too large a proportion of their borrowing comes from this market – as is almost certainly the case – and some of their other borrowing has been in a better currency from their point of view, the damage could be limited. Moreover, one of the main purposes of making an issue in a market such as this is to achieve credibility and the chance of using the market at a later stage. In the short term these objectives may well override the desire for an initial loan to be commercially as attractive as possible.

Maturities in this market are normally lengthy, although a Norwegian issue in 1978 had a maturity of only five years. Few issues are for under ten years; there have been several of 15 years for the World Bank and many others at 12 years. Amounts have generally been about 20bn yen or less, but all but the first one have been at least 10bn yen with the largest single borrowing so far being 75bn yen for the World Bank in 1978.

By the end of 1978 the exchange rate had appreciated by some 33 per cent in relation to the dollar since 1976; thus the true cost to the borrowers of raising funds in this way has been very high, even given that the dollar interest rates have been significantly higher than yen interest rates for this form of credit.

The greater proportion of yen foreign bonds has been placed within Japan and a selection of issues illustrating the distribution of this placing is given in Table 5.5; this shows the constant proportion held by Japanese banks and other financial institutions. Holdings by individuals have amounted to around 40 per cent in each case. The table covers only the period up to 1976, and the position changed during the exceptional circumstances of 1978, when there was a very sharp rise in issue volume

TABLE 5.5: Distribution (by Holders) of Yen-denominated Foreign Bonds

	Banks (%)	Financial institutions (%)	Individuals (%)	Others (%)
ADB – first series	80.0	—	20.0	—
IBRD – first series	35.0	27.0	32.6	5.4
IBRD – second series	34.7	24.4	38.3	2.6
ADB – second series	34.4	22.4	40.7	2.5
IBRD – third series	33.9	20.3	41.8	4.0
ADB – third series	34.4	18.9	43.0	3.7
Australia	34.4	23.1	39.3	3.2
IBRD – fourth series	33.9	24.9	37.2	4.0
Province of Quebec	34.4	22.0	39.9	3.7
IBRD – fifth series	33.4	22.5	40.8	3.3
IBRD – sixth series	33.4	9.9	54.2	2.5
Mexico	33.8	18.5	40.4	7.3
Brazil	30.0	27.5	32.3	10.2
Finland	30.3	18.5	48.6	2.6
New Zealand	30.0	11.0	55.9	3.1
ADB – fourth series	34.6	12.2	47.7	5.5

Source: *The Banker* (May 1977).

(see Table 5.3) associated with the dollar's decline and the strength of the yen. Domestic absorptive capacity became strained and for some issues as much as 25 per cent (the maximum allowed to foreigners for new issues) was placed abroad.

One of the main issues which has faced the Japanese authorities in handling this market has been the need to prevent too much competition with domestic capital demand when the conditions were relatively tight: at times the foreign bonds have had to give way to domestic demands. Moreover, in order to avoid the use of the yen as a reserve currency – and taking into account that most of the foreign bonds are for official borrowers – the authorities have requested governments borrowing yen to convert the proceeds as soon as possible into other currencies, although there have been occasional exceptions to this rule, notably one of the earlier Australian issues. The market also, of course, has to be regulated in accordance with balance of payments considerations, but that is not an important factor for the time being.

Although recording substantial growth in recent years, foreign bonds still represent only a very small part of the total Japanese capital market,

TABLE 5.6: Number and Amounts of New Issues in Japan

	Financial year 1970/71		Financial year 1974/75		Financial year 1975/76		Financial year 1976/77	
	Issues (number)	Amount issued (yen bn)	Issues (number)	Amount issued (yen bn)	Issues (number)	Amount issued (yen bn)	Issues (number)	Amount issued (yen bn)
Government and municipal bonds	3201	2343	7913	7483	6252	10977	7313	13941
Corporate bonds	483	739	369	1303	479	1872	278	1259
Bank debentures	206	3173	218	6516	206	8080	204	9437
Foreign bonds	1	6	—	—	3	35	6	62
Total	3891	6261	8500	15302	6940	20964	7801	24699

Source: Bond review by the Bond Underwriters' Association of Japan.

TABLE 5.7: Amounts Outstanding in Japanese Bond Market

	March 1973		February 1978	
	yen trillion	%	*yen trillion*	%
Government and municipal bonds	17.3	53.9	57.3	63.8
Corporate bonds	4.1	12.9	7.8	8.7
Bank debentures	9.7	30.4	20.6	22.9
Foreign bonds	0.1	0.4	0.7	0.7
Other	0.8	2.4	3.5	3.9
Total	32.0	100.0	89.9	100.0

Source: Nomura Research Institute.

which is one of the largest in the world. Tables 5.6 and 5.7 show the number and amounts of new issues of various types of bonds in recent years in relation to total capital raised in the market and the proportion of total capital outstanding. In 1978 foreign bonds represented less than 1 per cent of this total. However, the effect of this programme of foreign borrowing has been to accustom many Japanese investors to international risks, and this has increased the acceptability of later offerings. As an indirect result the secondary market has improved, there being more participants and more stock available. Although most investment in the primary market is by Japanese organisations, the commercial banks in particular often sell their stock into the secondary market where it may in certain cases be acquired by non-residents. Most of these issues are quoted on the Tokyo stock exchange. As in the US and certain other countries Japanese legislation (represented by Article 65 of the Securities and Exchange Law) separates investment and deposit banking; thus issues are underwritten by the securities houses, with Nomura Securities playing a part in most issues.

Many issues have been placed in the Japanese market by private placement, and these have included bonds denominated in US dollars, Canadian dollars, French francs and some other currencies. This is one way of obtaining capital exports from Japan and the procedure is simpler than a full public flotation.

EURO-YEN DEVELOPMENTS

A further stage in the development of the international yen capital market was the first euro-yen issue by the EIB in April 1977. This was thought to solve many of the problems caused by the Japanese foreign bond market in that interest rates were allowed to differ from those in the Japanese domestic market, and the direct competition and crowding out problem in the Japanese domestic market could be avoided. Eurobonds may well involve no capital export from Japan itself, as far as many investors may be international organisations, who will be buying the yen with other currencies. The yen will be used merely as a unit of account, and the direct effect on the Japanese economy be relatively slight. The euro-yen market is still extremely small and there have been only two issues – by the World Bank and the ADB – since the EIB loan. A precondition for the extensive issuing of long-term euro-yen bonds will be the creation of a large-scale short-term market in yen, so that this currency can be used for trading and warehousing the bonds. The euro-yen currency market has so far expanded significantly, but it is still a very small part of the total international currency market.

The first syndicated yen loan was in November 1971 for the Inter-American Development Bank. The market reopened in December 1975 for the Republic of Indonesia and by mid-1978 issues totalled over 110bn yen.

TABLE 5.8: Selected Syndicated Yen Loans

Signed	Borrower	Amount (yen bn)
Dec. 1975	Bank Indonesia	15.0
Apr. 1976	Inter-American Development Bank	2.0
May 1976	Central Bank of the Philippines	15.0
July 1976	The Korea Development Bank	5.0
Sept. 1976	Banco Nacional de Cuba	5.0
Jan. 1978	Sonatrach	12.5
Feb. 1978	CIA Siderurgica Brasileira	15.0
Feb. 1978	B C Nacional de Cuba	10.0
Mar. 1978	CIE Nationale Algerienne de Navigation	15.0
Mar. 1978	Autopistas Del Atlantico SA	10.0
June 1978	Central American Bank for Economic Integration	2.5
June 1978	Agricultural Development Bank of Iran	10.0

Source: World Bank, *Borrowing in International Capital Markets* (various issues, 1975–8).

A major issue arising for the Japanese authorities – given the increased use of the yen internationally both in bank and bond markets – is that the activities of the Japanese banks, companies and securities houses, are becoming less and less under the direct control of the Bank of Japan and the Ministry of Finance. Although the banks accept substantial guidance from the Bank of Japan (as evidenced in 1978 by their refusal to participate in a eurodollar loan at margins which were too fine), the principle of loss of control over financial organisations, and correspondingly less control over the yen and the exchange rate, must arise inasmuch as the yen is used extensively outside Japan. This problem becomes more acute as Japanese organisations acquire substantial interests and investments elsewhere in the world.

FOREIGN INVESTMENT IN JAPAN

Foreign investment in yen-denominated assets takes three main forms. The first is investment in 'free yen' bank deposit accounts; the second, investment in yen-denominated fixed interest rate securities (both domestic bonds and yen-denominated foreign bonds); the third, investment in Japanese equities. There have also been convertible issues by Japanese borrowers issued in euro and US markets which are sometimes also included because of their link with the underlying Japanese equities.

There are no precise data available on the amount of yen-denominated assets held by non-residents. Estimates range from $5 to 7bn for non-resident free yen accounts. For yen-denominated bonds the cumulative total of net acquisations since 1972 amounted to $8.7bn by the end of March 1978, excluding short-term government securities. The calculation of figures for equity investment by non-residents is complicated by the difficulty of accounting for capital appreciation, but an estimate, subject to a wide margin of error, by Nomura Securities around the middle of 1977 put the figure at $4bn. All in all it seems reasonable to assess total non-residents' holdings of yen assets to be about $15–20bn.

Free yen deposits are the main vehicle available to non-residents for short-term investment in yen assets. The interest paid on such deposits is controlled by the Temporary Interest Rates Adjustment Law which sets maximum interest rates on different types of deposit account. There are other well developed short-term money markets, such as the call market and the bill discount market, but these are interbank and are not open to non-bank outsiders. Since 7 March 1979 the rapidly growing Gensaki Market, widely used by Japanese companies for bond transactions based on re-purchase agreements, has been reopened for use by foreign banks. Thus foreign bank branches in Tokyo may now purchase from specified securities companies government or government-guaranteed bonds or first class-debentures on a buy-back basis, at a fixed future date; this provides them with a profitable investment for surplus yen funds.

Non-residents' purchases of bonds for maturity of less than five years and one month in the Japanese bond market was prohibited since March 1978. Until then the interest of non-residents was mainly in short-term paper, whose short supply created dislocation from time to time. However, the ban did not curb the inflow of international funds into the Japanese bond market, since funds moved into the long end of the market as currency speculation continued in the following months. The ban was lifted in January 1979 in response to the weakening of the yen. Purchases of Japanese securities and bonds by foreign investors have been very volatile from year to year for a variety of reasons.

TABLE 5.9: Purchases of Japanese Securities by Foreign Investors
(*$ million*)

	Stocks			Public and corporate bonds		
	Acqui- sition	Dispo- sition	Net increase	Acqui- sition	Dispo- sition	Net increase
1968	393	177	216	—	—	—
1969	1467	790	677	—	—	—
1970	1020	864	156	98	55	43
1971	1579	1149	430	652	174	478
1972	2762	2410	352	507	250	257
1973	1699	2337	−638	222	241	−19
1974	605	1738	−1133	423	185	238
1975	2064	1472	592	2437	1513	924
1976	2960	3068	−108	2986	1274	1712
1977	2671	3446	−775	4853	2758	2095
1978	n.a.	n.a.	n.a.	10740	8276	2464

Source: Ministry of Finance, *Quarterly Bulletin of Financial Statistics*.

Investment in Japan has depended extremely heavily on expectations of movements in the stock market itself, which have of course been linked with cyclical events in the world economy, expectations in other stock markets, expectations about the yen exchange rate and the regulations and controls imposed by the Japanese authorities. This combination of factors has made for sharp movements between investment and disinvestment and fluctuations have often been substantial in both directions.

The Japanese authorities have steadily moved towards adopting the attitude that transactions in long-term equities and bonds should be relatively free because these movements are not a fundamental threat to the exchange rate. They are not an efficient instrument for short-term regulation of the exchange rate and, although large amounts of funds are involved, the leverage which may be exercised through them is limited. The authorities have thus been much more willing to allow freedom in investment in long-term assets than in short-term assets and in particular in the banking markets themselves.

There has, of course, been a correspondingly heavy acquisition of foreign securities by Japanese investors which has to some extent compensated for investment in Japan itself. The type of policy in effect has been regularly influenced by the state of the Japanese balance of payments, but in general the authorities have moved towards relative freedom from exchange control for outward, as well as inward, long-term portfolio investment.

TABLE 5.10: Investment in Foreign Securities by Japanese Residents (*yen bn*)

	Stocks			Bonds			
Year	Acqui-sition	Dispo-sition	Net in-crease or decrease (−)	Acqui-sition	Dispo-sition	Conver-sion etc.	Net in-crease or decrease (−)
1972	42	26	16	93	73	7	13
1973	130	76	54	151	73	9	69
1974	58	68	−10	36	61	46	−71
1975	82	81	1	13	9	4	—
1976	72	79	−7	16	15	6	−5
1977	32	28	4	172	19	31	121
1978	30	25	5	792	113	556	123

Source: Securities Dealers' Association.

INTERNATIONAL BANKS IN JAPAN

As a centre for international banks Japan has developed significantly over the period with which we are concerned. In 1970 there were only nineteen foreign banks in Japan, of which the longest standing were Algemene Bank Nederland (1920) and Hong Kong and Shanghai

Banking Corporation (1924). There was a gradual increase in numbers until 1971, since when a steady flow of banks into Japan has taken place and the total number of foreign banks is now (early 1979) sixty one. The vast majority of the world's major banks are present as well as some with special regional trading connections with Japan.

The foreign banks come under the same strict control as domestic banks, and in particular are subject to 'window guidance'. This control is operated to an extent hardly envisaged in Western countries, and in many cases the authorities indicate the amount or proportion of business to be done in particular markets, and also the interest rate at which this should be done. For the period April/June 1973–January/March 1974 the Bank of Japan provided guidance on the maximum amount per quarter of loan increases to major foreign bank branches. This step was taken because credits given by foreign bank branches had increased remarkably since the latter half of 1972, and it was thought that if left uncontrolled they could undermine the tight monetary policy. As the lending of the foreign branches became more moderate, after the period April/June 1974, the Bank began to loosen its guidance and in 1975 lifted its guidance of foreign bank branches completely as far as currency lending was concerned. Increases in yen loans are still controlled, at the time of writing, but on a monthly basis.

There is no foreign exchange market of the scale known in London or New York and spot and forward foreign exchange transactions are controlled very closely. The foreign banks bring their capital into the country in the form of a swap transaction which provides the banks with some free yen which may be used until the swap has to be reversed.

The limit on the banks' overall foreign exchange positions is determined on the basis of objective indicators, such as the scale of exchange transactions undertaken for customers. The limits, which are revised from time to time, are higher for foreign bank branches than for those Japanese banks conducting a similar size of foreign exchange transactions; this is in recognition of the fact that foreign bank branches have more active overseas business.

Foreign bank branches are allowed upon application to open current accounts with the Bank of Japan. Japanese and foreign banks have the same rights of access to the facilities of the Bank of Japan and both have to go through the same procedure of screening and a certain length of time before they are eligible to borrow from the Bank. Loans and advances are not normally accorded to foreign bank branches, as is also the case with most Japanese banks except city banks, although there is a facility of last resort. If foreign bank branches face a liquidity problem, they are able to borrow from the Bank of Japan; this has happened on several occasions in the past.

In operating the commercial bill market no distinction is made as to whether the bills are for local banks or foreign ones. On occasions when the yen was subject to depreciation, the foreign banks have sold very substantial amounts of bills much more than in proportion to their other business.

The foreign banks are encouraged to finance their activities in the financial bill market, rather than in the call money market where transactions are very short term and much more volatile. The possibility of foreign banks widening their yen resource base emerged early in 1979 when it was announced that in common with the city banks they would be given permission to issue three to six-month yen certificates of deposits. The move, made in the face of strong opposition from the long-term credit banks, the securities houses and Japan's sixty-three regional banks, should offer increased flexibility and better funding opportunities for foreign and local banks.

While the conversion of foreign exchange into yen by Japanese banks is in principle prohibited, foreign bank branches are allowed to make a net conversion into yen up to a certain amount (swap limit) that is increased from time to time (the last increase was in March 1979). This is determined for each bank on the basis of subjective criteria such as the scale of yen transactions with customers in Japan and the relative volume of the banking operation as a whole. This treatment stems from the recognition of their limited ability to obtain domestic deposits, as they are less competitive than Japanese banks when they first begin operations.

One of the major sources of business for foreign banks in Japan in recent years – and at times a significant means of financing the Japanese balance of payments – has been impact loans. These are long-term loans made to Japanese companies in foreign currency. The only currency used up to 1977 was the dollar, but now any currency may be used if approved by the Ministry of Finance. Impact loans are supposed to be used for capital spending, but there is a general suspicion in the banking community that they are used for operating funds and as a currency hedge as well as for capital development. Any foreign bank may offer foreign currency loans, provided it receives permission, but Japanese banks have been precluded from this type of operation.

For the Japanese company the impact loan may provide funds over and above those available from a Japanese bank. Such loans may also be cheaper, the pay-back schedule more favourable or the security demanded easier. Impact loans are closely controlled; each one is screened according to the law of 1953 on foreign investment and the Foreign Exchange Trade Control Law 1949. The monthly inflow from this source is regulated by a series of measures, of which the most effective is a ceiling on the total amount of impact loans that may be made. This limit is not published but is frequently changed in line with the balance of payments position. Thus the sharp increase in 1974 was attributable mainly to the oil shock and the resulting balance of payments problem. As the balance of trade worsened the Government encouraged capital inflows to improve the total balance of payments; they were willing to change the flow of funds to meet domestic needs. The quality of borrowers in this market is monitored, and is limited largely to the major companies. Any large company which is sound and can obtain a Japanese bank guarantee can usually eventually receive official approval for an impact loan. A new non-guarantee type of impact loan was introduced after the oil shock. This type is closely screened by the Ministry of Finance and amounts to about one-quarter of all impact loans granted each month (roughly $70m during 1978). Only the very strongest corporations have been allowed to borrow on this basis, and usually between 50 and 100 have done so.

Japan's position as a financial or banking centre seems assured. The vast majority of foreign banks make significant profits in Tokyo. The Japanese are fundamentally risk averters, and regard cordial relations with the main financial centres and institutions around the world as a precaution in case times should become difficult for them. They thus have no rooted objection to foreign banks and institutions being allowed to operate profitably in their markets: it is a kind of insurance premium. Nevertheless Tokyo is not an easy market for foreign banks. The local banks have very substantial competitive power in the yen markets, and have available deposits, particularly when times are liquid, which the foreign banks cannot match, or match with adequate prudence. Further difficulties arise at times of large balance of payments surplus, when the justification for impact loans seems somewhat less. The Bank of Japan closely controls the markets in which foreign banks operate. Nevertheless, the banks have been able to operate profitably and in any case would regard the Tokyo presence as a very important means of making contact with the head offices of the major Japanese companies that have multinational operations.

THE JAPANESE BANKING PRESENCE ABROAD

Japanese banks have remained relatively domestically oriented and international earnings have accounted for only 10 per cent or so of their total profits. The situation is slightly different for the securities houses which have been strongly represented abroad for many years and have much more globally diversified structures. The first stage of the internationalisation of Japanese banks was the facilities offered for foreign exchange transactions and short-term trade finance for the export–import business of the commercial houses.

From immediately after the war until about 1954 the major Japanese city banks opened overseas offices in key international money centres, such as New York and London, and established foreign bank relationships. In line with the policy then adopted by the Japanese Government few more overseas offices were opened until the end of the 1960s. But along with the rapid activation of direct investments abroad by Japanese enterprises since the early 1970s, Japanese banks again started positive moves towards internationalisation. This was the second stage. They created international investment banks in key cities in industrial nations in order to take part in medium- and long-term loans for Japanese enterprises operating overseas. Six leading Japanese banks made capital investments in the Banque Européenne de Tokyo SA which was opened in Paris by the Bank of Tokyo in 1968. The Associated Japanese Bank (International) Ltd was established shortly afterwards as a joint venture of several Japanese banks and securities houses, and the Japan International Bank was founded in London on a similar basis.

The third stage started in 1972 when the banks became independently involved in overseas consortium banks or with foreign multinational banking agencies – for example Mitsubishi joined up with the Orion Group and the Bank of Tokyo with Western American Bank. In this stage medium- and long-term loans were extended by Japanese banks not only to Japanese enterprises operating overseas but to multinational enterprises in Western countries, as well as to governments and governmental agencies of developing countries in the form of syndicated loans.

Overseas merchant banks were also established at this stage by major Japanese banks through links with Western counterparts: Sanwa Bank joined with Baring Brothers and the Fuji Bank with Kleinwort Benson. Through such a medium Japanese banks aimed at advancing into securities underwriting which, as mentioned above, is not open to them in Japan. Internationally the Japanese banks are intent on obtaining a diversification of financial resources for supplying funds for Japanese enterprises abroad, commission income and participation in groups of managers and underwriters. The Japanese securities houses have resisted this development, but the banks have forced their way into the markets.

In the fourth stage – from 1974– Japanese banks have advanced into the field of retail business in overseas markets by purchasing local banks as subsidiaries, such as in California. No fewer than 8 city banks featured among the top 25 banks in the world, ranked by assets in 1978, and a ninth Japanese bank was in 16th place. This achievement owed something to the appreciation of the yen against the dollar in the year in question but is nevertheless a clear indication of the significant internationalisation of the major Japanese banks during the 1970s.

Medium- and long-term loans of Japanese banks increased to $7bn at the close of 1973, compared with only $200m at the end of 1971. This rapid increase was principally caused by participation in syndicated loans as the Japanese banks extended their financing from Japanese companies to partake in a wider spread of loans in order to obtain greater profits: they were also aware that size is a very important means of determining the ranking of banks in the international league. After the Herstatt Bank failure, however, the Japanese banks faced difficulty because of their substantial roll-over requirements at a time when the eurodollar market was relatively weak. To prevent further difficulty the Ministry of Finance placed a ban in principle on the extension of long-term loans overseas by Japanese banks. This was later modified as conditions changed and by 1977 and 1978 the Japanese banks had a compelling need for international activities because of both their very low earnings domestically and the vast surplus of dollars with the Japanese Government. Strenuous efforts are being made and will be made to give the Japanese banks an orthodox and well balanced international structure, and the international divisions will be of greater importance in their own global banking situations.

INTERNATIONAL BORROWING BY JAPANESE ENTITIES

In the immediate aftermath of problems caused by the OPEC action in 1973 and the sharp swing into current account deficit, Japan began to borrow substantially in international capital markets through foreign and eurobond issues. Japan also raised significant amounts in the

TABLE 5.11: Internationalisation of Japanese Banks

Business operations		Branches, overseas subsidiaries	Representatives
1970	1st stage	(Mainly trade and other short-term financing) Banque Européenne de Tokyo SA (1968)	New York, London	European continent, West coast of US, South-east Asia
1971	2nd stage	Associated Japanese Bank (International) Japan International Bank and Investment Co., Ltd. (issues of medium- and long-term loans, eurobonds, CDs to Japanese affiliated firms) Investments in and joint ventures with merchant banks in Australia Purchasing of privately-placed foreign bonds	West coast of US	European continent, New York
1972	3rd stage	Participation in syndicate-loans (full-fledged advance to suppliers of medium- and long-term loans to multi-national corporations and various governments) Establishment of consortium banks	European continent	South-east Asia
1973		Investments in and joint ventures with merchant banks in London, Hong Kong etc. (advance to underwriting of medium- and long-term loans as well as to securities acceptance business)	South-east Asia	Brazil
1974	4th stage	Joint ventures with Arab-affiliated banks Bought into US bank in California Established overseas subsidiaries in California (advance to the field of retail)	Chicago	Mid-East
1975		Acting as associate underwriters in securities issuances	Establishment of new overseas branches banned	

syndicated medium-term market. Syndicated loan issues totalled just under $400m in both 1975 and 1976.

In the bond markets the amount raised by Japan increased from $246m in 1974 to $1.6bn in 1975 and $2.1bn in 1976. In 1977 and 1978 figures of around $2bn were again recorded. The substantial increase in recourse to the bond markets reflected not only the swing into current account deficit, but also the need for Japanese companies to have finance to pay for their investments abroad, and the difficulty they faced at that time in exporting capital from Japan to do so. Thus a further stage in the internationalisation of Japanese operations took place through this means.

In 1976 for the first time the amount of convertible stock floated by Japanese companies in the international markets was more than that in the domestic market. Coupon rates were attractive, with a wider choice

TABLE 5.12: Japanese Bond Issues in Foreign and International Markets

Market	1974 No.	$ million	1975 No.	$ million	1976 No.	$ million	1977 No.	$ million	1978 No.	$ million
Eurodollars	8	110	14	340	31	819	33	915	10	380
Deutschemarks	1	42	12	344	14	348	6	250	35	1050
Swiss francs	4	64	21	413	22	569	18	362	46	1130
US bonds	2	30	5	260	4	285	2	350	2	75
Other	—	—	10	230	3	50	—	—	1	25
Total	15	246	62	1587	74	2072	59	1877	94	2660

Source: World Bank, *Borrowing in International Capital Markets* (March 1978 and March 1979).

TABLE 5.13: Japanese Bonds and Eurocurrency Bank Credits in Relation to Industrial Countries' Total (*$ million*)

	1974	1975	1976	1977	1978
Japanese bond issues	247	1651	2008	1929	2787
Industrial countries total bond issues	5774	16056	23215	22826	22654
Japanese eurocurrency credits	326	332	368	68	86
Industrial countries total eurocurrency credits	17270	5069	8307	11055	30352

Source: World Bank, *Borrowing in International Capital Markets* (March 1978 and March 1979).

of terms and conditions, and there was greater flexibility, less dependence on bank loans and an increased variety and sources of funds. There was also the chance that any foreign exchange losses stemming from this borrowing might be avoided by the investors' conversion of their loan into equity.

In 1976 Japanese issues amounted to $2bn and accounted for 7 per cent of total international bond activity. The issues were widely spread among different currencies: $819m in eurodollars, the equivalent of $348m in deutschemarks, $569m in Swiss francs, and $285m in US bonds. The Japanese accounted for as much as 15.5 per cent of the Swiss franc market and 12.7 per cent of the deutschemark market. Many of the issues were for Japanese companies, for unlike the British or French governments, the Japanese authorities had no need to borrow in their own name in international capital markets. This phase in Japanese companies' history had the effect of drawing them further away from the Japanese government and away from purely Japanese nationalistic considerations. Japanese companies were becoming multinational.

YEN INTERNATIONALISATION

'Yen internationalisation' is a phrase which has been heard often in recent years but one which must be treated with some caution. The main reason for this is that the whole basis of Japanese policy in the post-war period has been to give priority to manufacturing industry and its interests. The major objective was to maintain the exchange rate at suitable levels for as long as possible. This objective was contrary to any idea of allowing purely financial forces to have too much influence over the economy and in particular over the exchange rate. Japan has now accepted that it must play the part of a mature industrial country with a strong exchange rate and low inflation, and provide the capital outflows that are appropriate to such a country. While this removes one of the main objections to allowing greater international use of the yen, there is still room for considerable doubt as to whether Japan will ever really wish to allow financial forces to roam too much unchecked.

The initial international development of the yen came in the long-term market, both inward and outward. Attempts were also made to use the yen for financing exports: at present over 90 per cent of Japanese exports and a similar proportion of imports are financed in dollars. The main problem facing this new policy in 1976 was simply that interest rates on that paper were too high at the time in relation to those that would be paid on financing in dollars. Thus there was no commercial incentive at that time for exporters and importers to shift their financing into yen.

A euro-yen market has also been created with yen deposits being placed in the international markets largely, but by no means exclusively, with the Japanese banks. There have also been syndicated loans in yen, although this market still accounts for only a very small proportion of the eurocurrency market. A disadvantage which the Japanese could face if this market became exceptionally large is that there would be the external pressure on domestic policy similar to that exerted on the US: that there is now some $600bn in the eurodollar market makes the task of managing the American economy significantly more difficult.

The main difficulties in using the euro-yen market are the inadequacy of the forward exchange market and the exchange risk taken by the borrower. It seems likely that for a considerable time ahead this market will be relatively thin without the widespread acceptance other eurocurrency markets have achieved. Nevertheless, providing there is willingness on the part of the Bank of Japan to provide the basic exchange control structure behind this market and allow it to operate, and providing international banks, particularly Japanese banks, are willing to give it support, then there is no reason why such a market should not develop steadily. It must be emphasised, however, that this market is entirely dependent upon the policies of the authorities in Japan: should their control cease to be accommodating then it would face extreme difficulties. It is not completely certain that the Japanese authorities view the long-term use of the yen in the short-term international markets on a major scale as desirable, and this must be a risk overhanging the market.

A further attribute of an international currency is its use as a reserve asset by central banks. Because the demands of domestic economic management and the international monetary system sometimes conflict, the Japanese have traditionally resisted any tendency for the yen to become an international reserve asset. In 1976 only 0.6 per cent of the official reserves of all countries were in yen, compared with 6.8 per cent for the deutschemark. The yen's status as a reserve currency, despite the size and influence of the Japanese economy, is thus comparable with that of the Belgian franc or the Dutch guilder. However, in recent years the authorities have adopted a more accommodating stance towards foreign central bank demands to hold reserves in yen and have sold, directly from the Bank of Japan's own holdings, government bonds to overseas central banks on several occasions. Despite this easing, the greater access for overseas borrowers in the Tokyo market and other signs of a less restrictive posture, only modest steps have been taken toward the full internationalisation of the yen, which in this regard is some way behind the deutschemark. The Japanese authorities have not entirely discarded their traditionally cautious attitude, although it is likely that the practicalities of international trade and finance will eventually result in much greater use of the yen in international transactions.

CONCLUSION

These last years have seen great changes not only in the underlying real economy of Japan, with its acceptance of the need to change its industrial structure, but also in the manner of thinking about the international markets and the policies that are required. Japan has now created the basic infrastructure for a strong currency based on a capital exporting nation. There is considerable parallel with the position of West Germany. Depending on the pace at which the Japanese wish to take this forward, Japan should be able to acquire new attributes in terms of the use and functions of the yen, without unduly risking unwelcome pressure. As far as internal policy is concerned the Japanese have now ceased the inconsistency which they pursued in the early seventies; at that time they thought they could both stop the exchange rate appreciating and tighten monetary policy as a means of curbing domestic inflationary pressures. Now they recognise that curbing inflation domestically involves letting the exchange rate appreciate and hence accepting the corresponding pressures. The Japanese strength, similar to that of West Germany in their industrial and their economic structures, is such that she can face with confidence this transition to a new phase of economic performance.

REFERENCES

A. Chiba, 'Japan's capital market reaches for maturity', *Institutional Investor* (November 1977).
N. Kagami, 'The new world economic order and Japan', *Annals of International Studies*, vol. VII (1976).
H. Moya, 'Euroyen bond issues: a growing market', *Finance and Development* (December 1978).
Nomura Securities, *An Introduction to the Japanese Bond Market* (September 1977).

Y. Terasawa, 'The Internationalisation of the Tokyo Bond Market', *The Banker* (September 1977).

Yamaichi Securities Co., *The Japanese Yen Bond Issue* (November 1976).

Bank of Tokyo, *Non-Resident Free Yen Account System and Yen Exchange*, pamphlet published March 1976.

R. Pringle, 'Report from Tokyo', *The Banker* (May 1977).

6 The United Kingdom

INTRODUCTION

The external financial policy of the UK over recent years has been very much affected by the country's historic situation involving the transition from a relatively strong economy with powerful links with the sterling area to a much weaker economy linked increasingly to the EEC. Changes have necessarily taken place regarding the links with the sterling area, in terms of sterling as a reserve asset, the limitation on the size of the sterling area and capital exports allowed to that area. The country's economic history, of relative weakness and substantial balance of payments constraints, has influenced the way in which external financial policy and exchange control have developed. Significant commitments to the EEC have been made in recent years, but the authorities have so far been unable and unwilling to adopt the full commitments of the Treaty of Accession.

ECONOMIC HISTORY OF THE 1970s

The UK entered the 1970s with a strong balance of payments position inherited from the later years of the Labour government of 1964–70, and the incoming government was able to apply their policies of monetary expansion and growth from a strong foundation. Growth was rapid through 1972 and 1973, but inflationary pressures were becoming increasingly evident, and the balance of payments was deteriorating significantly, partly as a result of financial pressures linked to excessive growth of the money supply. By the time the oil price rises took place at the end of 1973 the British economy was over-extended, with high and still increasing inflation and the balance of payments in substantial deficit.

This transformation in the economic situation coincided with a change of government, and in order to deal with massive labour unrest at the time the new administration decided to finance expansionary wage

TABLE 6.1: Main Economic Indicators, the UK, 1972–8

	1972	1973	1974	1975	1976	1977	1978
Change in GNP	+2.4	+6.9	−1.9	−1.4	+2.9	+1.8	+3.0
Inflation (%)	7.1	9.2	16.0	24.2	16.5	15.9	8.2
Current account ($m)	+338	−2592	−8575	−4106	−2043	+520	+470
Effective exchange rate[a]	90	82	79	73	61	66	66

[a] National Westminster Bank calculations.
Figures are 'end year' (18 December 1971 = 100).

claims. Monetary and fiscal policy remained expansionary and the balance of payments was allowed to deteriorate further. This policy was maintained with the 'moral' justification that the UK was playing its part in keeping world demand up, thus offsetting the deflationary tendencies of the OPEC-induced recession. By mid-1975 inflation was rampant, running at an annual rate of over 30 per cent for a six-month period, and the government at that point introduced a statutory wages policy and tighter monetary measures in order to bring this under control. At the same time the balance of payments remained in substantial deficit, although during 1976 it showed signs of improving. The financial markets were unimpressed, however, regarding domestic financial policies as still too lax, and sterling deteriorated steadily throughout 1976. By October – with sterling having fallen to the record low of £1 equalling approximately $1.55 – the government was forced to enter into negotiations with the IMF.

The next phase of economic policy was that in the period after the government accepted the IMF conditions. A much tighter monetary policy was adopted and sterling recovered to over $2, with the effective trade-weighted index rising to 67 during the first quarter of 1979, compared with 57 in October 1976. Despite the tighter monetary stance, relatively rapid growth was registered in 1977 and 1978 and the balance of payments position improved, helped by the substantial contribution of North Sea oil.

The UK economy over this period was thus characterised by expansion and balance of payments strength in the early 1970s, followed by a rapid inflation and a sharply deteriorating balance of payments, and then orthodox financial policies, a reduction in inflation and a stronger balance of payments towards the end of the decade. Exchange control policy followed the same pattern, being tightened when the balance of payments was weak and relaxed when it was strong, but there were also substantial underlying changes in the direction of policy.

The traditional structure of British exchange control has been until recently (mid-1979) to offer considerable freedom for non-residents in dealing in the British economy and in sterling markets and to use exchange control to prevent outward movements: this was based on the fundamental assumption of a weak currency. Concessions were made within this framework firstly as regards the sterling area, later regarding the EEC, while in 1979 a more extensive relaxation took place.

THE STERLING AREA

Policy towards capital exports to the sterling area countries has varied in accordance with both the liberalism of the government at the time and changes in the composition of the area itself. As this period began, policy was determined by a programme, introduced on 3 May 1966, of voluntary restraint on investment in developed overseas sterling area countries. Under this programme companies planning direct investment in Australia, New Zealand, South Africa and the Republic of Ireland had been asked to consult the Bank of England about certain aspects of the financing. However, on 22 March 1972 the government announced – in accordance with its more *laissez-faire* framework of policy – the termination of this programme of voluntary restraint. This coincided with a period of strength in the UK balance of payments. However, after a brief period of membership of the European 'snake', sterling suffered speculative pressure in June 1972, and on 23 June the government announced that sterling would be allowed to float as a temporary measure. This had the effect of breaking the links between certain sterling area countries and sterling itself, because it by no means followed that the other countries would be able to ensure that their currencies floated exactly in line with sterling, or even that they would wish to preserve the link. It was thus announced at the same time that there would be an extension of exchange controls to cover transactions between the UK (including the Channel Islands and the Isle of Man) and sterling area countries other than the Republic of Ireland. Controls, and in certain cases restrictions, were imposed on resident capital outflows from the UK to other overseas sterling area countries, although current payments were not restricted. Accordingly, the scheduled territories were redefined as consisting solely of the UK (including the Channel

Islands and the Isle of Man) and the Republic of Ireland. Gibraltar was readmitted to the scheduled territories on 1 January 1973. The external account area henceforth comprised all other countries, divided into (i) other EEC countries (other than Eire); (ii) Rhodesia; (iii) the overseas sterling area (OSA), i.e. those countries which prior to 23 June 1972 were treated as scheduled territories; (iv) all other countries. This announcement marked a major landmark in British external financial policy, and detailed regulations implementing the new principles of policy were issued, concerning both the controls to be applied within the sterling area itself and the differences remaining between OSA countries and the rest of the world.

The other main changes on exchange controls with the OSA occurred on 27 March 1974 as a result of pressure on the UK external account because of the OPEC price rises. The main effect was to tighten the rules regarding direct and portfolio investment, terminating certain long-standing preferential arrangements for the OSA and similar treatment accorded since early 1972 to the EEC.

THE FINANCE OF INTERNATIONAL TRADE

This structure of exchange controls still left sterling as an important trading currency, mainly but not solely for the sterling area countries. However, the pressure on the balance of payments and in particular on the reserves which developed during 1976 because of the lack of confidence in the government's policies on the foreign exchange markets, led to a further diminution of sterling's use for these purposes. There was also a wide-spread suspicion that some of the banks' facilities for financing trade had been used by speculators to take short positions against sterling. Thus on 24 August 1976 the rules governing the provision of sterling finance by UK banks to overseas sterling area residents were further tightened so as to allow banks to provide such finance only against original documents relating to the specific current movement of goods, either into or out of an OSA country. On 19 November UK banks were advised that the merchanting of goods between non-scheduled territories by UK residents could no longer be financed in sterling; UK residents would be allowed to pay non-residents for goods on-sold to other non-residents only with foreign currency borrowed for this purpose. However, no change was made immediately in the arrangements for the long-standing London commodity market schemes. Thus sterling credit facilities for overseas sterling area trade were brought into line with those available to other non-residents, and were restricted to the financing of trade between the rest of the world and the scheduled territories. These measures were designed to terminate the use by UK residents of official exchange to finance trade with any of the non-scheduled territories, and they were expected to produce a substantial inflow of foreign currency as drawings under the previous facilities were repaid; contemporary estimates put the likely reflow of funds from these changes at up to £1bn. Sterling's role as a trading currency was thus diminished significantly.

STERLING AS A RESERVE CURRENCY

The past few years have seen the virtual demise of sterling as a significant reserve currency with the UK government no longer taking upon itself obligations in the interests of the foreign holders of sterling. As the period under consideration began policy was dominated by the Basle Agreements of September 1968, under which countries in the sterling area undertaking to hold a fixed minimum proportion of their reserves in sterling obtained in return a UK guarantee, in terms of the US dollar, for any official sterling above 10 per cent of that country's reserves. These agreements had been undertaken at a time of sterling weakness, following the devaluation of 1967, in order to calm the fears of sterling reserve holders that their assets might diminish in value. The agreements were also intended to diminish the risk of pressure being exerted on the British reserves if sterling area countries tried, or wished, to diversify out of sterling. If such moves were to cause a fall in sterling or produce excessive pressure on the reserves, then an atmosphere of cumulative fear might have become established and the situation become increasingly difficult to control.

These guarantees did not become operative until 24 November 1972 when the UK became liable to make up the difference between the old par value of £1 = US$2.40 and a middle rate of US$2.3506, the rate at which sterling closed on 23 November. Under the agreements compensation was necessary if the middle sterling–dollar rate in London remained below its old lower limit of US$2.3760 under the Bretton Woods arrangements for thirty consecutive days. Such compensation, due in sterling in London and not in foreign exchange, was in the event paid to the relevant sterling holders. A new problem emerged as regards these agreements in that they had originally been established in a period of fixed exchange rates, whereas the pound was floating in the second half of 1972. The scheme was, however, extended on two occasions (September 1973 for six months and March 1974 for a further nine months), and then on 12 November 1974 it was announced that the sterling guarantee arrangements would be discontinued at the end of the year. This had been an implied commitment as part of entry into the EEC, when the UK had agreed that the reserve role of sterling would be phased out.

TABLE 6.2: Exchange Reserves in Sterling Held by Central Monetary Institutions (£ *million*)

1971	1973	1975	1976	1977	1978
3220	3689	4102	2639	2835	2610

Source: *Bank of England Quarterly Bulletin.*
Note: Dates refer to 'end of period'.

During 1975 exchange reserves in sterling increased significantly as some OPEC countries invested in sterling assets, an increase the UK was not averse to as a means of financing the balance of payments deficit caused very largely by the impact of the OPEC price rise itself. However, in early 1976 when doubts had begun to develop over the financial policy of the UK funds were withdrawn by some OSA countries, and this became one of the sources of pressure on the sterling exchange rate. Thus, when at the end of that year the government was forced to apply to the IMF for credit, and to accede to their terms, one of the significant features of the settlement, reflecting considerable pressure from continental countries, was that the role of sterling as a reserve currency should be even further phased out.

As a result of this agreement the Bank of England offered OSA countries the option of non-sterling currency bonds, of varying maturities and in different currencies. Countries that used sterling as a reserve currency thus had the opportunity to escape from so doing if they wished. However, the fact that the UK was changing its policies to accord with IMF terms meant that the outlook for sterling had improved considerably. Holding investments in sterling became a much better financial option and only $680m of the non-sterling bonds were sold. But the main significance of this offer was the underlying implication that from then on the British government was relieved of the moral obligation to pursue a sterling exchange rate policy which would give considerable importance to the attitude of sterling reserve asset holders. Having been given the option of getting out of sterling, any countries which henceforth decided to hold their reserves in sterling would be clearly doing so of their own free will and they had to expect to bear the consequences of their own successes or failures of judgement.

Sterling is now only the third most important reserve currency, behind the dollar and the deutschemark (see Table 1.3, p. 4). Table 6.3 shows that reserve holdings in sterling have fluctuated around a declining trend and now are small in relation both to the UK's total liabilities and to world reserves. At the end of 1977 overseas official holdings of sterling accounted for a negligible proportion of total currency reserves, compared with a 10 per cent share in 1971.

TABLE 6.3: Official Holdings of Sterling compared with Total Foreign Exchange Reserves (*SDR billion*)

	1971	*1972*	*1973*	*1974*	*1975*	*1976*	*1977*
Official sterling claims	7.3	8.1	6.5	8.3	6.4	3.2	3.3
Total foreign exchange reserves	75.0	96.2	102.0	127.1	137.5	160.7	201.1
Sterling as percentage of total	9.7	8.4	6.4	6.5	4.7	2.0	1.6

Source: IMF *Annual Report* (1978).

An important feature in the decline of sterling as a reserve currency was the ceasing by certain OPEC states (including Kuwait) to accept payment for their oil in sterling – they changed to dollars – in 1975. This coincided with those countries' transfers of their reserves elsewhere, severing what had been an exceptionally close link with sterling.

UK CAPITAL FLOWS AND THE EEC

A major change occurred in the UK's position and attitude towards international financial markets on 22 January 1972 when membership negotiations were completed with the EEC. On 22 March that year it was announced that official exchange would be made available up to £1m for all new approved direct investments in member countries of the EEC and in Denmark and Norway, two countries which had also negotiated entry. At the same time it was announced that UK companies controlled by residents of member countries of the EEC, Denmark and Norway would, subject to certain conditions, henceforth normally be allowed to raise unlimited sterling finance for direct investment in the UK. The foreign currency proceeds of the sale and liquidation of direct investments in member countries of the EEC, Denmark and Norway would no longer normally be treated as investment currency. On 24 October, however, the new exchange control concessions introduced as regards EEC members and prospective members were withdrawn as far as they were related to Norway and Norwegian residents because the Norwegians in a national referendum had rejected EEC membership.

Accession to the EEC obliged the UK to liberalise exchange control on capital movements over a period of five years up to the end of 1977, with the first measure in this respect due in January and July 1975. However, the UK balance of payments at the time could not afford these relaxations, which related mainly to outward direct investment and personal capital transfers, and, starting on 23 July 1975, the UK was given periodic dispensations from compliance with these rules. At the end of 1977, there was some liberalisation of the exchange control regulations, reflecting the strength of the UK balance of payments. Personal allowances for capital movements were raised. For direct investment into other EEC countries official exchange would be made available up to the equivalent of £0.5 million or 50 per cent of the total investment whichever was the larger, if the balance of payments benefit was likely to occur within three years.

However, the new Conservative government which assumed office in May 1979 favoured exchange control relaxations. The strength of sterling at the time no doubt encouraged the government to accelerate the implementation of its plans for major changes. Although the formal structure of controls was retained, the measures taken in the June budget and in a separate package in July, amounted to a substantial removal of restrictions on outward capital flows. Henceforth currency could be made available without limit at the official exchange rate for all outward direct investment, and foreign currency borrowing to finance such investment could be repaid at the official rate. The relaxations on portfolio investment were limited to securities denominated and payable in the currencies of other EEC countries (with the exception of unit and investment trusts), and foreign currency securities issued by international organisations of which the UK was a member, including EEC institutions and the World Bank. The measures represented a further substantial move towards meeting in full the UK's obligations on capital movements imposed by the EEC treaty.

On 16 December 1972 the Bank of England announced that policy on banking mergers and acquisitions would be modified. Among other things, a bank from an EEC member country would be treated the same as British banks as regards participation in other British banks. Each case would be considered on its merits, but the authorities' attitude elsewhere in the EEC on local participation by British banks would be taken into consideration. The general liberal practice as regards the establishment of third country banks, branches and subsidiaries in London would continue, and the attitude to participation by third country banks would remain unchanged.

EUROMARKETS

(1) EURO-STERLING CURRENCY

Euro-sterling is only a small proportion of the total eurocurrency market ($7bn out of a total of $800bn), and is largely based in Paris. Euro-sterling trading in London is forbidden, but British banks operate in this market through their subsidiaries and branches abroad. Interest rates are professionally arbitraged in line with forward rates and interest rates of other currencies, so the market is often volatile and is used mainly for professional dealing. There has been a certain development of longer-term investment in euro-sterling and some long-term commercial business, but this is a small proportion of total activity. One of the functions of this market has been as a vehicle in which the government have operated at times in order to curb speculation against sterling, or to operate a bear squeeze. It is not, however, a major market in the sense of being an important source of funds for medium or short-term commercial activity.

(2) EURO-STERLING BONDS

For much of the post-war period non-residents who wished to hold sterling long-term assets held gilt-edged stock. They were able to do this and receive interest gross, either automatically or after making certain declarations and were thus able to benefit from the high domestic interest rates – interest rates which had been too high for the continuance of the domestic corporate debenture market. The first post-war eurobond in sterling was issued in 1972 in the form of a £10m guaranteed debenture issue for Amoco at 8 per cent. This sold fairly well, but the pound was becoming so weak that it was not possible to make further issues, so for several years the market was dormant. However, with North Sea oil money beginning to flow into the UK, the restoration of the British balance of payments, and the fall in inflation, the possibility of reviving the market was tested towards the end of 1977, following several months in which sterling had appreciated steadily. Although the Bank of England was committed to reducing sterling's role as an international currency, the Bank was prepared to allow the market to develop as long as it was based off-shore, and British resident investors were forbidden from investing in the bonds directly. Although residents could buy through the investment currency pool, the bank assumed that external holders of sterling would be the main purchasers.

At the time of the proposed revival of the market long-term interest rates in the UK were still historically high, but the issuing houses thought non-residents would be willing to forfeit the higher yield obtainable on sterling gilt-edged stock for the benefit of being paid anonymously and gross. This proved to be the case, and the issues were all offered at less than the domestic long-term rate of interest on government stock. The first of several issues in November 1977 was for the European Coal and Steel Community (ECSC) and was finally sold with a $9\frac{5}{8}$ per cent coupon. The bonds were bearer certificates, but labelled clearly as foreign currency securities to be treated as such under the Exchange Control Act 1947. This led to a problem in financing the trading in the bonds in the secondary market. Because the bonds were foreign currency securities, British dealers would have to borrow foreign currency to finance their portfolios, which would subject them to both interest and exchange rate risks. Because of the problem that would cause for the development of the necessary secondary market, the Bank of England relaxed its rules and permitted dealers to borrow euro-sterling to fund their positions.

At the time of the Amoco issue the Bank of England had laid down few restrictions, but in the next wave of issues strict guidelines were in force. British companies could borrow on this market for virtually any purpose, but foreign companies were barred unless the proceeds were to be invested in the UK. These rules thus tended to lead to capital imports into the UK, because all the funds had to come from abroad and some borrowers would use the proceeds in the UK.

The ECSC issue was announced on 8 November 1977 and was an outstanding success. The sum was increased from £15 to £20m and the coupon cut from 10 to $9\frac{5}{8}$ per cent. Nevertheless it was still over-subscribed. It was followed by several other issues that month and in

TABLE 6.4: Euro-sterling Bond Issues

Borrower	Date announced	Size (£ million)	Coupon	Issue price	Maturity
Amoco	Apr. 1972	10	8	98.0	1987
European Coal and Steel Community	Nov. 1977	20	$9\frac{5}{8}$	par	1989
Total	Nov. 1977	25	$9\frac{1}{8}$	par	1984
Finance for Industry	Nov. 1977	20	$9\frac{3}{4}$	99.50	1987
European Investment Bank	Nov. 1977	25	$9\frac{3}{4}$	99.75	1992
Fisons	Nov. 1977	10	$10\frac{1}{4}$	par	1987
Courtaulds	Nov. 1977	20	$9\frac{3}{4}$	98.0	1989
European Investment Bank	Jan. 1978	25	$9\frac{3}{4}$	par	1988
Rowntree Mackintosh	Jan. 1978	18	$10\frac{1}{4}$	100.25	1988
Sears	Feb. 1978	15	$10\frac{1}{4}$	par	1988
INA	Feb. 1978	20	10	par	1988
Allied Breweries	Feb. 1978	15	$10\frac{1}{4}$	99.50	1990
Finance for Industry	Feb. 1978	12	10	par	1989
Citicorp	Mar. 1978	20	10	99.50	1993
Gestetner	Apr. 1978	10	11	par	1988
Whitbread	Apr. 1978	15	$10\frac{1}{2}$	par	1990
General Electric	Mar. 1979	50	$12\frac{1}{2}$	par	1991
Finance for Industry	Mar. 1979	15	13	par	1991

Source: *Eurocurrency* (April 1978 and press announcements).

January, February and March 1978. Problems arose, however, from various sources. On 25 November the Bank of England announced a surprise 2 per cent increase in the minimum lending rate, which put up the cost of financing inventories of bonds, and raised the spectre that short- and long-term interest rates might have to increase further – thus affecting both the cost of holding the inventory of bonds and also implanting in the minds of bond holders the risk of falling capital values. Further interest rate rises took place during 1978 and these led to severe indigestion in the market. To make matters worse there was severe bunching of issues with no fewer than three being announced within hours of each other on 28 November 1977. These were a £25m issue for the European Investment Bank, which may have been over-priced, and others of £10m for Fisons and £20m for Courtaulds. It became clear that few of these bonds had been firmly placed and many, or most, were still in the hands of the dealers or selling groups. There was a certain panic in the market which might have been avoided had there been a queue for bringing forward investments, as happens in the domestic sterling market and in many foreign capital markets. Moreover, there was a lack of experience in the secondary market, which had just been re-established and had no history of confident and successful trading. Further issues were announced early in 1978, but by the late spring the market was dead, killed by very substantial rises in domestic sterling interest rates, a fall in sterling during the early part of the year, and further uncertainty about domestic inflation. Both the fall in sterling and the increases in domestic interest rates made sterling eurobonds unattractive to foreign asset holders, and this problem was compounded by the lack of liquidity and scale in the secondary market. Thus during late 1978 the possibility of further sterling eurobonds seemed remote, as inflation and interest rates increased. However, in early 1979, with interest rates past a temporary peak and the pound appreciating, the market was revived, in particular with a £50m issue for the General Electric Company. This company had very large net sterling assets and had a compelling need in relation to its total balance sheet to acquire sterling-denominated liabilities as a means of financing its international expansion. The issue of sterling eurobonds was almost the only way of achieving that objective. For the future the sterling eurobond market is likely to suffer marked changes of sentiment, and to remain at times a significant minor international capital market.

UK PUBLIC SECTOR BORROWING ABROAD

A major change in Britain's attitude to the international financial markets, in common with that of various other countries such as France and Canada, is exemplified in that she herself has become a very substantial official borrower. Over much of the post-war period the main external debts were in sterling in the form of reserves held by the sterling area countries. But there were also the American and Canadian loans, the lend–lease debt outstanding from the end of the Second World War and the external private sector holdings of sterling for trading purposes.

The rise in the price of oil at the end of 1973 caused the British serious problems, as the economy was already overheated and running a current account deficit which reached $8.6bn in 1974. To finance this the UK drew on two large eurodollar loans, the first of $2.5bn in 1974–5 and the second for $1.5bn in 1977. It also used the IMF oil facility and drew on its first IMF credit tranches. In addition, at the end of 1976 arrangements were made with the IMF for a $3.9bn standby credit to be available during 1977 and 1978. Including the $680m of foreign currency bonds issued as a contribution to reducing sterling's role as a reserve currency the Government's own foreign currency debt reached $11.5bn by April 1977.

TABLE 6.5: UK Government Foreign Currency Debt Outstanding, 1 April 1977
($ billion)

$2.5bn government loan	2.5
$1.5bn government loan	1.0
Drawing on IMF oil facility	1.2
May 1976 drawing on IMF first credit tranche	0.8
January 1977 drawing on IMF $3.9bn standby	1.2
Foreign currency bonds	0.7
Long-term debts	4.1
Total	**11.5**

Source: Treasury Economic Progress Report (May 1977).

Other public sector organisations have also been encouraged at various times to borrow on the international markets; by April 1977 the amount of foreign borrowing by nationalised industries, local authorities and other public sector bodies such as the National Water Council totalled $10.7bn. The greater part of this – $8.2bn – was accounted for by the nationalised industries and most of these borrowings were under the exchange cover scheme, which was in force from 1969 to 1971 and re-introduced in 1973. This scheme provides borrowers with cover against exchange risk, against payment to the Exchange Equalisation Account of a corresponding charge. The borrower surrenders most of the interest differential between the rate on the foreign currency loan and the appropriate rate on sterling loans from the National Loans Fund (or in the case of local authorities the Public Works Loan Board), but keeps an interest benefit of about 1 per cent.

A variety of methods has been used for loans by public sector bodies; public bond issues, private placements and bilateral loans, loans from European institutions, such as the European Investment Bank and the ECSC, and credits from banks or groups of banks. Use is also being made of the US domestic commercial paper market. The currency composition of the debt is mainly US dollars, but there are small proportions in Canadian dollars, Swiss francs and deutschemarks. Given that in 1977 a large proportion of HMG's debt was from the IMF,

TABLE 6.6: Foreign Currency Borrowing by Public Sector Bodies and Methods
Used

Amounts outstanding at 1 April 1977 ($ billion)

Nationalised industries	8.2 (7.3 under exchange cover scheme)
Local authorities	1.3 (1.2 under exchange cover scheme)
Other	1.2 (all under exchange cover scheme)
Total	10.7
Public bond issues	0.8
Private placements and bilateral loans	3.4
European institutions	1.8
Other (syndicated credits etc.)	4.7
Total	10.7

Source: *Treasury Economic Progress Report* (May 1977).

and such drawings are denominated in Special Drawing Rights, the SDR played a prominent role in the government's debt at that time.

The initial rationale for British borrowing was to cover a short-term balance of payments deficit of some severity, so as to finance the British government in the 'valley' before the balance of payments improved with the onset of North Sea oil production on a large scale. However, financial markets became impatient at the progress made by the government in rectifying the balance of payments and in managing domestic policy, and the government was forced to apply to the IMF in 1976. Moreover, the balance of payments has improved to a lesser extent than might have been hoped with the flow of North Sea oil revenue, as the rest of the economy has continued to suffer a lacklustre performance. Thus the UK still has substantial debts outstanding, despite the fact that early repayment of some IMF debt and some public bodies' debt was possible during 1978 and 1979. An objective of government policy has been to reschedule debt so as to even out the bunching of debt repayments and interest.

In addition to this debt, there is a substantial amount of official sterling liabilities amounting to the equivalent of $5.2bn at end 1978. There are also substantial sterling liabilities to overseas holders other than central monetary institutions, the equivalent of over $10bn at the same date. Against all these obligations, UK official reserves, reinforced very heavily during 1977 by the influx of funds into the UK, have risen from a low point of below $5bn in October 1976, to $20.8bn in January 1978, subsequently declining to around $16bn in early 1979. The UK has a relatively weak short-term liability and asset structure given the heavy debt and the sterling liabilities. One of the main objectives in the coming years will be to maintain confidence in the British government's policy so that they may handle the repayments, the rescheduling and the raising of new funds in an orderly manner which does not impinge too greatly upon domestic policy. By holding such large reserves – even though more than offset by liabilities – the British government has achieved flexibility and a better defensive situation with which to face uncertainties in the financial markets. If there were to be a severe crisis of confidence in domestic financial policy, however, then the fundamental weakness would become apparent and pressure could still be exerted very substantially indeed upon the exchange rate.

EXPORT FINANCE IN FOREIGN CURRENCIES

In the latter part of the period under consideration the UK embarked upon a fairly novel policy for financing exports of fixed-rate export credit. It was announced in February 1977 that foreign currency financing of certain export contracts involving buyer credit could be financed in foreign currency with the support of the Export Credits Guarantee Department (ECGD). These arrangements were extended in July 1978 to include certain contracts involving supplier credit. This was a deliberate attempt at reducing the role of sterling in financing UK exports and was the first time any major industrialised country had actively taken steps to reduce the use of its own currency in such a way.

Hitherto the basic procedure had been that the banking system through the clearing banks agreed to make available funds at certain fixed or concessionary rates of interest for medium- and long-term credits. Because of the concessionary nature of this business and the illiquidity it implied for the banks' balance sheets, the proportion of assets to be deployed in this way was limited. This proportion was increased on various occasions. In Chancellor Barber's period (1970–4) it was agreed that the banks would make available sums equivalent to 18 per cent of their current accounts for this purpose; this was subsequently raised to 20 per cent in December 1977. Amounts over this figure were refinanced by the Bank of England, so that the banking system obtained the fees for the negotiation of this business, but the credit was in effect granted by the Bank. There was also an interest rate adjustment on the part not refinanced. The whole scheme involved a charge on public expenditure, as the government had to raise the corresponding sums and so contributed to the public sector borrowing requirement (PSBR). Extending substantial export credit in sterling also had the effect of diminishing the reserves correspondingly, as repayment did not take place for many years. Thus two problems had stemmed from this earlier system, the charge on the PSBR and the charge on the reserves.

In the context of the negotiations with the IMF at the end of 1976, in which an important feature was the IMF's desire for greater control over the PSBR, decisions were taken to deal with these problems by shifting a proportion of export credit finance into foreign currency. On 15 December 1976 the Chancellor of the Exchequer announced the intention to reduce public spending on export credit refinancing and stated that steps would be taken to encourage export credits in foreign currency which up to that point had not been feasible. There would also be tighter controls on the rate at which the ECGD would approve new fixed-rate sterling finance. At the same time the clearing banks agreed to provide from their own resources an extra £100m of fixed-rate sterling lending for each of the next two years. Measures to facilitate the switch to foreign currency financing followed on 23 December, when the ECGD was authorised to use the powers of Section 2(2) of the Export Guarantee Act 1975 to make loans directly in foreign currencies to overseas borrowers. In the future the ECGD would underwrite larger projects only where these were financed in foreign currency. In addition foreign currency financing would be required for all project business with certain countries and would be actively sought in a number of others.

On 13 January 1977 the International Finance, Trade and Aid Bill was published which, apart from increasing the statutory limit of ECGD sterling commitments, also contained the measure to enable ECGD to take on commitments in foreign currencies. A separate statutory limit of initially SDR10bn was proposed, with provision for staged increases to SDR25bn. Other arrangements were subsequently made with the intention of phasing out the use of sterling for this business, in particular as regards financing non-UK components and costs.

The actual development of this process has depended upon the rate at which UK exporters obtained contracts suitable for this kind of financial support, but the amount of ECGD currency commitments (in effect dollars) increased significantly once the structuring of these contracts had been ironed out. It thus became the standard practice for the major UK exports on long-term credit to be financed through dollars. The effect of this was of course to give a greater competitive advantage to non-UK banks in financing such transactions, although British banks were also able to take part, and thus deliberately to push business away from sterling and from London.

THE CAPITAL ACCOUNT OF THE BALANCE OF PAYMENTS

Table 6.7 indicates the main features of UK investment and other capital transactions in recent years. The capital account has moved between surplus and deficit on a substantial scale over the period since 1971, starting with a large net inflow in that year, a further large inflow in 1974 and a major deficit in 1976. In 1977 there was again a large inflow. Two steady large sums in this generally unstable situation are overseas direct investment in the UK private sector, and UK private direct investment abroad. While the net figure has varied from year to year, it has been small in relation to the large sums flowing in both directions. In 1976, for example, the flows were over £2bn each way, yet they differed by only £93m. A further substantial but volatile figure has been the change in external sterling liabilities, which has tended to reflect changes in sterling's performance. Because of the relative smallness of the net position recorded by most other items in the accounts, this figure has dominated the final net outcome of capital transactions. The change in external sterling liabilities was substantially positive in 1971, when the UK economy was seen to be responding well to the measures adopted in the preceding two to three years, and in 1974 as much of the OPEC surplus found its way into sterling. A substantial deficit was registered in 1976 when confidence in the British government's financial policy deteriorated sharply, but in 1977 there was a correspondingly large inflow back into the UK. Trade credit has also been a significant capital outflow over the years, reaching £1bn in 1976, and it was partly for this reason that the authorities chose to denominate as much trade credit as possible, particularly longer term, in currencies other than sterling.

A stable basis for the capital account for sterling under modern conditions would almost certainly have large private direct investment flows each way, a fairly stable figure for changes in external sterling liabilities, a significant but not too large outflow of official long-term capital and some overseas investment in the UK public sector. The country would be in difficulty if the direct investment figures became too ill-balanced, although until mid-1979 policy was for British direct investment abroad to be financed in such a way as not to affect the reserves.

TABLE 6.7: UK Investment and Other Capital Transactions (£ million)

	1971	1972	1973	1974	1975	1976	1977	1978
Official long-term capital	−274	−255	−254	−276	−288	−158	−291	−348
Overseas investment in UK public sector	+107	+120	+175	+252	+43	+203	+2182	−81
Overseas investment in UK private sector	+1052	+773	+1652	+2278	+1719	+2063	+3096	+2835
UK private investment overseas	−836	−1383	−1848	−1149	−1383	−2156	−2167	−3288
Overseas currency borrowing or lending (net) by UK banks	+471	+471	+525	−294	+235	−106	+384	−599
Changes in external sterling liabilities	+1422	+196	+154	+1558	−67	−1152	+1452	+185
Trade credit	−233	−213	−226	−650	−346	−980	−229	−490
Other short-term transactions	+107	−399	−152	−48	+290	−608	+175	−441
Total investment and other capital transactions	+1816	−690	+26	+1671	+203	−2894	+4602	−2227

Source: Derived from *UK balance of payments 1967–77* (The Pink Book, HMSO); Treasury press release for 1978.

Notes: Assets: increase −/ decrease +.
Liabilities: increase +/ decrease −.

THE INVESTMENT CURRENCY POOL

An important feature of the British structure of exchange controls and the way this influences capital flows and the world markets is the rule regarding the financing of investments through the investment currency pool. When British residents wish to invest abroad they are, except in the circumstances mentioned earlier (i.e. UK capital flows and the EEC), required either to obtain funds from that pool, which means from the sale of corresponding external assets by somebody else, or to finance the investment by borrowing abroad. As confidence in sterling waxes and wanes the premium payable for sums bought from this investment currency pool varies. In view of the cosmopolitan multinational nature of many British companies and financial institutions, the effect of these rules has been to force them to borrow heavily in other national and international bond and banking markets. Thus British policy has had the effect of enhancing the development of the international markets. A side effect has been to give companies a very complicated multi-currency gearing structure, as investments around the world have been financed by borrowing abroad in a variety of currencies. Many companies would wish to tidy up their internal financial structure by consolidating in one currency and reducing their external currency gearing, if that were permitted. But the effect of allowing such a relaxation would be a once-and-for-all substantial drain on the UK's currency reserves, which could easily be of the order of £1bn or more and the British government was until the exchange control changes of mid-1979 reluctant to accept this cost.

During the period under study, various relaxations and modifications have taken place in the application of the investment currency rule, and in particular the rule whereby sellers of investment currency had to surrender 25 per cent of the proceeds to the government at the official rate was abandoned towards the end of 1977. This rule had had the effect of diminishing steadily the size of the investment currency pool and the return to the seller. It also had the effect of making it very difficult for investment companies to trade stocks abroad, because if they bought and sold abroad regularly in the investment currency market the surrender of 25 per cent of the proceeds acted as a tax on such transactions. The size of the investment currency pool has never been stated publicly. It is a relatively small and volatile market, and most serious portfolio investors use the alternative method of financing foreign investment by borrowing abroad.

LONDON AS A FINANCIAL CENTRE – INVISIBLE EXPORTS

One way in which Britain's position in relation to the world's financial markets is unique is the importance of London as a financial centre, and the importance of invisible exports to the British economy. London initially became the major home of the eurodollar market and a predominant proportion of business was done there. In recent years London's share has declined, but it is still by far the largest single centre. Its share of European eurocurrency deposits has remained high, at over 40 per cent, and it accounts for over a quarter of the worldwide total of eurocurrency deposits.

TABLE 6.8: Foreign Currency (Eurocurrency) Liabilities of Banks

		$ billion		UK as % of	
	UK	Total European reporting countries	Total all countries	European reporting countries	All countries
1974 December	111.5	220.8	392.1	50.5	28.4
1975 December	128.2	258.7	448.1	49.6	28.6
1976 December	148.6	310.7	544.0	47.8	27.3
1977 December	171.4	396.2	671.2	43.3	25.1
1978 December	213.4	510.8	864.4	45.8	24.7

Source: Bank for International Settlements, *Press Release on International Banking Developments* (18 June 1979).

The rise of other financial centres has been in many ways natural and has stemmed from a variety of causes. First, other centres have arisen purely for conducting transactions which contain no local management content at all – or virtually none. In this category are the Bahamas, the Cayman Islands, other Caribbean centres and certain areas in Asia, all of which have deliberately encouraged international banking business and turned themselves into important 'off-shore' centres. Other financial centres have arisen because of the importance of basing management locally to meet effectively the rise in local demand, and in many cases the growth of these centres has been fostered by time zone considerations. This applies, for example, to Bahrain, Singapore and Hong Kong. In other cases new centres have arisen because of the growth in importance of local currencies, or because of the effects of conditions in neighbouring countries, or because of new institutional links. For example the rise of Luxembourg has been heavily influenced by the importance of German banks' subsidiaries there and the German banking system using it – in effect – as an off-shore centre.

Despite these challenges there seems no reason why London should not remain a very important financial centre. It has two particular sources of strength. It is an excellent centre for communications and transport and is well placed for the European time-zone countries, which include Africa and the Middle East. It is also a good centre for management, for centred there is a sophisticated machinery for implementing decisions and a large pool of educated, capable professional workers. Nevertheless, it would be unwise to assume that London's pre-eminent position can be maintained unless policies are geared to that end, particularly that no policies are pursued which in effect are destructive.

The attraction of London as a financial centre is highlighted by the presence of some 300 foreign banks, employing 25,000 people. The financial services industry as a whole employs about one-quarter of a

TABLE 6.9: Invisible Earnings of the City of London (£ *million*)

	1971	1972	1973	1974	1975	1976	1977
Insurance, of which	341	367	364	384	442	795	909
Companies	137	160	157	148	138	307	345
Lloyd's	149	149	147	160	200	334	379
Brokers	55	58	60	76	104	154	185
Banking	106	151	146	122	215	416	254
Investment trusts	31	31	33	40	41	47	51
Unit trusts	3	5	6	8	9	11	12
Pension funds	4	6	9	10	16	14	17
Commodities	n.a.	n.a.	n.a.	140	209	201	109
Merchanting	64	66	97	54	90	108	120
Brokerage, etc. of which:	61	79	107	160	227	245	275
Baltic Exchange	25	35	53	103	146	147	155
Stock Exchange	10	15	18	19	19	16	20
Lloyd's Register of Shipping	4	6	7	10	14	18	23
The City of London	610	705	762	918	1249	1837	1747

Source: Derived from *UK Balance of Payments 1967–77* (The Pink Book, HMSO).

million people; much of this employment benefits from external business and contributes substantially to the country's invisible exports.

The main elements of the City's invisible earnings have been insurance, various services such as the commodity markets, the Baltic Exchange and other such markets, and appreciable earnings from banking and related fields. The City of London's invisible earnings have increased sharply in recent years and have approached £2bn in 1976 and 1977. Most of the markets which support these earnings have been able to hold their own in world competition, but competition has in many cases become more severe, particularly from dollar markets in commodities and from the rise of other insurance centres, such as New York and on the continent.

The UK's customary trade deficit is to an appreciable degree offset by the country's large invisible earnings, which in addition to those of the City derive from interest, profit and dividends to the private sector and public corporations, shipping and tourism. The recent slump in world shipping, coinciding with the excess capacity in shipbuilding, has slowed down the growth in earnings from this source and may have an adverse effect on shipping earnings over the longer term. Tourism, on the other hand, has boosted total invisible earnings enormously in recent years; this has stemmed partly from the fall in sterling. It was a net earner for the UK to the tune of £1077m in 1977. Part of the improvement in the invisible position has, however, been offset in recent years by government expenditure which has begun to rise very substantially indeed, and is increasingly outweighing the surplus on other items. Government expenditure has always been large on, for example, the British Army of the Rhine, but has recently increased particularly sharply as a consequence of membership of the EEC. The net budgetary contribution is expected to be about £800m in 1979, and the forecast is that it will later increase to well above that figure. This should be compared with the base of zero before membership of the EEC. Thus while in 1977 the UK's invisible earnings accounted for one-third of gross foreign exchange earnings and registered a net surplus of almost £2.5bn in 1976, future net earnings are likely to be substantially lower and may even disappear. They have already started to decline as shown in Table 6.10.

CONCLUSION

Over the period the UK has been in a state transition from its traditional links with the Commonwealth and the sterling area to new ones with the

TABLE 6.10: UK Invisibles (Net), 1971–8 (£ million)

	1971	1972	1973	1974	1975	1976	1977	1978
Services								
General government	−315	−351	−409	−538	−620	−757	−782	−786
Sea transport	− 52	− 75	− 99	−122	+ 56	+ 25	+ 21	−292
Civil aviation	+ 57	+ 77	+ 75	+ 96	+116	+241	+244	+331
Travel	+ 47	+ 19	− 1	+154	+245	+627	+1078	+857
Financial services	+471	+529	+601	+777	+1014	+1287	+1426	+1482
Other services	+327	+387	+455	+436	+340	+563	+888	+1272
Interest, profits and dividends								
General government	−204	−142	−199	−352	−514	−648	−685	−452
Private sector & public corporations	+709	+676	+1419	+1634	+1277	+1963	+1077	+1004
Transfers								
General government	−205	−210	−359	−320	−379	−784	−1111	−1686
Private sector	− 6	− 53	− 99	−121	−154	− 53	−114	−301
Invisible balance	+829	+857	+1384	+1644	+1381	+2464	+2042	+1429

Source: UK Balance of Payments 1967–77 (The Pink Book, HMSO), and Treasury press release for 1978.

European Economic Community. At the same time the use of sterling as a trading and reserve currency has diminished, although there has been a recent recovery in its use in the international (euro-sterling) capital market. It is a major objective of British policy to maintain London's position as an international financial centre. The British government will itself continue to be a major borrower in the international markets – banking and bond – and thus help stimulate their further development.

7 France

INTRODUCTION

France has had a unique position in the international economic order and to a lesser extent in international financial markets in the post-war period. She has been the strongest opponent of American or Anglo-Saxon views upon economic and financial matters, standing up for the rights of Europe against the US. In this era the French have consistently opposed what they regarded as the abuse of the international monetary system by the Americans, such as the way in which they bought European assets with money borrowed in the eurodollar market. The French opposed the creation of SDRs in the late 1960s. They have been strong advocates of a return to gold, or at least giving gold its due prominence in the system.

France's intellectual approach to economic and financial policy has been a sophisticated mixture of dirigism and the use of markets. The French have applied the weight of the state machinery to achieve their economic ends, while never accepting fully socialist doctrine regarding the paramount role of the state in such matters: on the other hand they have also used domestic and international markets to achieve economic and financial objectives, while never adopting fully a *laissez-faire* attitude about the ultimate value of such market operations. This sophisticated intellectual approach, combined with a determined and active state policy, has enabled the French to ride extremely well the changes and uncertainties in the post-war economic situation, and they are one of the post-war economic success stories.

ECONOMIC HISTORY

In the early 1970s France showed strong growth performance, averaging over 5 per cent in both 1972 and 1973. Inflation was, however, relatively high at about 7 per cent, and the current account of the balance of payments was moving into deficit. The economy benefited from the general strength of European currencies against the dollar, and the exchange rate remained relatively stable, but France was hit hard by the OPEC oil price rises, having little in the way of domestic energy capacity. The balance of payments moved into substantial deficit – $6bn in 1974 – inflation increased to over 13 per cent and the growth rate fell. Stabilisation measures were taken with the result that in 1975 real GDP fell by 0.1 per cent, and although inflation remained high, the current account showed a substantial improvement to just a small deficit. Since then France has managed to restore growth to some extent nearer past levels at over 5 per cent in 1976 and 3 per cent in 1977 and 1978, but at the cost of a more substantial current account deficit. Inflation has remained near double figures, although the fear of it accelerating much beyond 10 per cent has diminished. The exchange rate has remained relatively stable over the period since 1971, but has fallen away from the peak reached in 1975.

TABLE 7.1: Main Economic Indicators, France, 1972–8

	1972	1973	1974	1975	1976	1977	1978
Change in GDP (%)	+5.9	+5.4	+2.6	−0.1	+5.6	+3.0	+3.0
Inflation (%)	6.1	7.3	13.7	11.7	9.6	9.5	9.5
Current account ($m)	+284	−675	−5980	−66	−6097	−3300	−2000
Effective exchange rate[a]	100	101	100	107	97	97	99

[a] National Westminster Bank calculations.
Figures are 'end year' (18 December 1971 = 100).

Determination of the appropriate economic policy – given the sometimes conflicting objectives of stability in the exchange rate, an adequate balance of payments, continued growth, and control of inflation – has not been easy, and this was compounded by the political uncertainties and the major elections in March and April 1978. Policies had to be such as to minimise the chance of the Left winning that election – this objective was in fact achieved – and since then the French have embarked on a more liberal policy. Price controls have been abolished, and the policy has rested upon determination to maintain a stable exchange rate, combined with firm monetary guidelines and an intention to restructure French industry.

A key feature of French economic performance has been a determination to maintain the momentum of growth, and this has to some extent been done. In 1978, however, emphasis moved to give at least equal attention to the exchange rate, and membership of the EMS reflects at least in part a recognition of the need to pay some regard to strengthening the financial situation. The French franc has for some time been regarded as a weak currency and French inflation has been much higher than, for example, German.

BORROWING ABROAD

In response to the OPEC price rises France embarked upon an active borrowing policy, partly as a means of buying time while other policy measures came into operation. But against the background of substantial current account deficits France has since continued to be a regular borrower on a persistent scale, both through the public and private sectors. French external borrowing through the international markets totalled almost $17bn in the period from January 1973 to September 1978, of which more than half was through bond issues and private placements. State and state-guaranteed borrowings accounted for approximately two-thirds of the total.

TABLE 7.2: French Borrowing in International Capital Markets (*$ million*)

	1973	1974	1975	1976	1977	1978 (*Jan.–Sept.*)	Total 1973–8
Foreign bonds	—	340	574	1501	793	477	3685
Eurobonds	104	332	1228	1316	1113	740	4833
Total bonds	104	672	1802	2817	1906	1217	8518
Eurocurrency credits	50	3331	506	734	1865	1870	8356
Total	154	4003	2308	3551	3771	3087	16874

Source: World Bank, *Borrowing in International Capital Markets* (various issues, 1973–8).

The dollar has been used as the vehicle for eurocurrency credit borrowing; in the bond market the predominant currencies have been the US dollar, followed by the Swiss franc and the deutschemark. Apart from these currencies others have been used on a relatively small scale, including the Luxembourg franc and the Dutch guilder. The French have also in the past, but not in recent years, been able to raise sums externally denominated in French francs.

TABLE 7.3: Currency Composition of French Bond Borrowing, 1976–8 (*$ million*)

	1976		1977		1978 (*Jan.–Sept.*)		Total		Total bonds	%
	Euro.	Foreign	Euro.	Foreign	Euro.	Foreign	Euro.	Foreign		
Deutschemark	173	—	258	—	186	—	617	—	617	11.0
Dutch guilders	28	—	—	84	—	—	28	84	112	1.9
French franc	50	—	—	—	50	—	50	—	50	0.8
Japanese yen	—	—	—	76	—	226	—	302	302	5.2
Luxembourg franc	—	—	—	—	—	15	—	15	15	0.2
Swiss franc	—	871	—	520	—	158	—	1549	1549	26.4
US dollar	1065	630	855	167	340	60	2260	857	3117	53.1
EUA	—	—	—	—	83	—	83	—	83	1.4
Total	1316	1501	1113	847	609	459	3038	2807	5845	100.0

Source: OECD financial statistics.

France has naturally regarded itself as a country of the highest credit rating and has demanded the finest terms in international borrowing. It has, in many ways like Britain, cultivated a wide range of international markets, including the eurocurrency banking market, the eurobond market, foreign bond markets and the US commercial paper market. The borrowing agencies have included a wide range of public sector corporations, as well as the central government: these borrowers include the French railways, the electricity utility, and the post and telecommunications service. For such a creditworthy borrower to use these markets continually on a wide scale has clearly had the effect of enhancing the attraction of these markets to investors, and thus helping their further constructive development. The effect on the external debt position has been to boost gross short-term debt to over $30bn and gross long-term debt to some $20bn – repayment of which could pose a problem in the future – but there appears to be little alternative, and as long as the international trade imbalance persists France is likely to be a major borrower on the international markets.

PARIS AS A FINANCIAL CENTRE

In view of the relatively low priority given in France to purely financial factors, in relation for example to agriculture, industry, tourism and other sectors of the economy, the French would find it impossible to establish the conditions in which Paris could become a major world-wide financial centre; that would essentially require that banks and other financial institutions be given the opportunity of participating profitably in a wide range of financial markets. The degree of control exercised by the Bank of France over the financial markets makes this impracticable. Nevertheless, Paris has carved out for itself a certain niche in the international financial markets, and non-residents are permitted to invest in certain domestic financial assets without requiring permission from the Bank of France. They may buy savings bonds without formality if the operation is made from a French franc external account or by the sale of foreign currency. Foreign banks and institutions may with the specific authorisation of the Treasury, given on a case by case basis, purchase treasury bills. Non-residents may also purchase quoted bonds under the same rules and formalities as holding savings bonds – that is against payment in foreign currency or to the debit of an external account. The acquisition of unquoted bonds requires the authorisation of the Bank of France. Purchases of quoted shares by non-residents, if the participation by the non-resident represents a maximum of 20 per cent of the capital of the company, is also free of control. Purchases of unquoted shares, again up to a maximum of 20 per cent of the capital of the company, may also be allowed, but requires the prior authorisation of the Bank of France, and satisfaction of more stringent conditions.

But although non-residents may operate in certain of the domestic French markets, these markets are much narrower and more volatile than in many other countries. They have, for example, nothing like the same depth or scale as in Germany, the UK or, even more particularly, the US. Thus, these markets do not offer non-residents a particularly attractive means of holding their international liquidity.

Paris has, however, an important role in certain aspects of the international financial markets. It is probably the most important centre of the euro-sterling market. It has also become a major home of Arab banks operating in Western Europe. Paris benefited from its traditional pro-Arab stance, the problems of Beirut and the lack of any substantial alternative financial centre in the Arab world itself. There are some twenty-five banks with Arab links in Paris, of which many are consortium banks with some shareholders from the Arab world. This has made Paris an important centre for placing power as regards bond issues and syndicated credits, and as a means of tapping the ultimate source of funds within the OPEC world.

This gives the French financial community an identity and also considerable importance in this particular area of finance. The capacity of the Arab countries to absorb bank credit and eurobonds is of course very substantial indeed. Apart from this, relatively few of the French banks play a major part in the international bond market. The main exception, however, is Paribas (Banque de Paris et des Pays-Bas) which has consistently been near the top of the league of international bond placers.

FRENCH FRANC EUROBONDS

A further distinctive feature of the French as opposed to the international financial markets in recent years has been the use of the French franc on various occasions as the currency of eurobonds. One of the main problems of this currency has been obtaining investor acceptance, particularly in view of the fluctuating interest rates of French francs, and also of the fear of inflation and hence capital loss.

But on occasion these fears have been allayed, generally coinciding with periods of strength in the French balance of payments and relatively low inflation, and the authorities have permitted such issues to be made. These have taken place in two main spells over the past six years – in 1972/73 and in 1975. The general performance is rather similar to that of sterling eurobonds. It has been a narrow market which has not played a major part in the flow of funds in the international capital market. The risk to the balance of payments or to economic control of France or Britain has been negligible given the small scale and the predictability of these capital issues, not to mention the rules regarding sources and uses of the relevant funds. The main problem has been one of investor acceptance, and in neither case has this been solved decisively.

TABLE 7.4: Eurobond Issues in French Francs, 1971–8 (*$ million equivalent*)

1971	1972	1973	1974	1975	1976	1977	1978
54	534	152	—	286	62	—	46

Source: World Bank, *Borrowing in International Capital Markets*.

EXCHANGE CONTROL

The French attitude towards financial matters is a mixture of dirigism and the proper use of free markets. This attitude pervades their policies towards exchange control, as regards both foreign purchases of French assets, or capital inflows into France, and French residents' purchases of foreign assets, or capital and credit flows out of France. There have been no major changes in the overall attitutde towards these matters over this period, except in connection with France's obligations as an EEC member. In general these policies have moved cyclically in accordance with the French balance of payments and the priorities regarding economic policy. One 'trend' change has been a series of measures designed to help exporters face world-wide competition, the un- certainties of fluctuating exchange rates and foreign countries' export policies. Like most other industrialised countries France has offered exporters generally a more substantial range of assistance. But areas in which cyclical changes have taken place include the ability of French companies to borrow foreign currencies, the rules regarding foreign purchases of French stocks and bonds and other financial assets, the rules regarding French purchases of real estate abroad and other foreign assets and lending by French banks to non-residents. In this area France is very much like other industrialised countries which have to tailor the detail of economic and exchange control policy to the changing circumstances of the time.

EXCHANGE RATE POLICY

The French have pursued an apparently inconsistent exchange rate policy; they are traditional advocates of a fixed rate system, but they have adjusted the exchange rate, usually downwards, when it has suited them in order to maintain the competitiveness of their manufactured exports. In addition to this source of exchange rate movement, the French were forced by market pressures to leave the European 'snake' no less than twice and have at various times been conducting an independent float. Their latest policy move has been to encourage the formation of a European Monetary System (EMS) to be based initially on a European Currency Unit (ECU). This system requires considerable firmness of exchange rates within Europe, with a margin of tolerance of only $2\frac{1}{4}$ per cent on either side. The EMS has been established, after being held up by the French who demanded changes in the Common Agricultural Policy which were not acceptable to all the other member countries. Considerable doubt has been expressed whether France would be able to maintain currency parity with Germany over a long period, given the two countries' different performances as regards both inflation and their balance of payments.

One major achievement of the French in the creation of the EMS has been in effect to re-monetise their gold holdings. In the composition of French reserves gold has always played an important part – as indeed it has in the private capital of individual Frenchmen. Given the more uncertain economic times at present a major priority of French policy has been to obtain a greater value from gold holdings.

IMF statistics showed that at the end of 1978 the gold component of France's reserves – valued according to IMF conventions at around $46 (SDR 35) per ounce – was $4651m, accounting for 30 per cent of total reserves. When valued at the then market price ($226 per ounce) the value of the gold rises some $23,000m to 71 per cent of the resultant reserves of $32, 390m. Valuing gold at the market price adds enormously to France's reserves, providing a basis for considerably greater flexibility and strength in the future. Revaluation at nearer the market price was also an important issue for Italy and certain other European countries.

The role of gold in the world monetary system, after declining since IMF moves to de-monetise it in 1975, has assumed greater prominence again in recent months. This is partly due to the decision of the participants in the proposed EMS to deposit with the European Monetary Fund in due course 20 per cent of their currency reserves plus 20 per cent of their gold in return for ECUs. Agreement has been reached that the gold component will be revalued at a price based on an average of the past six months' market prices. Thus hitherto unusable gold reserves will become a significant addition to the liquidity of those countries as backing for the new ECU. These developments have obvious effects on the long-term health of the world gold market and on gold's value as an investment medium both for central banks and private investors. Moreover, now that the EMS countries have in effect a vested interest in favour of maintaining the price of gold relatively high, the risks of a sharp downward movement in that price have become considerably less. While gold has now been excluded from the legal structure of the IMF and of the formal international monetary system, in practice its importance in world finance is at least as great, if not greater, than it was, say, twenty years ago. When gold was linked to the legal structure of the international monetary system, and was under-valued, it could be said that it fulfilled two of the three functions of money. It was a unit of account and a store of value, but it was not a medium of exchange (because countries were not willing to settle accounts in this undervalued gold). In the present system gold also fulfils two of the three functions of money. But in this case it is a store value and a medium of exchange, but not a unit of account (because currencies are not formally denominated in it).

CONCLUSION

The main changes in French policy over this period have been the very substantial use of the international financial market for borrowing, achieving an increase in the status of gold, particularly among central banks, reviving on occasion the French franc eurobond market, setting under way further steps towards a European Monetary System, and hence perhaps a European monetary bloc, and acquiring a special niche in the international financial markets, in particular as a location for substantial Arab banking. France has needed the international financial markets and has helped develop them. Her policy towards gold and the EMS has helped push the world system in new directions: how much further the system will go in those directions, and whether that should be regarded as adaptation or a diversion of effort, are issues on which only time can adjudicate.

REFERENCES

D. Cudaback, 'French banks; sleeping giants', *International Herald Tribune Supplement* (December 1977).
J. Ennuyer, 'The French money market', paper given at Investment and Property Studies Ltd. Conference, 19–20 June 1978.
M. Kolbenschlag, 'Petrodollars create a Camelot on the Seine', *Business Week* (18 April 1977).
J. Thomson, 'How France bridged the oil deficit', *The Banker* (February 1978).

8 Belgium, Luxembourg and the Netherlands

BELGIUM

INTRODUCTION

Since the war Belgium has adopted an international stance on economic matters, partly because of its geography and size but also for more positive reasons. It has attempted to become the headquarters of significant international organisations, of which the outstanding example is the EEC, but it also attracted NATO when it left France. As a small country it has the advantage of being a compromise choice between more powerful rivals.

Since 1921 Belgium has been in monetary union with Luxembourg; this has required co-ordination of monetary and foreign exchange policies to ensure that leakages or loopholes in Luxembourg do not invalidate the effect of Belgian monetary and fiscal policy. Belgium has also been in the Benelux economic union with Luxembourg and the Netherlands. The mutual trade concessions in Benelux were more comprehensive than, and predated, those of the EEC, while the exchange rate commitments were also tighter. Belgium joined the EEC exchange rate system, the 'snake', at its inception and has remained a member ever since. The Belgian franc has never been formally devalued against the unit of amount of the 'snake', but on occasions the deutschemark has been revalued upwards against it and the other Benelux currencies.

Belgium also chose to offer itself as an attractive location for multinational companies setting up in Europe for the first time, and in this its geographical position was a considerable advantage. Brussels is a suitable location for administrative functions for international business and has become the European headquarters for many substantial household names. Banking and finance were similarly attracted to Belgium, and financial developments particularly of international wholesale business were encouraged. Nevertheless, Belgium's attitude towards international economics differs from what one might term the 'doctrinaire liberalism' of the US. Her approach to international economic issues is more pragmatic.

Belgium's economic history since the war has largely vindicated her strategic approach to economic policy. Growth was very substantial until 1974 and in line with the enormous success of the EEC. The currency has normally been strong and the level of living standards exceptionally high even within the EEC. Like other countries Belgium benefited from the boom of the early 1970s, with rising activity, upward pressure on its exchange rate and increasing inflation. This was followed by world recession, and the need to counter the existing domestic inflationary pressures. As the recession intensified Belgium faced special problems, stemming from the large share which structurally ailing industries (steel, textiles) had in total output, and the system of wage indexation which meant that Belgium was unable to obtain the conventional benefits from a devaluation because the level of real wages is very rigid. The authorities have thus found it more attractive to try to defend the exchange rate whenever it has shown signs of weakness. The economic recovery since 1976 has thus been rather slower than in the surrounding large countries.

TABLE 8.1: Main Economic Indicators, Belgium, 1972–8

	1972	1973	1974	1975	1976	1977	1978
Change in GDP (%)	+ 5.8	+ 6.5	+ 4.7	− 2.1	+ 5.7	+ 1.2	+ 2.3
Inflation (%)	5.5	7.0	12.7	12.8	9.2	7.1	4.5
Current Account ($m)[a]	+ 1142	+ 1155	+ 911	+ 705	− 296	− 373	− 600
Effective exchange rate[b]	102	99	105	102	113	116	118

Note: [a] Belgium and Luxembourg Economic Union.
    [b] Figures are 'end year' (18 December 1971 = 100).
Source: National Westminster Bank calculations.

MONETARY SYSTEM AND POLICY

The Belgian monetary system is characterised by a lack of specialisation; this is in direct contrast with the situation in London in the 1960s when financial institutions tended to remain in particular 'compartments'. This de-specialisation reinforced by doubts on some basic principles of monetary theory has meant that the authorities have considered that no single monetary variable, such as the money supply, could by itself be a suitable means of controlling the monetary situation. Consequently the authorities have armed themselves formally since a change of law in 1973 with an array of powers intended to act upon particular features of the situation.

The central bank has used its extended powers mainly to act upon private loan demand. It has rarely used instruments which affect directly the monetary base. Thus interest rate policy still remains an essential feature of central bank policy, and credit ceilings and controls over the direction of lending have been in operation for much of this decade. In periods of tighter money and credit the banking system has been under an obligation to invest a substantial part of its resources in public sector securities in order to prevent a liquidation of these assets in favour of an expansion of loans to the private sector, and also in order to meet the chronic and accelerating deficits of the Treasury. The central bank, however, has taken some cautious steps to a more monetarist policy by imposing quantitative controls over the amount of bills and bank acceptances which the banks may rediscount with the monetary authorities, and by introducing (from 1972 until 1975) monetary reserve requirements in the form of non-interest bearing assets with the National Bank, calculated in relation to financial institutions liabilities.

In view of Belgium's close economic and financial integration internationally, domestic monetary policy is determined largely by external considerations. A degree of autonomy for domestic policy is provided by the existence in Belgium of a two-tier exchange rate under which current payments are settled through the 'official' market using the commercial rate, while capital transactions are settled in the 'financial' market. While rates are allowed to move freely in the financial market, the authorities intervene in the commercial market to maintain the exchange rate within the margin agreed with partners in the European monetary arrangements.

The exchange rate was under upward pressure during 1972 and 1973 and the authorities had to adopt measures in order to defend it. These included increased reserve requirements and negative interest rates on non-resident holdings of Belgian francs and controls over the net foreign exchange position of the banks. During the initial part of the recession the Belgian franc retained its international relationship without great difficulty, but by 1976 the developing disequilibrium in the Belgian balance of payments, the deutschemark's appreciation together with the dollar's decline and Belgium's relatively high inflation rate in relation to West Germany led to speculation against the exchange rate. Domestic interest rates were the main means of defending the rate in 1976 and in two phases, early in the year and in August–September, they had to be raised to high levels because of the external situation. This aggravated the internal problems. After the deutschemark was revalued by 2 per cent in the 'snake' in October 1976 speculation disappeared, but the Belgian franc remained a relatively weak member of the currency agreement, and a further 2 per cent revaluation of the deutschemark occurred in October 1978.

EUROMARKETS

In the financial field Belgium's original international prominence came through her early development as an investment medium in the eurobond market. Exceptionally for a European country, Belgian individuals who own substantial savings have been, largely for tax reasons, large-scale purchasers of international bonds. Thus the Belgian banks had the opportunity of benefiting from this placing power and were able to offer bonds in the Benelux area, through either Brussels or Luxembourg. The Belgian banks played a prominent part in the initial development of the eurobond market and for many years they were at the top of the list of issuers of such bonds (see Table 1.11, p. 11). In recent years Swiss and German banks' placement power has reduced the relative importance of Belgian banks in the placement of international bond issues. In 1977 Kredietbank (the combined operations of Belgium and Luxembourg) was in sixth place in the table of international bond underwriters, Société Générale de Banque was thirteenth and Bank Bruxelles Lambert twentieth. One of the most successful innovations of the Belgian banks in this market was Kredietbank's development of issues denominated in units of account, particularly the European unit of account (EUA). These units were intended to make eurobond issues more attractive to both the borrower and the lender by limiting the exchange risk on both sides. The EUA was almost the only unit of account or composite currency cocktail to be used for a substantial number of bonds and was particularly successful in 1975 when issues totalled the equivalent of $371m, more than 50 per cent of which is estimated to have been placed in Belgium. Kredietbank itself has participated in almost all eighty-two EUA issues in the past fifteen years.

The original initiative taken by the Belgians in developing the eurobond market led to the establishment first of a eurobond clearing house in Brussels and then to a rival being established in Luxembourg. A subsequent section of this chapter deals with these two institutions.

TABLE 8.2: Eurobond Issues Denominated in European Units of Account
(*$ million*)

1974	1975	1976	1977	1978
174	371	99	28	165

Source: Morgan Guaranty, *World Financial Markets* (March 1978 and June 1979).

TABLE 8.3: Investment Abroad by Belgian Enterprises and Individuals
(*francs billion*)

	1972	1973	1974	1975	1976	1977	1978 (*11 months*)
Portfolio	36	31	15	36	13	18	20
Direct[a]	7	7	15	6	11	13	7
Deposits	1	6	13	3	18	17	15
Total	44	44	43	45	42	48	42

Source: National Bank of Belgium.
Note: [a] Excluding real estate.

Issues of foreign bonds on the Belgian market have been on a limited scale ($84m in 1975, half that amount in 1977, and some $140m in 1978), and the Belgian franc has not been used for eurobond issues or eurocurrency credits. Belgium's borrowing from the markets amounted to no more than $500m in the five years 1974–8. The most important relationships with the international markets have been through the placement of bonds by Belgian banks particularly with residents, and in Brussels' role as a centre for eurocurrency business, with some $5\frac{1}{2}$ per cent of European deposits (4.0 per cent of total eurocurrency deposits – see Table 1.13, p. 13). This share represents about half Luxembourg's business. High domestic interest rates in recent years have reduced Belgium's significance in the placement market. Table 8.3 shows that portfolio investment in 1976–8 was considerably lower than in earlier years, particularly 1975. For the future, demand will depend ultimately on the level of domestic savings, which in turn must be influenced by the prosperity and growth of the Belgian economy.

In comparison with the enormous accretion of funds in OPEC countries and elsewhere, the absorptive capacity of the Belgian market must be re-evaluated, although the Belgian market and the Belgian banks will remain very prominent participants in the eurobond capital markets.

FOREIGN BANKS

A useful development of the international structure of Belgium's finances was the influx of foreign banks. Their main interest has been in taking part in the eurocurrency and foreign exchange markets. For these purposes the proximity of major international company headquarters was an attraction. The banks have also taken part in the domestic commercial markets, a development aided by the presence of large multinationals, which account for 45 per cent of the total sales of Belgian industry. But the need to fund themselves from the relatively thin interbank market made the cost and availability of funds somewhat volatile. A steady if not spectacular presence in the domestic markets has however been achieved over time.

At the end of 1958 there were fourteen branches or subsidiaries of foreign banks in Belgium accounting for 8.2 per cent of the global assets of the banking system; by the end of 1978 there were no fewer than fifty-four foreign institutions and they accounted for one-third of the total business. Their share of the wholesale market is significantly larger, and the competition for corporate business is intense. Most of the foreign banks are represented by branches, which gives a more convenient legal structure for that market. The law limits strictly the use that may be made of a representative office. The Belgian authorities have recently been exerting pressure on the banks to give their Belgian offices more autonomy. Given that most of the international banks in Brussels are also represented in London and other European centres and that interest rates in the eurocurrency market are inevitably the same, it is to some extent a technical matter where business is booked. But Brussels has some tax advantages and its status has been enhanced in recent years. However, the most recent movement in exchange rates has largely restored London's competitive advantage. A parallel development to the growth of foreign banking in Belgium has been the international-isation of Belgian banks, both through their participation in foreign currency business in Brussels and Luxembourg and also by the establishment of subsidiaries and branches abroad.

The Brussels Stock Exchange has also developed internationally with a substantial increase in the number of foreign companies quoted, and with the foreign shares being much more actively traded than domestic ones. In 1976 the 150 foreign listings (compared with 227 Belgian shares listed) put Brussels well within reach of overhauling Paris in this field and not far behind Amsterdam. However, the Stock Exchange is not a major source of new funds either for Belgian or foreign companies. The Belgian capital markets are dominated by government bond issues and the role of private equity shares is limited.

A change in Belgium's basic international attitudes does not seem to be likely in the future. The authorities will be keen to see Brussels remain the headquarters for international and corporate organisations, although fiscal regulations and high costs may reduce its attractiveness. Other adverse factors include the restrictive attitude of the authorities towards the use of the Belgian franc on international markets and the narrowness of the domestic market which makes it unattractive for foreign investors. Nevertheless, the Stock Exchange and the eurocurrency market in Brussels will remain internationally active and the Belgian banks will be prominent in the eurobond market, particularly through Luxembourg where special factors apply. The relative absorptive capacity of Belgium may however be diminishing in relation to other areas. Belgium has very substantial social and economic problems stemming from the language difficulties, adjusting to the world recession, structural changes in industry round the world and the country's very high level of real wages. The extent to which the social pressures generated by these problems may impinge upon the growth of the financial markets has yet to be seen, but in the long run they may be counterbalanced by the possible growth in transactions in the ECU, the presence in Brussels of the EEC monetary decision centre and the gradual extension of the international network of the big Belgian banks.

LUXEMBOURG

INTRODUCTION

The economy of Luxembourg is closely linked with those of Belgium and the Netherlands with whom it participates in the Benelux economic union. The association with Belgium has been particularly strong since the 1921 monetary union and the foreign exchange and foreign trade systems are conjoined in the Belgium–Luxembourg Economic Union (BLEU). There is, therefore, no institution in Luxembourg which has been formally established to perform the functions of a central bank. Supervision of the exchange regulations is entrusted to the Institut

Belgo-Luxembourgeois du Change, monetary policy is applied by the National Bank of Belgium, and most other aspects of control of the monetary system are retained by the Luxembourg authorities and are exercised by the State Savings Bank (Caisse d'Epargne de l'Etat). Supervision of the banking system is carried out by a separate body – the Banking Control Commission (Commissariat au Contrôle des Banques) set up in 1945 for this purpose.

Traditionally, the economy has been dominated by the steel industry, which accounts for a quarter of GDP and absorbs almost half industrial manpower. Despite the current difficult conditions in this industry, the major Luxembourg company, Arbed, has recently undertaken a large investment and modernisation programme. For many years the authorities have followed a policy of diversification, notably by developing the Duchy's financial sector. Their success in this direction may be judged by the fact that banking has emerged as the second industry in Luxembourg, employing over 6000 people, representing over 4 per cent of the total labour force and contributing 75 per cent of all corporate taxes and 12 per cent of the government budget.

TABLE 8.4: Main Economic Indicators, Luxembourg, 1972–8

	1972	1973	1974	1975	1976	1977	1978
Change in GNP (%)	+4.4	+7.1	+3.4	−7.7	+2.9	+1.3	+2.5
Inflation (%)	5.2	6.1	9.5	10.7	9.8	6.7	3.1
Effective exchange rate[a]	102	99	105	102	113	116	118

[a] National Westminster Bank calculations based on data for the Belgian franc. Figures are 'year end' (18 December 1971 = 100).

Growth of the economy was steady in the early part of the decade but showed a substantial decline (7.7 per cent) in 1975 reflecting the decrease in foreign demand for steel. Modest increases have since been registered, but are only sufficient to raise the level of national output to that existing in 1974.

LUXEMBOURG'S POSITION AS A FINANCIAL CENTRE

A number of factors have combined to make Luxembourg attractive to foreign financial institutions. The country shares borders with Belgium, France and West Germany in the industrial heart of Europe, affording easy access for continental bankers. It possesses a bilingual – in fact largely trilingual – population and a healthy political and social climate. Of more direct importance is the fiscal and legal climate, dating from the Holding Companies Act of 1929. The application of this law encouraged the establishment of holding companies, of which there are over 4500 in Luxembourg, and liberal rules on taxation and international capital movements have also made the Duchy attractive. These advantages have been supplemented by the establishment (also in 1929) of a stock exchange which was internationally orientated from the start and the absence of a need for institutions to make detailed returns on operations. Moreover, in contrast with the Belgian and US positions for example, banks are permitted to carry out all banking activities and are not limited to either commercial deposit or security investment business.

A main concern of the government is to maintain the competitiveness of the financial sector, which means that the banks established there must be offered the same – or better – legal and financial conditions as elsewhere. Luxembourg has been designated as the financial centre of the EEC – for example it has the European Investment Bank (since 1968) and the European Monetary Corporation Fund (since 1972). This latter institution was set up as the formal administrative body to implement the short-term credits created in the maintenance of the 'snake' currency arrangements. The European Monetary System, which came into operation in March 1979, includes the establishment of a more ambitious European Monetary Fund to replace the EMCF.

THE BANKING SYSTEM

The banking system of Luxembourg is characterised by the presence of large numbers of foreign banks, but the authorities are very much concerned to maintain the quality of banking in the Grand Duchy. The requirements for establishing a subsidiary in Luxembourg are very tight. A minimum equity capital of LuxFr250m (LuxFr350m from 1 July 1979) is required and the sponsorship of two existing Luxembourg banks. The philosophy of banking supervision was described in the review of the Commissariat's operations in 1975 on the occasion of its thirtieth anniversary as being essentially to develop Luxembourg as a financial centre paying regard to the due protection for national and international savings and to guarantee by all necessary control the harmonious operations of financial markets by leaving all possible freedom to private initiative. The Commissariat has considerably expanded its powers since its establishment, particularly since a 1965 law which widened its control over banks, granting it power to set solvency and equity ratios. This type of authority, akin to that exercised by a central bank, was thought necessary because some newcomers from abroad were obeying the letter but not the spirit of the previous regulations. As a result of this legislation the Banking Control Commissioner may, with the approval of the Minister of Finance, impose regulations fixing a solvency ratio for banks and savings banks. This ratio is defined as the proportionate relationship between a bank's own funds and its current liabilities, and may be fixed by the Banking Control Commissioner at between 3 and 10 per cent. At present this ratio is at the minimum of 3 per cent.

The balance sheet internationally of banks in Luxembourg has increased very substantially in recent years, and totals about $40bn. This is a far more rapid rate of growth than the market as a whole and Luxembourg's share is about a fifth that of London (see Table 1.13, p. 13). This growth has taken place almost entirely in the euro-deutschemark market, discussed in somewhat more detail later.

TABLE 8.5: Estimated Size of the Luxembourg Eurocurrency Market (*$ billion*)

	1971	1972	1973	1974	1975	1976(*Sept.*)	1977 (*Sept.*)	1978 (*June*)
Luxembourg's eurocurrency deposits	5.4	8.5	14.2	20.1	26.6	33.5	39.8	48.6
Percentage of gross size of eurocurrency market	3.7	4.3	4.7	5.4	5.8	6.0	6.5	6.6
Percentage of European centres	4.6	5.3	6.1	7.3	7.9	8.4	9.2	9.6

Source: Morgan Guaranty, *World Financial Markets* (March 1978 and January 1979).

The number of foreign banks in Luxembourg has increased to nearly 100, with Luxembourg being used prominently by the German and Scandinavian banks. The American presence is less now than some years ago, because the Americans find that their existing structures in London, plus the possible use of Nassau for booking transactions, make the Luxembourg presence somewhat superfluous. US banks nevertheless provide the second largest contingent, after the West Germans who account for nearly a quarter of the foreign bank presence.

TABLE 8.6: Banks in Luxembourg by Geographical Ownership, 1977

Luxembourg	9
Belgium	2
France	6
West Germany	21
Switzerland	6
US	13
Scandinavia	9
Other	15
Consortia	11
Total	92

Source: Commissariat au Contrôle des Banques.

The entry of German banks has been a more recent development, the first German bank in Luxembourg having been established there for little more than a decade. Indeed, Dresdner Bank's decision to open in Luxembourg in 1967 made it one of the first German banks to be established anywhere outside Germany itself. The underlying rationale for German banks operating in Luxembourg is to avoid reserve requirements on international business. German regulations are such that these requirements apply to business looked in Germany even if in foreign currencies and international on both sides of the balance sheet, deposit and borrowing. Luxembourg is near German head offices, communications are excellent and German is widely spoken. Because of the difference in reserve and other requirements most international companies which wish to borrow deutschemarks would find it cheaper to do so in Luxembourg than in Germany. German banks are now thought to be responsible for about half of all Luxembourg's euromarket business, and in total the balance sheet volume of German banking subsidiaries in Luxembourg represents 14 per cent of that of the parent banks, or the equivalent of DM63bn.

Relations with the German authorities over supervision of German banks' subsidiaries in Luxembourg have now become more orderly, but pose difficult problems still. Representatives from German parent banks are carrying on discussions with the Federal Supervisory Office of Credit Institutes about achieving greater transparency in the banks' international operations. The German authorities and the Commissariat have agreed to a certain co-operation which would allow the German agency to get figures of the German subsidiaries' operations through the parent bank. The German supervisory authorities have also concluded a 'gentlemen's agreement' with the Luxembourg authorities in order to control the affiliates of German banks there.

THE EUROPEAN INVESTMENT BANK

Luxembourg's status as a financial centre was recognised and enhanced by the transfer to the city in 1968 of the European Investment Bank (EIB), previously located in Brussels. The EIB was established in 1957 under the Treaty of Rome and began its financing operations two years later. It is a self-governing institution within the Community with independent legal status and is afforded financial autonomy in order that it may exercise independent banking judgement in the selection of investment projects. The bank's prime purpose is to make long-term loans available for financing projects in less developed regions of the EEC, modernising or converting industries in decline, and realising ventures of common interest to several member states, although lending for operations outside the EEC is also permitted. The EIB has expanded rapidly in recent years, its annual financing operations having almost doubled since 1973 (the year that the UK, Denmark and Ireland joined the Community) to reach almost 1.6bn units of account (£1.04bn) in 1977.

From its founding up to the end of 1977 the institution had provided 8.506bn EUA in financing, 87 per cent of it to the EEC member states. The EIB is now expanding its lending in two main areas: to industry to help resolve the problems of slow growth and for regional and infrastructure development. Lending to industry increased 43 per cent in 1977 to 426.2m EUA, almost half to the steel industry. As part of this lending the EIB has boosted its global loans, credits to national intermediary bodies for onlending to small- and medium-size industry, by 50 per cent to 91.3m EUA.

The growth of the bank's financing operations has entailed a corresponding increase in its borrowing requirement, supplied principally through the capital markets. As a result the EIB has become the EEC's major borrower. In the past the EIB has raised the bulk of its funds on the national markets of member countries, but in recent years it has turned increasingly to national markets outside the EEC and to the international capital markets. The EIB now borrows on most world financial markets. Non-EEC currencies have recently accounted for up to 65 per cent of borrowing. At the end of June 1978 outstanding borrowings were denominated in a total of twelve currencies, the main ones being the US dollar (44 per cent), the deutschemark (21 per cent) and the Swiss franc (9 per cent).

EUROMARKETS

(a) Eurocurrencies

Since 1971 Luxembourg has increased its share of eurocurrency business in European centres from 5 to almost 10 per cent (see Table 8.5). In the deutschemark sector, which accounts for 15 per cent of the gross eurocurrency market, it is the leading centre, conducting almost half the transactions in that currency. During 1978 the Germans were forced to strengthen their national exchange control defences against appreciation of the deutschemark, resulting in a further expansion of the substantial holdings of liquid deutschemarks outside Germany. The holdings provide non-residents with the opportunity to buy deutschemark securities without dealing in the German domestic market, boosting the business of banks located in Luxembourg. The four main euromarket subsidiaries of German banks in Luxembourg, which have a combined balance sheet of about DM40bn ($19bn) would naturally expect considerably enhanced business in Luxembourg whenever attempts are made to tighten significantly the exchange control regulations on dealings in Germany itself.

In April 1978 a euro-deutschemark credit for the Bulgarian Foreign Trade Bank for the first time offered an interest rate linked to the Luxembourg inter-bank offer rate, dubbed 'Luxibor', instead of to the more traditional LIBOR (London inter-bank offer rate). This reflected Luxembourg's growing prominence as a euro-deutschemark centre; this development made it reasonable to peg eurocredits in that currency to the local offered rate. The move was pioneered by a relative newcomer to the Luxembourg scene, but more established German banks are not particularly impressed with 'Luxibor' and warn that for borrowers, if liquidity dries up and a thinner Luxembourg market develops, a higher rate of interest may be charged.

(b) Eurobonds

Despite uncertainties in the early 1970s and the lower protection there than in national stock markets, over the past few years there has been a sharp increase in the number of borrowers using and of lenders willing to place funds in the eurobond market. Whatever fears there may have been at one time about the long-term development of this market, these have now been overtaken by events, and growth in the period 1975–8 was massive. The increasing maturity of the market has merited and generated a more sophisticated infrastructure. Luxembourg has been well placed to provide this, and has taken full advantage of the opportunities. Perhaps the first major step towards improving the trading capability of the market was the foundation of Euroclear by Morgan Guaranty in Brussels in 1968. This was followed, three years later by Cedel, founded jointly in Luxembourg by seventy-one banking institutions on a non-profit making basis. These two clearing systems have continued in competition since then, with neither completely dominating the other. By 1977 the annual turnover of Euroclear had reached $47bn, that of Cedel $38bn.

Another measure of the relative scale of the two systems shows that at the most recent count Cedel had some 860 participants: Euroclear had somewhat fewer, but claims that something like three-quarters of all market makers use it. The range of services has increased since the early seventies. This growth has been fostered by the active competition between the two systems; for instance Cedel has offered its participants overdraft facilities, thus catching up with a service offered by Euroclear for some time. A bond lending service may also be introduced by Cedel, in a move to match Euroclear.

The basic structural difference is that Cedel has only one main depository – in Luxembourg – while Euroclear uses sixteen depositories in many centres. Both clearing centres offer fungibility, which means that bond owners are credited with a certain number of bonds in the system, but do not necessarily receive back exactly the same bonds, when liquidating their holdings. This is analogous to banking where one's deposits of bank notes are fungible. One will receive different bank notes – but of course to an equivalent sum – when withdrawing. Cedel offers non-fungibility as well, and this may be a slight advantage in that France and Italy do not allow their nationals to deal in fungible accounts. But euroclear reports that this is a relatively slight disadvantage since in practice there is very little demand for non-fungibility.

Both clearing houses have been highly profitable. The duopolistic situation appears to have had the effect of stimulating the development of new services and other forms of beneficial competition. Morgan Guaranty sold its original investment to a syndicate of banks in 1972 and manages Euroclear on a contractual basis. There would be legal complications and considerable costs in attempting to unite these two systems and it seems unlikely that it will be done.

The Luxembourg stock exchange plays an important role in the eurobond market in that it is the exchange upon which are quoted virtually all eurobonds. More than 1100 eurobond issues were listed at the end of 1977, some three-quarters of all public eurobond issues. The main exception are deutschemark bonds which are listed on the German stock exchanges, where naturally most of the dealing takes place. (Foreign bond issues, such as all Swiss franc issues and virtually all international yen issues, have of course to be quoted in the corresponding national markets.)

The main reason for using this stock exchange is to comply with legal requirements for institutional investors in many countries, and little actual trading takes place on the bourse itself. Luxembourg is important in trading eurobonds largely because of the trading departments of the banks who operate an over-the-counter – or, more precisely, over the telephone – system. Although many of the banks in Luxembourg are involved in eurobond trading in this way, they are not, with the possible exception of Kredietbank SA Luxembourgeoise, major forces in the market.

The administrative procedures of the Luxembourg stock exchange are quick and flexible – one reason why listing takes place there. The authorities will often accept the accounting practices of the home country of the borrower, thus making it unnecessary for the borrower to go through complicated, expensive and perhaps embarrassing special audits. In some cases applications are processed in as little as two weeks. The bourse also publishes the most comprehensive list of price and yield indices in the eurobond market. A computerised system for dealing came into operation in January 1979. Known as Eurex, the system is in someways analogous to the Ariel system for stock exchange dealing in the UK. It is owned by an international group of banks and will be used by the stock exchange as a means of keeping its services fully up to date and increasing its efficiency. Eurex is intended to match user orders with the best market maker quotes, execute the trade, confirm the exchange and then clear the transaction. A running service on yield and price developments is also provided.

Luxembourg's significance in the eurobond new issue market originally derived almost entirely from the importance of Belgian investors. The importance of Luxembourg in the primary market has varied enormously from year to year; the main determinant is still the behaviour of Belgian investors and in particular what they can earn on Belgian franc investments. When Belgian interest rates are high investors are tempted to invest domestically rather than in the euromarket. For example in 1976 Belgian interest rates were extremely high in relation to dollar rates, as the Belgians needed to defend their currency, and Luxembourg banks were in the management groups for only 27 per cent of eurobond issues, compared with 40 per cent in the previous two years. More recently the situation has changed; there have been substantial falls in Belgian interest rates, so Belgian investors have been returning to the eurobond market. As far as management of new issues is concerned the only domestic institution of any significance is Kredietbank, the Luxembourg affiliate of the Belgian bank of the same name.

Luxembourg is clearly concerned to match the facilities offered by other major financial centres, but is equally conscious of the need to avoid provoking opposition. As a small country it would run the risk of being overrun if other countries decided to act in concert against it. The delicate approach that needs to be adopted was illustrated in October 1977 on the occasion of the introduction of a fiscal package designed to remedy some of the competitive disadvantages which faced banks in Luxembourg. Even though the measures did no more than create conditions which already existed in London or Zurich, the package aroused suspicions that Luxembourg was attempting to create a tax haven, encouraging private investors to take their business to Luxembourg-based banks. In fact Luxembourg has never been a tax haven for foreign banks, and with corporate taxation at 40 per cent, plus a 15 per cent withholding tax on income paid out on dividends, it hardly offers the necessary attractions.

The October 1977 package contained five points which had long been sought by foreign banks: (i) the removal of the 10 per cent VAT on gold trading; (ii) compensation for Luxembourg's lack of double-taxation agreements by the introduction of tax credits for foreign withholding tax on interest payments; (iii) elimination of a 5 per cent coupon tax on bond issues; (iv) elimination of stamp duty on CDs denominated in foreign currency; and (v) a global value adjustment of up to 1 per cent on secured credits, allowing Luxembourg banks to create general reserves (previously global reserves of 1.5 per cent could be created only for unsecured credit).

INVESTMENT TRUSTS

Luxembourg has been attempting in recent years, particularly through its regulations on holding companies and trusts, to rival Switzerland in portfolio management. Nevertheless, at present the position of Luxembourg is well behind and it is most unlikely to catch up in the foreseeable future.

Attempts have been made to weed out the number of dormant investment trusts, leaving only those of significant scale, whose total balance sheet is roughly $2bn. Luxembourg has substantial advantages from this point of view, in that holding companies pay no capital gains tax and there is no withholding tax on dividends. They pay directly to the Luxembourg Exchequer an initial 1 per cent of their capital and an annual 0.16 per cent of their capitalisation. For our purposes it is sufficient to record that Luxembourg does derive some benefits from certain aspects of its tax arrangements, but is unlikely to develop as a financial centre purely from this point of view.

THE NETHERLANDS

INTRODUCTION

The Netherlands may be described as a country with a major minor currency. Thus although operations in the guilder markets are not on the same scale as in the dollar, deutschemark or yen markets, the guilder has been used actively over the period in question, and the Netherlands authorities have always had a positive and accommodating international financial policy recognising the benefits and value as well as the problems stemming from these markets. This in turn reflects a fundamental internationalism of the Netherlands economy arising from various factors, of which perhaps the most important is its relatively small size and its geographical position. The important Rhine waterway makes Holland a substantial entrepôt, with many of Germany's exports physically flowing through. Moreover it is a major oil terminal; Rotterdam is the largest port in the world. This internationalism led it to join the Benelux union, which gives it a much greater degree of integration financially and commercially with Belgium and Luxembourg than accrues from commitments to the EEC, or than the overall commitments accepted by many countries in relation to each other. The Netherlands is the home of three of the world's major multinational companies – Unilever, Royal Dutch Shell and Philips. In the post-war period economic integration with West Germany has proceeded apace and prices and exchange rates in the two countries have largely moved together. The Netherlands was a member of the 'snake' from its inception and maintenance of its position in the joint float has been a dominant element in monetary policy. One commentator has suggested that as much as 80 per cent of interest rate movements engineered by the authorities in recent years in the Netherlands have been concerned primarily with international factors. Table 8.7 illus-

TABLE: 8.7 Main Economic Indicators, the Netherlands, 1972–8

	1972	*1973*	*1974*	*1975*	*1976*	*1977*	*1978*
Change in GDP (%)	+3.8	+5.9	+4.2	−1.2	+4.6	+2.5	+2.3
Inflation (%)	7.8	8.0	9.6	10.2	8.8	6.4	4.1
Current account ($m)	+1278	+2353	+2060	+1986	+2668	+245	−1127
Effective exchange rate[a]	101	105	111	111	119	121	126

[a] National Westminster Bank calculations.
Figures are 'end year' (18 December 1971 = 100).

trates some of the main developments in the Netherlands economy in the 1970s.

Growth was fairly rapid in the sixties and early seventies in line with Holland's full participation in the post-war boom. While overheating resulted in an acceleration of the rate of inflation the exchange rate experienced continued upward pressure, and the balance of payments remained healthy. Indeed, over the period of the oil crisis and three years of its aftermath one of the strongest elements in the Dutch economy was the strength of the balance of payments, caused very largely by the development and exploitation of massive reserves of natural gas. These have given the Dutch considerable energy self-sufficiency, and at the same time improved the balance of payments by cutting energy imports and boosting export earnings. In 1977 and 1978, however, the current account deteriorated progressively, as a result of a combination of factors: an increasingly adverse position on invisibles, a high ratio of imports to domestic consumption, the effect on exports of the appreciation of the guilder and reduced natural gas deliveries reflecting self-imposed restrictions on the amount of gas exports in order to husband resources. Looking at the immediate future, the benefit to the balance of payments from energy is likely to continue to decline because peak levels of production have nearly been reached, but the Netherlands like the UK should retain energy self-sufficiency until well into the 1990s. The OPEC price rises affected the Netherlands severely, not least because that country was singled out for an oil boycott at the time the price rises were put through. This occasioned the authorities to reverse some of their exchange control policies. Since then the authorities have given greater attention to cutting back inflation and growth has been weak. The policy against inflation has on the whole been successful with the rate down to 4.1 per cent in 1978. The periods of currency unrest, and in

particular the weakness of the dollar, which led to substantial speculation in favour of the deutschemark in 1978, necessitated moves to
boost the guilder, and interest rates had to be increased accordingly.
The economic situation towards the end of the seventies shows steady
growth and relatively low inflation, but also a weakening in the balance
of payments and possibly in the exchange rate in the longer term as the
extra benefit from the gas revenue diminishes. The Dutch accept that
they have to follow the world as far as growth possibilities are concerned
and a period of slower growth is inevitable.

FINANCIAL MARKETS AND EXCHANGE CONTROL

Over this whole period the underlying attitude of the Dutch authorities
to the international financial markets has remained relatively constant,
being affected from time to time more by temporary factors than any
fundamental reassessment of policy. There are many financial assets in
the Netherlands in which non-residents may invest freely. Conspicuous
by their absence are markets for short-term money instruments such as
treasury bills or CDs, which are in limited supply; this aspect of the
money markets is not developed even for domestic operators. But non-
residents may hold deposits with Dutch banks outside the Netherlands
for periods up to five years. These are of course euro-guilder deposits,
and are subject to the euro-guilder interest rate.

There are also euro-guilder notes issued by foreign governments,
Dutch firms and Dutch banks, also traded in the secondary market, that
receive the same rate of interest as euro-guilder bonds rather than
whatever happens to be the interest rate in the domestic market. Non-
residents are also able freely to invest in the domestic capital market
obtaining whatever are the yields on those domestic instruments. It is
possible to buy a long-term investment instrument with the plan of
holding it for only a short period, and thus use it as a short-term
investment. But in that case the non-resident takes the risk not only of
the exchange rate changing over the period of his investment, but also of
the capital value changing. Possibilities include government and local
authority bonds, turnover in which annually exceeds some $4bn. The
mortgage letters (bonds) of the big mortgage banks, in which there has
been an annual turnover of more than $1bn, may also be used for non-
resident investment, as may the bonds and saving certificates of the main
Dutch banks. All these instruments are available through the intermediary of the Dutch banks and security brokers, and are quoted on
the stock exchange. Dutch policy is to allow at present very free non-

resident investment in the domestic long-term capital markets, but investment in the short-term money markets is confined to deposits receiving euro-rates of interest.

The situation changed significantly after the abolition of what was called the '0-guilder' circuit, which existed from 1971 to 1974. Under this procedure, developed in order to prevent upward pressure on the guilder by preventing capital inflows from abroad, the non-resident pool of investment in the domestic capital market was maintained constant. Non-residents could increase their holdings by buying from other non-residents or by selling to residents as much as they bought from them. The '0-guilder' market was thus the reverse of the British investment currency premium in which residents of the UK are able to buy certain assets abroad only when another holder sells (or alternatively through borrowing abroad) in order to prevent a capital outflow from the UK. The '0-guilder' exchange rate naturally could move at a discount or premium against the official guilder rate and at one time in July 1972 it reached a peak premium of $8\frac{1}{2}$ per cent. But it was the policy of the authorities to maintain the two rates relatively close to each other – in contrast with the UK where the investment currency rate has moved very far from the normal exchange rate and the premium has exceeded 50 per cent on occasion.

The '0-guilder' circuit was abolished in February 1974 at a time when the guilder exchange rate was under downward rather than upward pressure and the authorities had more reason to encourage a capital inflow. At the time it was abolished the premium was a fraction of 1 per cent – negligible in effect. This policy instrument, the '0-guilder' circuit, was unique to the Netherlands. It is a limited form of multi-exchange rate system. It remains doubtful to what extent the policy measure achieved the desired effect upon exchange rate movements themselves, since the guilder did suffer upward pressure at that time and other policy instruments had also to be used to try to protect the exchange rate. Indeed it was probably the fact that the '0-guilder' system had only a limited effect in achieving the desired policy objective that led to its abolition. In this case the response of the Dutch authorities is not entirely unlike that of the German authorities who found that the *bardepot* scheme was not particularly effective as a means of preventing upward pressure on the deutschemark. Moreover, the '0-guilder' system, by limiting activity in the capital market, could have had no particular benefits to those markets, and there may well have been advantages in terms of liquidity and strengthening the secondary market in allowing the system to lapse. Since then non-resident investors have maintained a healthy and active interest in the Dutch capital markets and non-resident holdings have been high and actively traded.

EURO-GUILDER MARKETS

The euro-guilder loan and bond markets have been active in recent years and the Dutch banks themselves have been able to play a leading role in the euro-guilder banking markets. Table 8.8 indicates the volume of euro-guilder bank loans and the euro-guilder bonds and foreign guilder bonds which have been issued 1974–8. Euro-guilder liabilities have been acceptable to international organisations with a wide currency diversification of assets and liabilities, and to companies with strong interests in the hard currency countries of continental Europe or the Far East. Thus Japanese, Scandinavian and continental borrowers have had no difficulty in placing their guilder issues in the long-term markets. Given the Netherlands' close links with Western Germany and the virtual compulsion on them to pursue fairly stable monetary policies, the guilder has been an acceptable long-term asset to international investors. Dutch residents themselves have not been able to participate in euro-guilder issues in the primary market (except in the case of an issue by a Dutch resident company), but have been allowed to purchase in the secondary market. Borrowers of euro-guilders have been required to make immediate use of the currency outside the Netherlands. Thus, as in the case of other currencies such as the deutschemark and Swiss franc, the guilder is used largely as a unit of account in these markets, although when Dutch residents purchase in the secondary market a capital export out of the Netherlands takes place.

There have also been guilder foreign bond issues in which residents have been able to participate at the primary stage. In 1970 for the first time a foreign bank was able to participate as a lead manager in a foreign bond issue.

Both foreign and euro-guilder bond issues are regulated under a

TABLE 8.8 International Bonds and Credits in Guilders (*$ billion equivalent*)

	1974	1975	1976	1977	1978
Eurocurrency credits	8	45	18	8	148
Eurobonds	382	627	467	363	313
Foreign bonds	4	235	692	182	387

Source: World Bank, *Borrowing in International Capital Markets* (various issues, 1974–8).

calendar (*calendrier*) under the control of the central bank, so the regulation of and participation in both the bond markets are totally integrated and under considerable supervision by the Dutch authorities. Moreover the Dutch banks play a very active part in the management of issues in both markets, and make sure that activity in them does not clash with that in other related capital markets, or with their relations with the Dutch authorities.

The fact that the Netherlands has managed to maintain a current account surplus over much of this period has facilitated its ready participation in the capital markets, and the situation might be more difficult if the Netherlands were to experience a protracted period of current account deficits, or the possibility of a major weakening of the guilder. But up to now the Netherlands has fulfilled many of the characteristics, on a relatively small scale, of traditional reserve currency or trading currency countries – a healthy underlying current account position, limited inflation, a willingness to supply some capital exports, and the controlled development of the markets which enable international activity in its currency to take place.

Euro-guilder rates of interest are more volatile than domestic rates, and are heavily influenced by expectations about future exchange rate movements. One of the main factors causing at times considerable discrepancies between euro and domestic interest rates is the central bank rule which in effect prevents banks from using non-resident deposits for domestic purposes by requiring banks' claims on non-residents to be at least equal to their liabilities to non-residents. This is aimed at avoiding a capital inflow. Thus when there is a period of speculation upwards on the exchange rate and non-residents wish to hold guilders, the Dutch banks are forced to reduce systematically and progressively the interest rate on euro-guilders to prevent this inflow reaching the point where it would be greater than their external assets, or they must augment their claims on non-residents. Thus euro-guilder rates are quickly forced well below domestic interest rates, although these will also decline as a result of the inflow into the money markets.

MONETARY POLICY

Domestic monetary policy has been used actively in the 1970s and comprises a variety of instruments, the main objective of which is to operate on the free liquidity of the banking system. In periods of tight money the banking system is forced to borrow from the Netherlands Bank, and each bank has a quota for its maximum borrowing under this last resort lending facility. When the banks are near this maximum quota, interest rates in the call money market may reach extremely high levels, as banks bid against each other to try to balance their books. When money market conditions are extremely tight the central bank may ease conditions by offering special short-term cash loans to banks or by using foreign exchange swaps: on the other hand, when liquidity is excessive the central bank may impose compulsory cash reserves, or also use foreign exchange swaps in the opposite direction. The Dutch situation is characterised by considerable intervention in the control of credit except for bank lending financed with long-term funds from the domestic non-banking sector, that is funds of a duration of at least two years which are free of restrictions.

The Dutch monetary system has to accept wide volatility of interest rates. In an economy in which exports and imports added together account to a sum equivalent to GNP, and the economy is being held within a very narrow exchange rate band to be in line with a currency such as West Germany's, external pressures (including leading and lagging) may have an enormous effect on domestic liquidity and on the exchange reserves. Because the influence over domestic interest rates is one of the main ways of reversing any adverse effects on liquidity or the exchange market, these instruments must be used very freely.

Up to 1973 it was possible to see some inconsistent elements of policy formation, similar to those taking place in Germany and Japan. By and large these countries like the Netherlands had a certain reliance upon administrative controls in the exchange markets, which they were later to decide were not as effective as had been thought. Moreover they were also trying to fulfil simultaneously two conflicting aims of policy. One was to prevent speculation in the foreign exchange market forcing the exchange rate upwards; the other was to tighten domestic policy as a means of reducing overheating in the economy. From 1969 to 1974 this was effected by the application of direct credit ceilings to the banks' short-term lending to the private sector. But the effects were contradictory in that by tightening the domestic policy the resultant pressure in the exchange market could only be upward. This line of policy came to an end in autumn 1973 with the OPEC price rises, the ensuing world recession and the changing appreciation of the expected fortune of the different currencies, including the guilder.

A new form of credit control was introduced in 1973 which would meet the requirements of the authorities for a mild form of monetary restriction, but would be flexible enough to accommodate severe restrictions when required. Bank lending was to be regulated through constraints on the available liquidity margin, rather than through direct ceilings; this would involve the application of a variable ratio of liquidity to deposits. Credit expanded strongly in 1974 and although the authorities were inclined to move to a more restrictive phase, two factors combined to induce them to take no immediate action. These were the economic recession of 1975, when GNP declined by over 1 per cent, and the fact that any sharp rise in interest rates – inherent in such a move – would lead to an appreciation of the guilder within the 'snake' and to undesirable capital imports. However, in 1976 liquidity ratios were increased quite sharply in a series of moves to curb credit in response to the 19 per cent rise in monetary growth (on the narrow M1 definition) in 1975.

Although the business situation remained difficult in 1977, the economy was showing modest growth and the authorities decided to reintroduce direct restriction to supplement the increase in the liquidity ratio which had occurred during the previous year. As in earlier periods of direct credit restriction, the system involves maximum monthly rises from a set base. As a consequence of these measures monetary growth in 1978 was much reduced – at around 6 per cent.

CONCLUSION

Belgium, Luxembourg and the Netherlands provide some of the most interesting examples of the interaction between changing international financial policies of countries and the structural development of the international markets. All these countries have long accepted that their geographical situation gives them no alternative but to accept substantial external and international pressures upon their domestic policies. All three countries have also long since decided positively to adapt to this situation by carving out special niches in the international financial marketplace and thus obtain economic benefits from this inevitably international orientation. The Netherlands has continued its policy of being a major minor currency and has allowed its currency to be used internationally in both the banking and bond markets. Its policy towards financial flows is fairly liberal and it has accepted that domestic monetary policy will have to be orientated to keeping its exchange rate in line with that of the 'snake', or in effect with that of the deutschemark. This policy has been maintained consistently over the period under study with economic benefit to the Dutch economy and its financial institutions.

Luxembourg has adapted even more positively to recent developments and has become the centre of the financial institutions of the EEC. It has fought to become a major 'off-shore' financial centre for deutschemark business and has attracted a major presence of international banks, in particular from Germany and Scandinavia. Its institutional structure in the banking and bond markets is now well established, and this should lead to further constructive development in the future. It has also striven to attract other international financial business, such as that relating to trusts and holding company operations. The momentum of Luxembourg's development in relation to the EEC and in association with the financial structure of West Germany has now developed to such an extent that further continued progress should be achieved.

Belgium also has a special place in relationship to the EEC, being the home of the Commission, and it has long been a significant centre of placing power in the eurobond markets. It has also become a minor centre for eurocurrency banking deposits, and has attracted a large number of international banks and financial institutions. Part of the basic infrastructure of the eurobond market has been established and developed there in the period under study.

The record indicates that the underlying financial policies of these countries were at the beginning of our period fundamentally sound. Many of these have continued relatively unchanged with considerable success for the countries concerned. On the other hand significant adaptations have taken place both in policy and in the institutional structures to meet the challenges and opportunities presented over the past decade. In general, too, these changes appear to have been soundly based and very few of the positive developments have had to be reversed or have caused serious problems. Further progress on the by now well-established lines should continue and these countries will also benefit from their strong position at the heart of the EEC, which would enable them to seize further opportunities provided by the increasing economic and financial integration of Western Europe.

REFERENCES

Amsterdam–Rotterdam Bank, 'Monetary policy in the Netherlands', unpublished paper.

'Luxembourg banking and finance', *International Herald Tribune Supplement* (May 1978).

J. M. de Jong, 'The Dutch market', paper given at Investment and Property Studies Ltd. Conference, 19–20 June 1978.

9 Scandinavia, Iberia, Austria and Italy

INTRODUCTION

This chapter is concerned with the countries of Europe which are least active as financial centres. There is a very limited use of their currencies for international commerce and finance, and by and large they are not capital exporters on a systematic basis. Nor is there much foreign investment in the domestic financial markets. The main link between these countries and the international financial market is their need for it as a means of helping with their adjustment processes in the recent more difficult and varied economic times. In the case of Italy a further link exists, for the euromarkets have been very important for the Italian banking system. Foreign currency liabilities amount to over $22bn, and are employed largely in lending overseas, but also somewhat – $6bn – to residents. In line with their widely varying economic structures the adjustment problems of these countries have differed greatly. The Scandinavian countries have had an exceptionally high standard of living based on very efficient production of a limited range of manufactured goods, a strong position in agriculture, resource endowment in forest and other products and, in some cases, a traditional strength in world-wide industries, such as shipping. Many of these industries have faced extremely severe cyclical or structural problems, reflecting the changing conditions in the world economy. This has applied in particular to shipping and shipbuilding, while commodity prices for forest products have remained low for a long period. But most sectors of export industry have suffered because allied to this is the fact that except for Finland the Scandinavian countries adopted the policy of fixing their exchange rates to those of the stronger European countries, in effect to that of West Germany, by joining the European 'snake'. While this has helped curb inflationary pressures in some countries, the resultant currency appreciations (despite the periodic devaluations which have been made) have made the adjustment of the Scandinavian economies even more difficult, and they are still in the process of making structural changes to find products which will give them an adequate added value, at an exchange rate which is appropriate. A further influence on the Scandinavian economies has been their advanced social legislation. This was a model for other countries during the substantial post-war boom, but in some ways has made for inflexibility at a time when it is necessary to adapt and to find new products.

On the other hand the countries of the Iberian Peninsula have been among the developing and industrialising European countries, with standards of living well below the average of Western Europe. During the post-war period growth in Spain in particular was exceptionally good and Portugal was becoming more integrated into Western European trade, such as through its membership of EFTA. Both these countries were hard hit by the slow-down in world trade after 1974, at a time when they were trying to adjust to political changes following the deaths of their respective dictators. In Portugal's case circumstances were made more difficult as these changes involved the loss of overseas colonies and the arrival of refugees from former territories. Portugal has now adopted a democratic constitution, but the political turmoil of those years had a very adverse effect upon the economy, and the economic problems are by no means over. Spain has also faced major political changes following the death of General Franco, but in this case the political transition has been made with enormous skill and has by and large been successful. Both Spain and Portugal face the twin problems of dealing with the social pressures and the high expectations of the population which inhibit social change, at the same time as they have to adapt their economies to a more competitive and changing international scene.

Austria is heavily influenced by German developments and while its economy is largely integrated into that of West Germany, the weight attached to various economic goals is not the same in the two countries. Austria is more concerned with stability in income distribution and less inclined to gear performance to the attainment of price stability. As a small country she has no choice but to accept the inevitability of severe external pressures conditioning the possibilities for domestic policy. The Austrians tried to run their economy at a high level of activity after the OPEC price rises, but this led to balance of payments weakness and a subsequent need to slow down the rate of growth. Economic expansion has since been relatively slow, but the government has managed to handle this transition, using significant external borrowing, and at the same time get inflation under control. The political stability of the country has hardly been in question over this period, and the social arrangements for a form of power sharing and semi-coalition have stood the test well.

Italy was for fifteen years one of the success stories in the Common Market, but problems stemming essentially from labour anarchy and the abuse of trade union power in the late sixties and early seventies brought her economic miracle to a halt. Since then she has been faced with very severe political uncertainty, a low rate of economic growth and a major continuing problem of capital flight, particularly into Switzerland. The Italian economic and political problems are by no means solved, but following agreements reached with the IMF, which in turn followed agreements within the EEC, Italy at least turned its balance of payments round, albeit at the cost of slow growth and extremely high unemployment.

Table 9.1 sets out some of the key features of the economic history of these countries over this period. For almost all these countries borrowing on the international markets was an essential part of their strategy for bridging the gap between the challenges of the mid-1970s and their response to it. This borrowing has taken place heavily in the eurocurrency syndicated lending market and in the eurobond markets, particularly for the Scandinavian countries. In addition both Portugal and Italy have had to obtain funds from the IMF through agreed programmes, and Italy has also borrowed funds within the EEC. The country with the greatest long-term problem to date as regards the balance of payments has been Portugal. But by and large the borrowing of these countries has in no way impaired the ultimate assessment of their credit rating, and none of these countries is excessively bound in their domestic policies by this consideration.

The growth, inflation and current account performances of these countries show the customary reaction to the events of 1973, but some points stand out from the general picture. Because of its oil potential Norway has been able to sustain steady growth throughout the period and run a current account deficit – aggregating $14bn in the period 1974–8 – covered by huge external borrowing as shown in the final portion of Table 9.1. Another interesting feature is the dramatic turn round in Italy's current account; deficits totalling over $14bn in 1973–6 have been converted into surpluses in the past two years, in 1978 as high as $6.3bn. The transformation began with the imposition of an import deposit requirement in 1976, and was continued by restrictive domestic demand management, the depreciation of the exchange rate and an improvement in the terms of trade. The combined effect of these

TABLE 9.1: Selected Economic Indicators, Scandinavia, Iberia, Italy and Austria

	1972	1973	1974	1975	1976	1977	1978
Real growth (%)							
Denmark	+ 4.3	+ 2.8	+ 0.2	− 1.1	+ 5.3	+ 1.9	+ 1.0
Finland	+ 7.0	+ 6.5	+ 4.3	+ 0.9	+ 0.3	+ 0.7	+ 2.5
Norway	+ 5.1	+ 4.1	+ 5.3	+ 3.5	+ 6.0	+ 3.6	+ 3.5
Sweden	+ 2.6	+ 3.5	+ 4.0	+ 0.9	+ 1.5	− 2.1	+ 2.8
Portugal	+ 8.0	+ 11.0	+ 1.1	− 4.3	+ 6.2	+ 5.4	+ 3.2
Spain	+ 8.5	+ 8.4	+ 5.3	+ 0.7	+ 2.1	+ 2.4	+ 2.9
Italy	+ 3.1	+ 6.9	+ 3.9	− 3.5	+ 5.6	+ 2.0	+ 2.6
Austria	+ 6.0	+ 5.3	+ 4.3	− 1.5	+ 6.2	+ 3.7	+ 1.5
Inflation (%)							
Denmark	6.6	9.3	15.3	9.6	9.0	11.1	10.0
Finland	7.1	10.7	16.9	17.9	14.4	12.2	7.8
Norway	7.2	7.5	9.4	11.7	9.1	9.1	8.1
Sweden	6.0	6.7	9.9	9.8	10.3	11.4	10.0
Portugal	8.9	11.5	29.2	20.4	19.3	27.2	22.6
Spain	8.3	11.4	15.7	16.9	17.7	24.5	19.7
Italy	5.7	10.8	19.1	17.0	16.8	17.0	12.1
Austria	6.3	7.6	9.5	8.4	7.3	5.5	3.6
Current account ($m)							
Denmark	− 58	− 467	− 910	− 513	− 1915	− 1646	− 1391
Finland	− 117	− 387	− 1212	− 2173	− 1169	− 159	+ 578
Norway	− 58	− 349	− 1103	− 2408	− 3733	− 4936	− 2134
Sweden	+ 264	+ 1221	− 950	− 1614	− 2089	− 2772	− 981
Portugal	+ 350	+ 351	− 829	− 819	− 1246	− 1496	− 776
Spain	+ 571	+ 557	− 3245	− 3488	− 4294	− 2449	+ 1509
Italy	+ 2043	− 2662	− 8017	− 751	− 2816	+ 2284	+ 6254
Austria	− 194	− 359	− 471	− 322	− 1510	− 2972	− 1506
Effective exchange rate[a]							
Denmark	103	104	108	107	114	110	115
Finland	99	100	100	100	101	94	88
Norway	102	111	115	116	126	123	115
Sweden	103	97	103	103	109	92	93
Portugal	102	100	99	95	85	65	51
Spain	103	106	104	104	93	75	82
Italy	100	87	76	77	60	57	55
Austria	101	106	114	113	123	126	129
Borrowing in international markets ($m)							
Denmark, total			525	555	1661	1672	3266
of which							
bonds			124	214	858	799	931
credits			401	341	803	873	2334

TABLE 9.1 (*Contd.*)

	1972	1973	1974	1975	1976	1977	1978
Finland, total			400	893	712	710	1556
of which							
bonds			81	494	412	396	1005
credits			319	399	300	314	551
Norway, total			730	1530	1915	3184	3817
of which							
bonds			84	1322	1445	2561	2627
credits			646	208	470	623	1190
Sweden, total			312	1350	1550	2939	2672
of which							
bonds			123	1068	1110	1563	811
credits			189	282	440	1376	1861
Portugal, total			182	34	50	137	615
of which							
bonds			17	—	—	50	—
credits			165	34	50	87	615
Spain, total			1134	1124	2268	2411	2514
of which							
bonds			25	117	244	531	324
credits			1109	1007	2024	1880	2190
Italy, total			2440	181	105	1078	2792
of which							
bonds			50	61	85	299	225
credits			2390	120	20	779	2567
Austria, total			697	1335	706	1587	1380
of which							
bonds			492	959	706	1433	1230
credits			205	376	—	154	150

Sources: OECD *Economic Outlook* (July 1979); World Bank, *Borrowing in International Capital Markets* (March 1978 and March 1979); National Westminster Bank calculations.
Note: [a]'End year' figure (18 December 1971 = 100).

developments has restored Italy's credit rating in the international banking markets – Table 9.1 shows the resultant increase in borrowing from this source in 1977/78 – and has enabled early repayment of West German and EEC loans. Spain and Finland have also managed to turn their balance of payments round, with less need to cover balance of payments deficits, but are still major borrowers in the international markets.

The use of the markets have given all these countries an extra policy option and extra room for manoeuvre in difficult times; despite the fundamental differences between these economies, the euromarkets have had to play an important role for each of them. But the nature of this role has varied according to different circumstances. Norway has borrowed for resource development, Austria to consume and avoid unemployment, Spain to develop and Sweden to gain time in dealing with structural problems.

Perhaps the main change in financial policy has come in the case of Spain and Portugal, as they have chosen to open up and liberalise their economies through a combination of economic and political pressures. Indeed given their desire to enter the EEC some liberalisation of these policies was required for that reason alone. But Spain has recently allowed the opening of foreign bank branches in Madrid for the first time in many years, and ten have initially been given permission to establish there.

In the case of the Scandinavian countries there has been a recent liberalisation in the use of their currencies in the euromarkets. The main specific change in international financial policy stemmed from Denmark's accession to the EEC. This has required certain liberalisation of capital markets, and at the same time of the right to establishment of banks in that country. Previously Denmark had been virtually closed for new banking offices.

THE USE OF CURRENCIES IN THE EUROMARKET

There is no use of lire, schillings, pesetas or escudos in the euromarket. Short-term investments in Scandinavian currencies are virtually limited to the eurocurrency markets, which are free of any exchange control regulations in force within the Nordic countries. Medium- and long-term portfolio investment opportunities may be fulfilled in some of the countries subject to the prevailing exchange control requirements. The high living standards in Scandinavia and the political stability have classed the area in the top rank of borrowers on the international credit markets. Yet Scandinavia remains an enigma in respect of her currencies, money markets and exchange control regulations. The tight control and cautious approach administered and monitored by their central banks protect their currencies to some extent from the uncertainties of the international markets, and also restrict their domestic markets from becoming over-banked. This protective approach is typified by the exclusion of foreign bank branches from Oslo, Stockholm and Helsinki, although a few representative offices have been allowed. Following its accession to the EEC, Denmark has been more liberal by allowing branches to be established and some banks, mainly American have opened in Copenhagen.

Scandinavian banks (with the exception since the end of 1978 of those in Denmark) have been precluded from opening branches abroad, and yet they have to provide clients with the full range of international services. Their response has been to form banks with shareholdings from banks within the Nordic area. In the 1970s closer trade with the EEC and the increasing need to attract capital to Scandinavia prompted the commercial banks to form not only further consortium operations, but also wholly owned subsidiaries. Luxembourg's established position as a key financial centre has attracted many of these. The consortium banks have tended to offer a comprehensive service in all Nordic currencies, while the wholly owned subsidiaries concentrate on their parent bank's currency. Free of regulations from their respective central banks these relatively new operations created and developed the euro-kroner deposit markets and assisted in improving the exchange market for spot and forward quotations. Unlike domestic money markets, all interest rates are determined by the premium or discount applicable for forward delivery against US dollars, that being subtracted or added to the dollar rate.

No deposit markets could have developed in euro-kroner without the freedom to operate in forward exchange markets against the dollar. But while Norway permits a relatively unhindered forward market, the forward markets in Sweden and Denmark face exchange control regulations which have hindered any rapid escalation in turnover. In Sweden not only are commercial bank dealings in the spot market related to a percentage of customer business but the forward markets are confined mainly to bilateral dealings. Should third countries be involved the central bank may require to know the names of importers, exporters and descriptions of goods before granting authorisation. In Denmark temporary restrictions are enforced during periods of intense specu-lation, and at all times banks are precluded from purchasing Danish kroner in the forward market from non-Scandinavian banks for amounts in excess of DKr1 million unless the movement of goods and the names of the traders can be disclosed.

The development of the euromarkets outside Scandinavia enabled the business community to benefit from the opportunity of covering trading commitments by forward delivery. The banks have also been able to expand their services in the euro-kroner markets. Investment is predominantly represented by deposits placed with these banks on a fixed-term basis, and the choice of maturity and scale is less flexible than in the markets for major eurocurrencies. Occasionally investors may be able to purchase bills, promissory notes or loan participations denominated in Scandinavian currencies, perhaps at slightly more attractive interest rates.

The Swedish domestic market offers little opportunity for portfolio investment by non-residents, permission being required from the Riksbank and seldom granted, but the euromarket in Swedish kroner probably accounts for the largest proportion of external Scandinavian deposits. In Norway too, opportunities for portfolio investment are unattractive. Sums in excess of NKr100,000 deposited with Norwegian banks are subject to licensing and approval from the Norges Bank, but the door is not completely closed for non-resident purchases of shares and stocks, and special arrangements are applicable to Norsk Hydro. Again, however, permission is required if the purchases go beyond a certain scale. Turnover in Norwegian kroner on the euromarkets is not large, but the relative ease of dealing in forward markets enables sizeable transactions to take place.

The euro-Danish kroner market is also limited, but in contrast with Sweden and Norway investment opportunities in the domestic market are attractive. Following EEC entry the rules governing the sale of Danish shares and bonds to non-residents have been liberalised to conform with provisions aimed at freeing capital movements. Bonds issued by the State and various credit institutions are open to purchase by non-residents. They are quoted on the Copenhagen stock exchange, ensuring good marketability, with a daily turnover estimated in 1978 at some DKr55m. Non-residents may also purchase bonds issued by the four Mortgage Credit Institutions. These are regulated by government legislation and their bonds are considered akin to gilt-edged securities. Total non-resident investment, of which 75 per cent came from EEC countries, amounted to DKr1.3bn in 1977, compared with only DKr27m in 1974.

The market in euro-Finnmarks is the smallest of these euromarkets. Rates are determined by forward prices, but the central bank is very influential in view of the small size of the market, and is active in the forward market from three months to one year. State bonds and Mortgage Credit Bonds may be purchased freely by non-residents, but marketability is insufficient to generate much interest.

CONCLUSION

This group of countries clearly illustrates the vital role of the international financial market as a buffer between countries and in giving them extra flexibility to determine their domestic strategy. Moreover by providing a large number of creditworthy countries keen to use these markets, their breadth and depth have been furthered. There have been some changes in the financial policies of these countries, tending to increase the use of their currencies in the euromarkets, to create openings for investment in their domestic capital markets and to liberalise capital movements – at least within Europe. These markets have provided the vehicle by which banks from these countries, and particularly from Italy, can generate extra international business and obtain funds to deploy abroad – thus operating on a scale not limited to that of their home country. All these countries are economically integrated both within the European economy and within world economic developments. They continue to pursue widely differing economic and social policies, but for each of them the international financial markets are very important.

These countries have not changed to any significant extent their underlying attitudes to the international financial markets, although their methods have changed according to the changing circumstances. The operation of such large creditworthy countries as these in the markets has helped to widen the markets and attract new lenders. On the other hand, they could by no means have had the flexibility they needed had they not had access to this developing pool of funds. These countries needed the markets. They also benefited from them by having greater choice and competition among lenders, as regards the sources, currency and maturity of funds.

REFERENCE

J. M. Hale, 'Short-term investments in Scandinavian currencies', Investment and Property Studies Ltd. Conference, 19–20 June 1978.

10 Australia, New Zealand, Canada and South Africa

INTRODUCTION

It is convenient to take these four countries together because they have certain interesting and important elements in common, apart from their historic links with the UK which still persist in various ways. These countries are mainly producers of raw materials and agricultural products, and in most cases, apart from New Zealand, have very substantial resource endowments of minerals. They have in many substantial respects the income per head (in South Africa at least among the white population) of the developed countries. Yet they are major net importers of capital with regular programmes of substantial borrowing on international and foreign markets. None of them is a capital exporter to any significant extent. Despite being part of the world trading framework these countries have fairly nationalistic attitudes regarding financial institutions, and most have severe restrictions on the activities of foreign banks within their borders. There are virtually no external holdings of their currencies, and these currencies are used very little in international trade or finance. They were all hard hit by the fall in commodity prices after the OPEC recession, so their economic histories in recent years have shown some common features. Nevertheless, their problems have differed considerably, as have their policy responses.

AUSTRALIA

The Australian experience over the past few years illustrates many of the traditional themes of their policy, plus some new and temporary ones.

RECENT ECONOMIC HISTORY

A survey of the main features of the recent economic history of Australia indicates clearly the major problems which have arisen since the oil price rises. Growth was substantial in the main years of the last boom, reaching 6.3 per cent in 1973. Since then it has decelerated sharply and was only 1.9 per cent in 1975 and 0.5 per cent in 1977, averaging only slightly more than 2 per cent in the period 1974–8. This recession has been accompanied by higher levels of inflation, 9.5 per cent at the end of the boom and exceeding 15 per cent in the following two years 1974 and 1975, although a significant improvement had been effected by 1978 when the rate declined to 7.5 per cent.

TABLE 10.1: Main Economic Indicators, Australia, 1972–8

	1972	1973	1974	1975	1976	1977	1978
Change in GDP (%)	+3.4	+6.3	+2.4	+1.9	+3.8	+0.5	+2.0
Inflation (%)	5.8	9.5	15.1	15.1	13.5	12.2	7.5
Current account ($m)	+556	+490	−2608	−616	−1460	−2512	−3888
Effective exchange rate[a]	105	115	104	104	90	87	79

[a] National Westminster Bank calculations.
Figures are 'end year' (18 December 1971 = 100).

The OPEC crisis also precipitated a substantial current account deficit, averaging $2.2bn in the period 1974–8, compared with surpluses of about $500m in each of the previous two years. The effect of this on the exchange rate is not difficult to envisage, and from a trade-weighted level of 115 at the end of 1973 the index reached 79 at the end of 1978. Although the economy is showing signs of improving Australia still faces severe balance of payments problems, inflation has not been driven out of the system and real growth is still very sluggish. Substantial current account deficits necessitated corresponding external borrowing as shown in Table 10.2.

Because of her strong credit rating Australia was able to borrow mainly in the bond markets, and nearly half of the total raised from that source was from the foreign bond market rather than the euromarkets. The bulk of the borrowing was in dollars on the New York market although in 1977 and 1978 the major part took place in European currencies, notably deutschemarks and Swiss francs, and on the Japanese market. This borrowing did not build up until 1975 and 1976, a full year after the main deterioration in the balance of payments. Moreover, during 1974 long-term capital inflows were not substantial

TABLE 10.2: Australia's Balance of Payments and International Borrowing, 1974–8 ($ *million*)

	1974	1975	1976	1977	1978
Current account	−2608	−616	−1460	−2512	−3888
Long-term capital	+ 833	+637	+1424	+2151	+3693
Short-term capital and other items	+ 152	−932	− 367	− 588	+ 105
Overall balance	−1623	−911	− 403	− 949	− 90
Borrowing in international markets	274	801	1076	1073	2266
of which					
bonds	147	690	1056	1024	1467
credits	127	111	20	49	799

Sources: IMF, *International Financial Statistics* (July 1979); World Bank, *Borrowing in International Capital Markets* (March 1978 and March 1979).

and Australia was forced to run down its gold and foreign exchange reserves. In recent years the combination of increased external borrowing and revived other long-term capital inflows has managed at least to maintain the level of international reserves at around $2.5bn. The external use of the Australian dollar in international financing is virtually negligible, although $18.7m of that country's borrowing in 1976 and $11.3m in 1977 was denominated in Australian dollars. These applied to two bond issues. No credits have been denominated in Australian dollars.

The flow of inward capital investment, attracted by Australia's massive natural resources, has been influenced heavily in recent years by political changes. The arrival in power of the Whitlam Labour government in 1972 led to a sharp change in the Australian attitude towards inward investment and in the regulations applied to it. Strong nationalism regarding the control of natural resources has always been a major feature of Australian attitudes, since the resignation of Prime Minister Menzies in 1966, and with a Labour Government this was strengthened by a desire that the public sector rather than foreign investors including multinational companies, should control resources. Symbolically one of the first announcements of the Whitlam administration after its election in September 1972 was that legislation would be introduced to prevent foreign takeovers considered by the Government to be contrary to the national interest. The administration's attitude to the country's natural resources was made manifest in legislation which became effective on 23 February 1973; export controls were applied on all minerals, whether in their raw state or partly processed. For real estate, it was announced on 20 March 1973 that foreign investment would be restricted; for the time being exchange control approval would not normally be given except for acquisitions purely incidental to other purposes, such as the establishment of a factory. The general tightening of control over inward capital remittances was carried a stage further when in August 1973 it was announced that the minimum amount of such inflow for which Reserve Bank approval was required before the underlying transaction could take place was to be reduced from Aus$250,000 to Aus$50,000.

Energy resources were of particular concern with full Australian ownership of development projects involving uranium, oil, natural gas and black coal seen as a desirable objective, although a lower level of Australian participation was acceptable in the exploration stage. As a step towards eventual full Australian ownership of these resources the Government announced on 29 October 1973 that it did not wish to see foreign ownership in the mining industry going beyond the existing level. Guidelines for foreign equity participation and control in the mining industry were announced in the following November; all enterprises, Australian or foreign, engaged in the industry were required to conform to Australia's national interest. The mechanism for achieving this was the residual powers of export and exchange controls. Where important existing ventures were under foreign control the promotion of Australian equity and control over resources and industries in the mining sector was viewed as a longer-term objective. On 24 September 1975 new policy guidelines on foreign investments were announced. Henceforth they would be screened irrespective of whether they involved exchange controls. A new committee, the Foreign Investment Advisory Committee, was established by merging the Foreign Investment Committee and the Committee of Foreign Takeovers. Special requirements would have to be observed in respect of proposed investments in the fields of non-bank finance, insurance and real estate.

The new guidelines also contained a further elaboration of the Government's policy towards foreign investment in minerals. It was no longer necessary for foreign companies to seek Australian participation at the grass-roots exploration stage, but they would be required to report to the Foreign Investment Advisory Committee on the exploration programmes. The development stage would be subject to the following requirements. For uranium 100 per cent Australian ownership was required for all deposits discovered under exploration licences granted after 24 September 1975. For other minerals proposals for new development projects could have no more than 50 per cent foreign ownership, with the foreign participants having no more than 50 per cent voting power on the board of the development company.

As an indication of the continuing strength of the Australian economy during the early months of the Whitlam administration the Australian dollar retained its par value in terms of gold at the time of the February 1973 currency crisis and in fact appreciated strongly in September. As a means of combating speculative holdings of Australian dollars, the variable deposit requirement (VDR) applicable to borrowing from abroad was increased on 26 October from 25 to 33 per cent but drawings under loan agreements already approved by the Reserve Bank were not affected. By the end of 1973 the Australian dollar, on a trade-weighted basis, was 15 per cent above its Smithsonian level.

By 1974 the economic climate had changed and on 25 June the VDR on borrowings from overseas lenders for periods greater than two years was reduced from $33\frac{1}{3}$ to 25 per cent. On 11 November this requirement was suspended, and at the same time a previous embargo on overseas borrowing for a maturity of two years or less was modified to apply only to overseas borrowings of less than six months. On 14 January 1975 modifications were made to the controls over indirect forms of borrowings and over transactions having a similar effect on capital inflows. In general these modifications were relaxations, making it easier to bring money into the country.

During 1977 and 1978 restrictions on foreign borrowing were eased progressively. The VDR, which had been temporarily reimposed in January 1977, was suspended in May and the required maturity on foreign borrowings was reduced from two years to six months before being waived entirely in June 1978.

In November 1975 the Whitlam government was dismissed and they lost the ensuing election. The present government has decided that while there should be no fundamental change in the basic policy objectives regarding foreign investment, a relaxation to the procedural requirements should be made wherever experience has shown this to be possible. The previously mentioned stringent control exercised over foreign investment in real estate has been relaxed, and since June 1978 it has been possible for foreigners to invest as much as Aus\$250,000 in Australian property without seeking government approval. Moreover, whilst the government continues actively to encourage increased

Australian ownership of industrial enterprises, it will now allow foreign-owned companies with 25 per cent or more Australian ownership to undertake new mining ventures, providing Australian ownership is ultimately to be increased to 51 per cent. Foreign takeover of companies with assets of less than Aus$2m is now allowed, in many cases without requiring government approval. Further relaxation of Australia's restrictions on foreign investment is evidenced by the decision in June 1978 to increase from Aus$1m to Aus$5m the limit of foreign investment that may be undertaken without government sanction except in the financial sector and uranium mining. Table 10.2 shows clearly the improvement in long-term capital inflows. While this is in part due to a revival in private flows – as a response to the less hostile attitude of the present administration and the substantial devaluation of the Australian dollar in 1976 (which removed fears of capital loss) – it mainly reflects official borrowing.

INTERNATIONAL TRADE AND FINANCIAL RELATIONS

Traditionally the UK had been a financial centre for Australia and a major supplier of capital but a series of changes in policy in the UK itself had reduced this capital flow in the early seventies and on 23 June 1972 Australia ceased to be a Scheduled Territory in terms of the 1947 UK Exchange Control Act. On 19 September the Australians announced that the trade agreement under which the UK enjoyed tariff preferences would cease to be in effect from 1 February 1973, with the tariff preference structure being gradually dismantled. Australia's trade policy has since then incorporated its preferential arrangements with New Zealand under the Australia–New Zealand free trade area, and the adoption of preferential arrangements with regard to developing countries, in line with general OECD policy. Nevertheless, special action has been taken regarding low-cost imports from certain countries, including Hong Kong, in as far as they harm Australian industry. The concessions Australia had granted under the sterling area system were generally dismantled, and the privileged position which Hong Kong had enjoyed was removed. In her trade policy Australia enjoys a position somewhat between the developing countries and the OECD countries, in that it has substantial resource interests, and a relatively small manufacturing base. A very important part of its whole trade posture is its relations with Japan, for whom it is the major supplier of raw materials. The opening up of the Chinese market in 1978 provides the potential for the development of stronger trade links with the Far East through additional sales of raw materials and agricultural technology.

TAX HAVENS

Over this period the New Hebrides has begun to develop as a tax haven in the Pacific area, and the Australians had to take action to ensure that their own domestic policies were not offset by transactions with banks in that country. On 25 October 1973 the Treasurer announced that the Taxation Office had begun screening exchange control applications for all transactions between Australia and the New Hebrides. Approvals have not been given to transactions between companies and persons in Australia and the New Hebrides unless the Reserve Bank was provided with evidence that the Commissioner of Taxation did not object to the proposed transactions. All exchange control applications to make portfolio investments in tax havens are now being screened.

Further modifications of these regulations took place over the coming months and years with the intention of keeping appropriate control of the relations between Australian nationals and regional tax havens.

MONETARY AND FISCAL POLICY AND THE EXCHANGE RATE

The domestic economic situation of Australia was broadly one of increasing inflation at the peak of the world boom in 1973, followed by attempts to spend the way through the recession of 1974 and 1975. On the coming into power of a Liberal government at the end of 1975 monetary and fiscal policy were tightened to reduce the excess liquidity in the system and bring down the rate of inflation. External considerations also required some curtailment of demand. Policies of restraint have continued since, with but only slight relaxation, as the economic situation of the country, including the mounting current account deficit, did not permit any other course.

On the fiscal side the budget deficit increased to Aus\$3.6bn in 1975/76 (5.1 per cent of GDP) compared with a deficit of only Aus\$0.3bn (0.6 per cent of GDP) two years earlier. Since then deficits have declined both in money terms and as a proportion of GDP. These reductions were consistent with slower growth in the monetary aggregates during 1976, 1977 and the first half of 1978, with the growth in the volume of money on the M3 definition declining from a peak 22 per cent (annualised rate) in mid-1975 to around 6 per cent in mid-1978. Since then, M3 growth has accelerated and the government acknowledged that its previous target of 6–8 per cent growth for fiscal 1978/79 was unattainable.

Because of the pressures on the Australian economy between 1974 and 1976 the exchange rate was devalued on several occasions, the largest being a devaluation of 17.5 per cent that had effect from 29 November 1976. At that time the government adopted a new exchange rate policy designed to make flexible adjustments on the lines of a managed float against an unspecified basket of currencies. Since the end of 1976 the Australian dollar's effective (trade-weighted) value has depreciated by some 11 per cent.

CONCLUSION

In general Australia shows many of the structural problems of European industrialised countries, having rigidities within the economic system and a well-organised labour sector which can generate cost pressures. The Australians are caught between relatively free market and left-wing ideologies, showing the same philosophical doubts as in many or most industrialised countries. This has almost certainly impaired the adaptability and efficiency of the economy, and because of the current account deficit, the room for manoeuvre has been reduced. But the international financial community is heavily involved in propositions for financing the development of Australia's natural resources, including uranium, oil and gas, and there is little doubt but that in the years to come substantial capital imports will be achieved, largely offsetting the medium-term current account imbalance and in the longer term generating export revenues through the development of mineral resources.

NEW ZEALAND

RECENT ECONOMIC HISTORY

The New Zealand economy relies heavily upon the export of agricultural products, in which it is very efficient but has limited resource endowment and manufacturing capability. Its small size makes it a difficult base for manufacturing output, and it is inevitably a high-cost producer. Its agricultural production faces trade barriers in important European and North American markets and competition from other temperate producers in the world; in particular the accession of the UK to the EEC reduced substantially the scope for agricultural exports, many of which may well be phased out in due course. The economic history of recent years shows good growth during the boom until the end of 1973, followed by severe structural problems to which there is no immediate end.

TABLE 10.3: Main Economic Indicators, New Zealand, 1972–8

	1972	1973	1974	1975	1976	1977	1978
Change in GNP (%)	+4.4	+7.2	+2.9	+1.9	−1.7	−0.5	+0.8
Inflation (%)	6.9	8.2	11.1	14.7	16.9	14.3	11.5
Current account ($m)	+252	+214	−1128	−1400	−751	−629	−395
Effective exchange rate[a]	99	111	104	88	84	84	82

[a] National Westminster Bank calculations.
Figures are 'end year' (18 December 1971 = 100).

Growth was as much as 7.2 per cent in 1973, but since then has averaged only 0.7 per cent and was negative in 1976 and 1977. Inflation was already 8.2 per cent by 1973 and then increased steadily to 16.9 per cent in 1976 before moderating somewhat during 1977 and 1978. The current account of the balance of payments moved substantially into deficit as a result of the oil price rises, going from modest surpluses in 1972 and 1973 to deficits well in excess of $1bn in the next two years. The average deficit in the five years 1974–8 was almost $1bn. The effect of this imbalance combined with persistently high inflation was predictably a fall in the exchange rate.

The oil price rises and the following recession thus hit New Zealand particularly hard and given the structure of her economy she had limited capability for fighting back. External financing was clearly necessary, and in September 1974 a $400m eurocurrency loan was announced.

Total borrowing was more than $600m in both 1975 and 1976, rising to over $1bn in 1977 and 1978. New Zealand was able to tap the bond markets for substantial amounts. As a result of this borrowing New Zealand has managed to maintain a high level of foreign exchange reserves, and at the end of September 1977 had eurocurrency deposits of $294m. Despite regular recourse to the international markets, New Zealand continues to enjoy the highest rating, and borrowings are negotiated at the finest rates.

In recent years New Zealand has experienced a substantial change in its pattern of trade. The most prominent feature has been a shift in the direction of trade away from Europe, and in particular from the UK.

TABLE 10.4: New Zealand's Balance of Payments and Borrowing, 1974–8 (*$ million*)

	1974	1975	1976	1977	1978
Current account ($m)	−1127	−1399	−750	−630	−395
Long-term capital	+389	+1004	+743	+601	+431
Short-term capital and other items	+328	+ 91	+ 91	− 58	− 61
Overall balance	− 410	− 304	+ 84	− 87	− 25
Borrowing in international markets	524	656	613	1083	1079
of which					
Bonds	34	543	413	544	619
Credits	490	113	200	539	460

Sources: IMF, *International Financial Statistics* (July 1978); World Bank, *Borrowing in International Capital Markets* (March 1978 and March 1979).

Although the UK's accession to the EEC on 1 January 1973 was an important landmark in the dismantling of New Zealand's long-standing special relationship with the UK, the first event in this process occurred in the previous year when on 23 June New Zealand ceased to be a scheduled territory of the sterling area. On 28 June, a few days after sterling's float, it was decided to maintain the gold par value of the NZ dollar, with the effective parity for the US dollar remaining unchanged. This was followed in July by the modification of the access provisions of the trade agreements with the UK. In September it was announced that the tariff preferences accorded to goods of UK origin would be phased out. As a consequence of the UK's accession to the EEC the New Zealand–UK trade agreements were terminated on 31 January 1973 and, with the UK tariffs being progressively aligned with those of the Community, New Zealand phased out its British preferential tariff in four stages by 1977. Within the structure of the new tariff arrangements provision was made for preferential treatment to be given to certain developed countries, notably Australia, and all developing countries (with Commonwealth developing countries receiving more favourable treatment for some items). The new tariff system aims to put industry in a position to obtain its requirements of components and machinery from the most favourable sources. Thus imports from the UK are now subject to increased competition from other European countries, Japan and the US.

EXCHANGE RATE AND MONETARY POLICY

As in the case of Australia, the exchange rate remained strong during 1973. When the US dollar was devalued in February of that year the New Zealand currency maintained its par value in terms of gold. A new fixed relationship with the US dollar was introduced lasting until 9 June 1973 when it was decided to fix the rate daily in a new relationship with major trading partners. In September the NZ dollar was revalued by 10 per cent and by the end of the year the trade-weighted index was 111 (100 at the Smithsonian settlement). Since then the NZ dollar has been under continuous downward pressure, the index falling to 82 by the end of 1978.

On 1 June 1973 a reserve asset system of control over trading bank operations in New Zealand replaced the lending ceiling and guideline system of control. The basis of the requirement was expressed in terms of demand and time deposit liabilities, without any distinction between liabilities to residents and non-residents. This system was extended in March 1976 when the government announced that it was to introduce a more open and competitive monetary system that would allow the operation of an orthodox monetary policy, making it a more effective instrument of overall economic policy. This involved the removal of direct controls on the deposit rates of financial institutions and on the trading banks' maximum average overdraft interest rate and their replacement by a flexible system of indirect controls over the whole financial sector using market forces. In July 1977 controls over savings banks' term deposit interest rates were also removed and the government raised rates on its own stock to compete actively with private rates, opening the way for the implementation of full open market operations. Some further changes need to be made before the authorities' objective of being able to apply a fully effective monetary policy is realised, but the changes already made have resulted in a more efficient and competitive financial system and one which involves a more effective role for monetary policy.

CONCLUSION

The problem facing New Zealand is that its traditional exports of meat, wool, butter and cheese are for the most part consumed in developed countries whose agricultural sectors are heavily protected. The problem is compounded by the fact that exports or surpluses generated by the EEC's Common Agricultural Policy compete with New Zealand's produce in other markets which New Zealand itself is trying to penetrate. The diversion of trade from Europe and in particular from the UK to North America and Japanese markets has merely shifted the problem of negotiating access to markets from one hemisphere to another. It is necessary to strengthen and diversify the structural base of the New Zealand economy and to encourage a substantial shift of resources to the export sector. In this context substantial overseas borrowing will be indispensable for the foreseeable future. Moreover, in order to maximise the benefit to New Zealand from the international transfer of capital, direct foreign investment will continue to be encouraged. New Zealand has generally operated a liberal system with regard to capital inflows (except where assets are taken over from local ownership); dividends and other income due to foreign shareholders have always been remittable without formality and capital repatriation is subject to few conditions. The authorities are keen to encourage foreign capital provided it makes a positive contribution to the country's wealth. Under the March 1973 Overseas Investment Act the Overseas Investment Commission was established, administered by the Reserve Bank of New Zealand, with the function of reviewing all proposed foreign investment in the country.

CANADA

RECENT ECONOMIC HISTORY

Although Canada has substantial resources of oil she suffered in the recession that followed the oil price rises with reduced demand for most of her other export commodities. Economic activity was maintained at a relatively high level during 1974 and 1975, but only at the cost of severe inflation and large current account deficits. The anti-inflation programme in October 1975 was a key watershed in economic policy formulation. Since then growth has been at about $3\frac{1}{2}$ per cent a year, well below the annual rates of 6–7 per cent to which Canadians had been accustomed. Growth continued below potential until mid-1978 with unemployment rising, but since then the trend has been stronger.

Inflation was accelerating during the boom of the early 1970s and reached 10.9 per cent in 1974. Little progress was made in the following year, and while in 1976 the rate came down to 7.6 per cent, the past two years have seen renewed acceleration with a rise of 9 per cent in 1978, caused partly by soaring food prices. The policy of maintaining spending and demand in the face of world recession had the inevitable effect of causing a sharp deterioration in the balance of payments, and from near balance in 1971–3 a current account deficit of $1.5bn was recorded in 1974 and deficits of around $4bn in each of the following years. Inevitably the exchange rate suffered, and having been relatively stable from 1972 to 1973, largely because of foreign borrowing, it fell by 10 per cent in 1977 and a similar amount in 1978, though it staged a modest recovery in the early months of 1979.

TABLE 10.5: Main Economic Indicators, Canada, 1972–8

	1972	1973	1974	1975	1976	1977	1978
Change in GNP (%)	+5.6	+7.2	+3.2	+1.1	+4.9	+2.7	+3.5
Inflation (%)	4.8	7.6	10.9	10.8	7.6	8.0	9.0
Current account ($m)	−388	+107	−1487	−4696	−3841	−3903	−4635
Effective exchange rate[a]	101	99	100	99	100	91	82

[a] National Westminster Bank calculations.
Figures are 'end year' (18 December 1971 = 100).

It was an inevitable corollary of the policy of maintaining demand that Canada should suffer a balance of payments deficit and need to borrow heavily in the international markets. Borrowing began to accelerate in 1974, and increased steadily in 1975 and 1976 to a massive total of over $10bn in the latter year. In 1977–8 the usual types of provincial borrowing fell away and were supplemented by federal borrowing. Very substantial use was made of the foreign bond markets, in particular the New York market, but substantial eurobond loans were also raised. Before 1978 only some 10 per cent or less of the total borrowing took place in the international banking markets.

The Canadians succeeded for a time – some eighteen months – in having a sizeable proportion of their borrowing denominated in Canadian dollars, nearly $1.5bn in 1976, but the increasing weakness of the Canadian dollar generated lender resistance in 1977. Nevertheless, total Canadian dollar borrowings in that year amounted to over Can$600m.

The invisibles account of the Canadian balance of payments has always been influenced by the fact that Canada is a traditional capital importer, with foreign direct inward investment being very large until the late 1960s. The provinces have substantial autonomy in in-

TABLE 10.6: Canadian Balance of Payments and International Borrowing, 1974–8 (*$ million*)

	1974	1975	1976	1977	1978
Current account	−1487	−4696	−3841	−3903	−4635
Long-term capital	+1120	+3621	+7981	+4087	+5759
Short-term capital and other items	+ 391	+ 678	−3585	−3123	−2874
Overall balance	+ 24	− 397	+ 555	−2939	−1750
Borrowing in international markets	2477	4641	10025	5885	14433
of which					
US bonds	1962	3074	6138	3022	3142
bonds other than US	440	1479	2952	2350	1710
credits	75	88	935	513	9581

Source: OECD, *Economic Outlook* (July 1979); Morgan Guaranty, *World Financial Markets* (March 1978 and June 1979); World Bank, *Borrowing in International Capital Markets* (March 1978 and March 1979).

ternational borrowing, and even when the government requested them (10 July 1972) to borrow temporarily at home, it set up an information centre to assist them to borrow in foreign markets in an orderly fashion, by spacing out such borrowings. Moreover, Canada is very close to the New York market, and because of the heavy American direct investment it is sometimes contended that it is dominated by the American economy. Exchange controls between the US and Canadian currencies are virtually non-existent and the Americans have tended to exempt Canada from whatever restrictions have been in force designed to discourage a capital outflow from the US. Thus Canadian borrowers have easy access to the US bond market, and use it and the eurobond market extensively, although the Ministry of Finance has from time to time requested Canadian borrowers to explore fully the Canadian capital market before floating issues abroad.

A new development in Canada's substantial borrowing abroad was that the federal government itself entered the international markets on a vast scale after the end of 1977. Until then the Canadian government had not borrowed abroad since 1968. But in order to boost reserves, which had fallen to $3.7bn, and to moderate the depreciation of the Canadian dollar during the last few months of 1977 and throughout 1978, substantial borrowing was undertaken. A further reason for this borrowing was the desire to fill the gap caused by the absence of provincial and private issues in foreign markets, and as such the federal borrowing was viewed as a temporary departure from the usual practice of raising all required federal funds domestically. The bulk of federal government borrowing has been in the form of stand-by bank credits rather than bond issues. By early 1979 a level of some $3.6bn of such foreign borrowing had been arranged and some $2.7bn drawn. The reasons for this shift to the eurocurrency bank credit market are not entirely clear. Canada remains one of the world's prime borrowers and had it chosen to do so the federal government would certainly have had no trouble in raising funds in the bond market. There are two possible explanations of the decision to rely on the credit market. First, the usual flow of provincial borrowing dried up in 1977 because of cuts in spending programmes and the federal authorities might have wanted to leave the bond market open for the provincial governments and their utilities in case they wished to return, as indeed they did briefly during the second quarter of 1978. The alternative explanation is that the federal government may have chosen the credit market for its greater flexibility, believing that it would not need to draw all of the funds available to it, and would be able to repay quickly and flexibly borrowing that became superfluous.

Although foreign capital has always played a prominent part in financing development, Canada has in recent years adopted a relatively nationalistic approach to foreign investment, particularly in the banking field, and foreign banks have not been allowed to set up branches, agencies or subsidiaries, no doubt reflecting Canadian awareness of the power of the big US banks just across the border. This restriction has not stopped banks setting up financial companies of various sorts to engage in certain banking markets, and between forty and fifty foreign banks are heavily involved in making commercial loans in Canada – though they are not permitted to call themselves banks, and operate under provincial, not federal, law.

Canadian bank legislation is reviewed every ten years. The latest review of the Bank Act is now underway; but delays in introducing the revised Act have caused considerable uncertainty. A federal White Paper was published in August 1976 and the review should have been completed by 1 July 1977. This date was missed and a new deadline fixed for 31 March 1978, but this date passed too without any new legislative proposals being presented. Draft legislation was finally presented in May 1978, including proposals to bring foreign banks under federal regulation, but with permission to establish banking subsidiaries. This legislation had not, however, been dealt with by Parliament at the time of writing.

EXCHANGE RATE AND MONETARY POLICY

The Canadian dollar was floated in mid-1970 and was relatively strong through most of 1970–6. The authorities were not unhappy with the modest depreciation of the Canadian dollar, as there was some concern that the dollar was over-valued; but when this decline gathered momentum during 1977 the federal government began to borrow heavily in order to moderate the fall. The markets were, however, unimpressed, and despite heavy official intervention the exchange rate continued to fall quite sharply in 1977 and 1978.

The underlying reason is that the Government miscalculated the country's ability to ride out the world recession. On the other hand, Canada's export competitiveness has improved significantly in line with the currency depreciation, although the effect has been reduced by the depreciation of the US currency, since the US accounts for 70 per cent of Canada's trade.

The rapid inflation of 1973 and 1974 forced the authorities to direct attention towards achieving better price performance, and as part of their strategy for a gradual reduction in inflation, to consider control of the money supply. This was included in the Anti-Inflation Programme introduced in October 1975, with explicit targets for limiting increases in incomes and prices and a clear-cut commitment for restraint in government spending. But in November 1975 the Governor of the Bank of Canada confirmed that the authorities were specifically seeking to control expansion in one particular measure of money supply, the narrowly defined M1. This consists of currency in circulation, plus Canadian dollar demand deposits (less private sector float) at the chartered banks, excluding Government of Canada deposits. This form of monetary targeting has been maintained ever since. The main method of achieving the targets set for monetary expansion was to act on interest rates, and thus on the total demand for money, rather than on the banks' reserve assets, and thus on their ability to create credit.

Monetary policy is now conducted to lessen the risk of a new round of faster inflation being set off at some point in the future. Its central purpose, facilitating a gradual diminution in the inflationary pressures that already burden the economy, and the experiment in the use of the money supply as a guide to policy have been showing mixed but on balance helpful results.

CONCLUSION

A special feature of the Canadian situation is the recent increased pressure since late 1976 for an independent Quebec. Such a separation would impinge upon Canada's relationship with the financial markets because Quebec is an independent borrower in the world capital markets. Quebec's need for investment in utilities, notably power, makes it a substantial borrower, which like other provinces, it undertakes without guarantees from the Canadian government. The direct access of the provinces to the outside capital markets makes it more difficult for the Canadian government to control what is in many ways a decentralised federal state; as the pressures for provincial independence or freedom become greater, the international capital markets will need to reassess the implications of this change in the Canadian political structure.

By tending to integrate the provinces more closely with the world economy, the markets impose external constraints directly at the level of the provinces. In contrast with Quebec, Alberta is in a very healthy economic situation, largely because of its vast energy resources; British Columbia and Saskatchewan are also strong. Such differing provincial performances add to the centrifugal pressures on the Canadian federal system. Canada's need to adjust to the 1973 oil price rises and ensuing global recession, which it succeeded in doing more slowly than many countries, was made the more difficult by the problem of widespread demands for greater provincial autonomy and in particular the pressure in some quarters in Quebec for that province to leave the federal structure. However, there are many other favourable elements in the situation, notably Canada's hydrocarbon energy resources and the much improved potential for both oil and gas.

SOUTH AFRICA

As a consequence of being by far the largest producer of gold in the Western world, South Africa has a strong interest in the development of the international monetary system. Its affairs are also greatly influenced by its particular and very difficult political problem. This has caused a substantial reduction in the normal traditional inflow of long-term capital and has made the balance of payments adjustment, which the country had to make after the OPEC recession more difficult.

RECENT ECONOMIC HISTORY

The growth of the economy was relatively strong in 1972 and 1973 and then increased sharply in 1974. But since then balance of payments pressurs – first on current transactions, later on capital account – have forced the authorities to make a very substantial cutback in real growth, which has averaged only 1.5 per cent in the period 1976–8. Inflation has been a problem too; it peaked at 13.5 per cent in 1975, and since then it has stabilised at 10–11 per cent. The current account of the balance of payments, in small deficit in 1972 and 1973, subsequently deteriorated sharply to deficits of $1.5bn and $2.4bn in 1974 and 1975 respectively. But the policy measures to reverse this trend began to have an effect in 1976. The deficit that year was less than $2bn, and in 1977 and 1978 current account surpluses were realised.

TABLE 10.7: Main Economic Indicators, South Africa, 1972–8

	1972	1973	1974	1975	1976	1977	1978
Change in GNP (%)	+3.2	+3.5	+7.1	+2.1	+1.3	+1.3	+2.0
Inflation (%)	6.5	9.5	11.6	13.5	11.3	11.1	10.2
Current account ($m)	−122	−90	−1457	−2444	−1871	+580	+1225
Effective exchange rate[a]	98	108	102	86	89	81	75

[a] National Westminster Bank calculations.
Figures are 'end year' (18 December 1971 = 100).

The strengthening of the current account was, however, accompanied by a sharp deterioration in the capital account. As Table 10.8, shows, long-term capital inflows, which amounted to over $2bn in 1975, had dwindled to $201m in 1977 and were negative in 1978.

The payments deficits of the 1974–6 period had to be covered by substantial borrowing, and from a figure of $500m in 1973 borrowing increased to $900m in 1975 and $950m in 1976. In contrast with the other ex-Dominions, a significant proportion of this borrowing took place in the international banking market rather than in the bond markets. Only in 1975 were bond issues as much as about 40 per cent of total international borrowing. The bulk of the bond borrowing took place on the eurocurrency market, rather than in foreign bonds, and much of this was by the public sector. The use of the rand as international currency is virtually negligible, and none of the in-

TABLE 10.8: South Africa's Balance of Payments and International Borrowing,
1974–8 (*$ million*)

	1974	1975	1976	1977	1978
Current account ($m)	− 1455	−2458	−1905	+ 512	+ 1623
Long-term capital	+ 1646	+ 2175	+ 982	+ 201	− 819
Short-term capital and other items	− 340	+ 221	+ 232	−1253	− 770
Overall balance	− 149	− 62	− 691	−540	+ 34
Borrowing in international markets	775	920	957	33	453
of which					
Bonds	50	372	85	33	453
Credits	725	548	872	—	—

Sources: IMF, *International Financial Statistics* (July 1979); World Bank, *Borrowing in International Capital Markets* (March 1978 and March 1979).

ternational bonds or eurocurrency credits was denominated in that currency.

Since 31 December 1959 South Africa has had severe exchange controls on capital transactions, both on foreign investment in the country and the repatriation of capital invested. The sale proceeds of all non-resident owned investments have been subjected to a blocking procedure. Such proceeds must be credited to a blocked account with a local commercial bank. These Securities Rands, known as such since 1 January 1976 before which they were known as Blocked Rands (a term now applicable only to the funds of people emigrating from South Africa), may be reinvested in locally quoted shares or rand-denominated bonds. But the redemption proceeds of rand bonds owned by non-residents are not convertible into foreign currency. A non-resident may however sell Securities Rands directly to another non-resident at a discount of 40 per cent on the free-rand rate. In a move aimed at reviving the inflow of foreign investment, the South African government announced a package in January 1979 which expanded the Securities Rand market, enabling foreign companies to buy rands for equity investment in plant and equipment at the Security Rand rate. This rate is determined by market forces and stands currently at a discount of 40 per cent. Dividends from investments will be fully remittable at the commercial rand rate thus providing the opportunity for a substantial yield.

THE EXCHANGE RATE

Sterling's float in June 1972 and the changes in UK exchange control resulted of necessity in an amendment to South Africa's exchange control regulations; in place of the distinction between sterling area and non-sterling area countries, the authorities applied a distinction between the rand currency area (comprising South Africa, Botswana, Lesotho, South West Africa and Swaziland) and the non-resident area. Initially, however, the South African government decided to maintain the existing relationship between the rand and sterling, with the result that the rand's effective exchange rate began to float downwards in line with the pound. The link was severed on 24 October 1972, when the Reserve Bank established a fixed rate with the US dollar instead of sterling, but this relationship initially lasted for less than four months. Following the dollar's devaluation in February 1973, it was announced that the par value of the rand was to be maintained in terms of gold, with the result that while the dollar's index since Smithsonian had fallen from 100 at the end 1972 to 94 a year later, the rand had appreciated from 97 to 108 over that period. The problems of the external economy resulting from the OPEC action at the end of 1973 and the effect of political fears on capital flows exerted increasing downward pressure on the rand, including a major devaluation in September 1975, with the result that South Africa's exchange rate experience has paralleled that of Australia and New Zealand. From a moderate appreciation at end 1973 the rand now shows a post-Smithsonian depreciation of over 20 per cent. The decline over 1977–8 owes much however to the re-linking of the rand with the dollar during 1974. While this link with the dollar has had the advantage of helping transform the current account deficit into a substantial surplus, it has also inhibited fixed capital investment. As a result the South African government in its January 1979 package severed the link with the dollar and introduced a two-tier exchange rate with an official commercial rate moving to a limited extent in response to market forces but under tight Reserve Bank supervision, and a financial rand entirely dependent on supply and demand although having a very limited range of functions for which it may be used. The ultimate intention of the proposals is for the financial rand and the commercial rand to move into line and for there to be a single exchange rate. The present dual system is a first step in what may be a lengthy process.

CONCLUSION

South Africa and the other countries considered in this chapter have largely maintained their traditional attitudes to the international financial markets – namely those of borrowers. The existence of these markets and their present substantial resources give these countries much greater freedom of manoeuvre and a wider variety of choices. The presence of such creditworthy borrowers has also helped expand the markets by improving the markets' acceptability to new international investors.

11 New Financial Centres

ASIA

The 1970s have seen the growth of substantial financial centres in Asia, notably in Singapore and Hong Kong, and more recently in the Philippines. The main purpose of this development has been to tap the sources of funds and the outlets in the region, and this has coincided with extremely rapid economic growth in the area as a whole, with South-east Asia being one of the world's fastest growing regions.

SINGAPORE

In Singapore's case this development reflects that country's traditional approach to international economic affairs. It is a natural service centre because of its geographical location and has long been a major trading centre. It has a much higher level of income per head than the rest of South-east Asia and would find it difficult to compete with the rest of that area in the manufacture of relatively simple products. Its objective is therefore to provide services both for South-east Asia and for the international industrialised world and its corporations. The development of international finance was thus a natural outgrowth from this underlying structural feature of the economy.

Table 11.1 shows that Singapore has now further attributes of a

TABLE 11.1: Main Economic Indicators, Singapore, 1972-8

	1972	1973	1974	1975	1976	1977	1978
Change in GNP (%)	+13.4	+11.4	+6.2	+4.1	+8.0	+7.8	+8.6
Inflation (%)	2.6	25.7	23.0	2.7	−1.9	3.2	4.8
Current account ($m)	−510	−573	−1105	−605	−704	−543	−661
Effective exchange rate[a]	100	104	111	108	109	108	109

[a] National Westminster Bank calculations.
Figures are 'end year' (18 December 1971 = 100).

monetary centre, notably a very low level of inflation and a strong exchange rate under fairly steady upward pressure. The trade account figures indicate a steady deficit; however, the Singapore authorities remain unconcerned by these figures on the grounds that the overall balance of payments position is always covered by unrecorded items, which could well include a significant amount of financial inflows from neighbouring countries.

In the financial area one of the aims of the Singapore government was to establish an external currency market, in dollars, which has become known as the Asian dollar market. To this end external deposits in dollars were to be attracted to Singapore by banks which were able to operate in the market with departments licensed as having Asia Currency Unit (ACU) status. Legislation to this end was passed in 1968, and the Monetary Authority of Singapore (MAS) has always carefully supervised the growth of this market, with full emphasis on the need for exceptionally high quality business. In order to stimulate growth in the market, tax concessions have been given at various times on the profits stemming from this external business of the banks. As a separate development reflecting the greater confidence the Singapore authorities have in the ability of their economy to maintain low inflation and a stable exchange rate, there has been a relaxation in exchange control regulations covering Singapore residents. Permission for Singapore residents, corporate and other, to operate in the Asian dollar market has been changed and relaxed over the years. However, in contrast with Hong Kong, a liberal fiscal regime does not apply to non-residents or to employees of these banks; the fiscal structure in Singapore on personal taxation and the supervision over foreign companies' expenses and fringe benefits to employees is strict and taxation is relatively high.

To ensure a successful take-off of the Asian dollar market, the authorities in 1969 scrapped the 40 per cent withholding tax on interest paid to foreign depositors. The government also introduced incentives to accelerate market expansion. It abolished from 1 January 1972 the 20 per cent liquidity ratio requirement for all ACU deposits. This put the market on a par with the eurodollar markets elsewhere, for which one of the main stimuli to growth had been the easier reserve requirements compared with banking activity in domestic markets. Stamp duties on certificates of deposit and bills of exchange have also been abolished and in May 1972 exchange control was liberalised to enable local corporations to borrow from the market and maintain accounts in external currencies. At the same time the MAS announced that it would be prepared to consider applications by insurance companies and approved provident and pension funds to invest up to 10 per cent of their funds in ACUs or in approved Asian dollar bonds.

On 2 July 1972 residents of Singapore and of Singapore scheduled territories were permitted to invest in securities or deposits denominated in specified currencies with authorised banks and ACUs with the following limits: individuals up to S$100,000, companies up to S$3m and approved unit trusts, mutual funds and investment trusts up to S$5m or 15 per cent of their funds. As a further incentive to the market the rate of corporate income tax on interest accruing from offshore lending by ACUs was reduced with effect from the beginning of 1973 from 40 to 10 per cent and since February 1978 the concession has been extended to cover additional areas of activity in the Asian dollar market, such as managing and selling bonds, transactions in currencies other than the Singapore dollar, advisory services and acceptance business.

On 4 February 1976 greater participation by residents was encouraged when the limits governing investment in specified currency deposits and securities were increased to S$250,000 for individuals and from S$3m to S$5m for companies. The provision was also extended for residents to take such investments in foreign currency deposits, dollar securities and properties outside the scheduled territories.

A further major step towards acquiring the attributes of a strong currency centre was taken on 1 June 1978 when Singapore lifted all foreign exchange controls. Henceforth Singapore residents could borrow in all foreign currencies without prior approval from the Monetary Authority of Singapore (MAS). Limits on the amount of capital investment an individual or corporation could make in foreign currencies were abolished. Transfers of interest, profits and dividends, royalties and fees, the repayment of principal on foreign loans and repatriation of capital were henceforth without restriction.

In January 1978 the market for Asian dollar CDs was revived. Permission to issue such paper was originally granted in 1970, but in view of the lack of interest authorisations were rescinded and a fresh start needed to be made. Licences to issue CDs were granted to twenty-six banks, although not all participated when operations began on 3 January. Maturities range from one month to five years, with a minimum amount of US$50,000.

The attraction of foreign banks to Singapore resulted from a legislative system that established a three-tier basis. Banks could come in order to participate in the offshore market, where most of the new foreign banks operate. In the second, and later, stage they could operate in a limited range of domestic markets but only under tight scrutiny and approval. In the third stage they would have the full ability to operate in the domestic markets on the same basis as the local banks. Clearly, there is an element of protection for the existing domestic banks in setting up such an obstacle course, but on the other hand the local market could be swamped if major world-wide banks were able to operate in a relatively small currency market which might have to bear the brunt of speculative flows. There are in mid-1979 thirty-two foreign banks with offshore licenses, thirteen banks in the second (restricted) category and thirty-seven fully-licensed banks undertaking the whole range of banking activities. All types of bank may apply for approval to set up an ACU of which there are eighty-five. Under this guidance the Asian dollar market has developed rapidly in Singapore.

The market is clearly primarily an interbank one. It appears that in line with the general liquidity of the eurodollar market as a whole there has not been sufficient outlet in the area for the funds available, and many funds have been placed elsewhere, notably in Europe. It is possible to exaggerate the distinctive nature of this market, which is merely one part of the world-wide second-tier dollar market, and is linked through interest arbitrage and trading to other dollar markets.

Conditions in this market may not differ significantly from those elsewhere, and arbitraging ensures that the flow of funds will move flexibly in relation to possible outlets. Nevertheless the potential sources and uses of funds in Asia, and the development of Singapore has made it convenient for a substantial market to be established there.

As a further strand of the development of Singapore, Asian dollar bonds have also been established, namely the issuing of eurobonds in dollars. The cost of the issue is normally about $2\frac{1}{4}$ per cent, comprised of a management fee of $\frac{3}{8}$ per cent, underwriting commission of $\frac{3}{8}$ per cent and selling commission of $1\frac{1}{2}$ per cent. Other expenses would also need to be reimbursed although there is usually exemption from all taxes. The development of this market is shown in Table 11.3.

In this case it appears that the placing power within the region may in some cases be less than required to float bonds fully, and commentators have expressed a strong view that the distinction in this case between the Asian dollar bond market and the rest of the eurobond market is even more artificial than in the case of the currency markets. These dollar bonds are traded and listed on the Singapore stock exchange, but the main trading is on a telephone market. There seems no reason why local consciousness and prestige should not allow this market to be maintained steadily in relation to the general conditions in the dollar eurobond market, and it should be a source of fees and finance to the

TABLE 11.2: Growth of the Singapore-based Asian Dollar Market (*$ billion*)

	1972	1973	1974	1975	1976	1977	1978
Total market	3.00	6.28	10.36	12.60	17.35	21.02	27.04
Assets							
Loans to non-banks	0.60	1.21	2.63	3.30	4.05	5.28	6.38
Interbank in Singapore	0.10	0.26	0.22	0.27	0.41	0.57	0.87
Interbank outside Singapore[a]	2.20	4.71	7.31	8.83	12.54	14.68	18.96
Other assets	0.10	0.10	0.20	0.20	0.35	0.49	0.83
Liabilities							
Deposits of non-banks	0.40	0.91	1.61	2.07	1.96	2.26	3.60
Interbank in Singapore	0.15	0.41	0.68	0.58	0.80	1.38	1.44
Interbank outside Singapore	2.40	4.84	7.86	9.71	14.26	16.97	20.55
Other	0.05	0.12	0.21	0.24	0.33	0.41	1.45

Source: Monetary Authority of Singapore.
Note: [a] Includes inter-ACU transactions; figures are 'end year'.

TABLE 11.3: The Asian Dollar Bond Market

	1971	1972	1973	1974	1975	1976	1977	1978
Amount (US$m)	10	60	70	—	47	267	366	454
No. of issues	1	2	3	—	3	9	13	12

Source: *Far Eastern Economic Review* (7 April 1978); MAS Annual Reports.
Note: Figures are 'end year'.

Singapore financial community. Although the majority of the forty-two issues have been denominated in US dollars, yen, deutschemark and Swiss franc bonds have also been issued.

In conclusion, the underlying economic structure of Singapore is consistent with its role as a significant regional financial centre, and it has pursued the basic monetary and legislative policies required to enable this to take place. In contrast with Hong Kong, however, Singapore is itself not a natural capital exporter and capital flows out of the country from its own markets into other currencies have been very limited.

HONG KONG

In many ways Hong Kong could not be a greater contrast to Singapore, operating as it does in an ultra free market capitalist economy without Singapore's strong socialist leanings. Hong Kong exists too in a symbiotic relationship with China which is both deeply puzzling and in many ways quite improbable to outside observers.

An important development in the structure and standing of Hong Kong is the absence of exchange controls. Traditionally the currency had been linked with sterling, and the authorities had had to apply sterling area exchange controls in order to prevent the leakage of funds. Sterling's float in June 1972 posed the Hong Kong authorities with a challenge, to which they responded first by floating with sterling and then by pegging to the dollar. As a result of the change in sterling area exchange controls which took place at that time (discussed in Chapter 6) the Hong Kong authorities were able to free their exchange control regulations virtually entirely from those of London. They responded by abolishing exchange control from 1 January 1973.

The freedom of the Hong Kong financial markets has made it unnecessary to evolve an artificially contrived legal structure such as exists in Singapore. Hong Kong has vigorous and active stock markets which have been able to raise funds for the country's own business people. It is a natural generator of capital. It is also an important regional centre; by the pure fact of geography it is a key management centre for international banking business in, for example, South Korea, Taiwan and the Philippines. From 1966 foreign banks were restricted to finance company status, as the granting of full licences to operate in Hong Kong was severely limited to prevent Hong Kong from becoming over-banked. But early in 1978 the authorities liberalised conditions allowing world-wide banks to acquire licences to operate in the domestic market if they so wished, although limiting them to one branch only. A total of 41 new licences was issued in the period up to August 1979, when the authorities imposed a moratorium on the issue of bank licences because the number of applications was far in excess of that originally envisaged.

Dollar banking business is booked substantially in Hong Kong. Figures comparable to those published by the MAS are not available, but a recent estimate puts the size of the Hong Kong Asian dollar market at around $14bn. The allocation between Hong Kong and Singapore depends a great deal upon the fiscal and regulatory arrangements in force. Most of the major international banks are represented in both centres, and the booking of a transaction is simply a technical matter. The fiscal competition between Hong Kong and Singapore has varied over the years as each has modified its taxation system, and at any given time one country offers some advantages over the other.

Hong Kong has also been used for formal capital exports as a few Hong Kong dollar foreign and eurobonds have been issued. These issues took place in 1975–7 at a time when the Hong Kong economy was in a particularly strong position, showing price stability and a strong currency. The equivalent of $180m was raised in Hong Kong dollars during that period.

TABLE 11.4: Main Economic Indicators, Hong Kong, 1972–8

	1972	1973	1974	1975	1976	1977	1978
Change in GDP (%)	+7.2	+14.2	+2.2	+2.9	+16.9	+11.6	+9.5
Inflation (%)	+9.0	18.1	14.4	1.2	3.4	5.9	4.5
Trade account ($m)	−421	−591	−809	−748	−356	−884	−1949
Effective exchange rate[a]	98	103	105	108	117	110	97

[a] National Westminster Bank calculations.
Figures are 'end year' (18 December 1971 = 100).

Hong Kong's economic performance in recent years has been rather more uneven that Singapore's with faster inflation at times, and a more volatile exchange rate. Hong Kong's problem economically is that it is much larger than Singapore and is dependent upon the export of manufactures – largely textiles – to industrialised countries. The increasing protectionism in Europe, Japan and North America thus continually narrows its markets and it has either to go 'up market' or to develop new products in order to keep its manufacturing base flourishing.

Hong Kong's future as a financial centre seems secure, and the reorientation of Chinese policy implying much greater trade with the West should help it further. The wind of change in China means that many things will be done there which could not have been done a few years ago, and there may be a loss of certain activities from Hong Kong. Nevertheless, the rigidities of the system in China and the politicisation of economics means that it will still be more convenient to do many things through Hong Kong. The new situation should mean that the total throughput in Hong Kong will be far larger than in the past.

PHILIPPINES

The other recently developing financial centre in South-east Asia is the Philippines, which in 1976 introduced legislation to establish offshore banking units, with the aim of creating in Manila a financial market dealing almost entirely in offshore currencies, notably dollars. The Philippine situation is different from that in Hong Kong and Singapore in as much as the Philippines has a much lower income per head and a currency which could not be used as a unit of account in international trade and is fundamentally a natural capital importer with a weak balance of payments. Given its income level and population growth the country must always give great priority to the expansion of real income, which means that it will always be forcing itself against its balance of payments constraint, but the economy has been successful with growth in the late 1970s on an adequate scale. The Philippine authorities want to create conditions which will enable banks to earn profits from offshore banking, and at the same time to use the presence of international banks to encourage the import of capital into the country.

The Philippines' market suffers from being in close proximity to, and at the same time in the same range as, Hong Kong and Singapore which have a very long headstart on it. Nevertheless sixteen banks have established offshore banking units. Combined assets total $1.2bn. In undertaking this financial course the Philippines are thinking years if not decades ahead and it is more important for progress to be steady than volatile. In this they have succeeded and offshore banking in the Philippines should be able to show continued progress over the years, although it will remain a relatively minor part of the Asian dollar market.

THE ARABIAN GULF

The Gulf states have risen to prominence in recent years as a result of the enormous financial influence exerted by OPEC since 1973 and at a wider level the great strategic importance of the oil resources of that part of the world. They have in their different ways played an important part in the evolution of the world's financial structure. The area includes some of the main countries whose earnings from oil exports are so great that they have virtually no possibility of spending the income received. The two most notable examples of this are Saudi Arabia and the United Arab Emirates, in which Abu Dhabi is the Sheikhdom with the greatest revenue in relation to spending capacity. Qatar also comes into this category, as does Kuwait, for a long time a rentier country needing to invest its accumulated financial assets for the time when its oil exports will run down. Other countries in the Gulf area do not have such an abundance of natural wealth and need to earn their living in other ways, including in some cases through establishing financial markets. In addition to its investment programme Kuwait has also adopted this strategy.

SAUDI ARABIA

The internal markets of Saudi Arabia are largely closed to international investors in the sense that there is little suitable paper, short-term or long-term, and the financial markets are heavily ill-balanced with the supply coming almost entirely from the Saudi Arabian Monetary Agency (SAMA) which acts as the central bank of Saudi Arabia. The Saudi riyal has, however, been used for a certain number of international syndicated loans and also since 1975 for eurobonds on a limited scale. Apart from the thinness of the market and the lack of familiarity with the currency on the part of participants, the main problem in this market, from the point of view of the borrower, is that the exchange risk is substantial and to a certain extent random. Given that Saudi Arabia's exports are virtually entirely oil, and she has almost no production domestically to compete with imported goods, the authorities have considerable flexibility in moving the exchange rate with a view to whatever other policy objectives they might have in mind, such as the control of domestic currency inflation. This makes the exchange movement of the riyal difficult to predict and a major source of concern for borrowers in that currency.

Most of the borrowers are those who were unable at that time to obtain credit on the terms they might have hoped for in the major currency markets of the world. The majority of the loans and issues are managed by non-Saudi banks, predominantly Banque Arabe et Internationale d'Investissement, and Indosuez, in Paris, but the local banks have participated in the co-management and have taken an active role in the placement of these issues, not a difficult operation given the enormous creation of Saudi riyals in Saudi Arabia itself, and the financial resources of that country. By the end of 1978 eight public and several private bond issues had been floated in Saudi riyals.

While SAMA is reported to be concerned at the apparent internationalising of the riyal and is opposed to any significant growth in this sector, there is no reason why Saudi Arabia could not eventually establish the infrastructure and regulatory techniques to give it and its currency a role similar to that of the Kuwaiti dinar. However, the internal financial structure does not exist and it probably does not have a particularly high priority, given the other considerations which the Government has to face in the modernisation of the country.

One way in which Saudi Arabia has played an enormous role in world financial markets is as a placer of funds. Saudi external financial assets, excluding oil and other industrial investments, are reported to amount to no less than $70bn of which by far the greater part are in US dollars in the domestic American market. Some have been placed in the open markets and others invested directly through the American government. But Saudi money has also found its way into most of the other financial markets in the world, whether through diversification of SAMA's assets, or through the investment of the massive private and corporate fortunes being accumulated. This Saudi money has been a major prop to the American dollar, and Saudi diplomacy has been a key factor in American policy towards the exchange rate and international markets. The Saudi Arabian present ruling group must be the governing body in the world with the most to lose and least to gain financially and this makes them an exceptionally conservative government. But the fall of the dollar in the late 1970s reduced both the real price of their oil exports and the value of their accumulated US dollar assets. The fall in the dollar also adversely affected in both ways other OPEC members, some of whom had a less favourable distribution of resources to needs than Saudi Arabia and could not afford to view with equanimity the falling value of their assets. Thus pressure built up within OPEC for increases in the price of oil, which the Saudi Arabians attempted to resist because they did not wish to rock the boat further and precipitate recession in the West.

Attempts to restrain extremist policies have however become less positive in 1978/79. It has become clear that the Saudi authorities will continue to adhere to production limits and will not raise output significantly to help meet consumer demand in times of pressure. This attitude may reflect, at least in part, an unwillingness among important factions of the ruling group to offend other OPEC (particularly Arab) producers. The Saudi Arabians are in a dilemma because of their size in world financial markets and they may indeed have become rather more prominent as a result of the oil price rise in 1973 than they expected at the time. The same could also be said of several other oil producers. It is, for example, widely thought that the oil price decisions of OPEC in 1973 were taken by the oil ministers of the countries concerned, who had little inkling of the financial consequences of that step, and the way in which these might rebound to affect, in some cases adversely, other goals of those countries. Tables 11.5 and 11.6 give figures for the accumulation of Saudi Arabian assets and their distribution.

TABLE 11.5: SAMA's Reserves and Other Foreign Assets (*$ billion*)

	1972	1973	1974	1975	1976	1977	1978
Reserves[a]	2.5	3.9	14.3	23.3	27.0	30.0	19.4
SAMA other assets[a]	na	na	na	15.4	22.6	25.0 (Mar)	na
SAMA foreign assets[b]	2.9	4.6	19.9	38.9	51.2	59.1	60.4 (Oct)

Source: IMF, *International Financial Statistics* (July 1979).
Note: [a] Published in US$.
       [b] Published in riyals.

UNITED ARAB EMIRATES

The United Arab Emirates have many characteristics in common with Saudi Arabia, one being that the domestic financial markets are extremely narrow, with a few banks dominating the interbank market, and the other banks dependent upon them. In contrast with Saudi

TABLE 11.6: Total*a* Saudi Arabian Overseas Investment, mid-1977 (*$ billion*)

United States	
US Treasury bonds	12.0
US oil-related industries	10.0
Other US industrial operations	9.0
Partnership operations with major US oil companies	10.0
Held on deposit with US banks	7.5
Special loans and deposits of at least three months' maturity	6.5
Total Saudi Arabian investments in the US	55.0
Investments in other countries	
France	18.0
Japan	13.5
West Germany	12.0
United Kingdom	7.5
Canada, Italy and Spain	15.0
Total investments in other countries	66.0
Total Saudi investments in the 'West'	121.0

Source: *Middle East Currency Review*, vol. 4, no. 3 (February–March 1978).
Note: *a* Excluding private holdings of the Saudi Royal entourage.

Arabia, however, the Emirates are excessively over-banked. Following the volatile cycle of 1974–7 many of the country's fifty-one banks became illiquid because of their loans to real estate and uncertainty surrounding the dirham. When the construction boom, which was based on growth assumptions that were impractical, began to falter in mid-1977, two banks were forced to cease trading. The authorities responded by declaring in May 1977 a moratorium prohibiting until further notice the opening of any new branches or banks, locally incorporated or foreign. Restrictive measures were also introduced by the Currency Board, the most important being that dirham deposits with the Board were increased from 5 to 7.5 per cent, and the ratio of deposits to advances was tightened. The Currency Board's efforts to bring a greater stability to the system also contain proposals to establish a proper central bank.

The international use of the dirham is extremely limited, but several bond issues have been denominated in it. In all cases they have been structured in the form of private placements and have been placed almost exclusively with the major governmental financial agencies. There is some possibility for this market to be reactivated, perhaps on the lines of Kuwait, given the natural advantages of the Emirates, but this would require considerable stability in the financing structure, including interest rates and inflation, and strenghthening of the institutional and legal framework. There is the potential to use this market to provide part of the financing for local borrowers, but for a long time yet first-class international borrowers would probably be able to obtain better terms elsewhere.

Although the UAE as a whole is extremely wealthy, a vast difference exists between Abu Dhabi and the other sheikhdoms. The constitutional structure financially is imprecise; there is no formal pooling of financial resources and the emirates operate independently in the world's financial markets, with or without guarantees from the UAE as a whole. Some of the smaller emirates, notably Sharjah, have experienced a situation of over building. Dubai, which has an appreciable oil income, has been operating independently with some success and appears to be in a satisfactory financial situation. However, this prosperity pales in comparison with Abu Dhabi which has a colossal income in relation to its size. Its annual income, entirely from oil, is of the order of $7bn in relation to a total population estimated at around 250,000, of which only some 30,000 are local nationals, the rest being immigrants of various sorts. This gives Abu Dhabi a vast surplus for investment. Some of the money is held in short-term assets by the National Bank of Abu Dhabi, but the bulk is transferred to two major investment bodies set up to handle the money on a long-term basis. These institutions – the Abu Dhabi Investment Authority (ADIA) and the Abu Dhabi Investment Council (ADIC) – are major purchasers of financial assets and investments around the world, with the aim of maximising investment income for Abu Dhabi in preparation for the time when oil supplies are exhausted. Some lack of satisfaction with their performance led to reorganisation in 1977, but they are now firmly established as major long-term investors.

BAHRAIN

The key financial trading centre in the Gulf is Bahrain, which has traditionally been a centre for trade and commerce. It is an island just offshore of Saudi Arabia, and there is a proposal to connect eventually the two countries by a causeway. While it has some resources of oil these are limited and production is already diminishing sharply. Bahrain has thus turned its attention to creating a banking business fully commensurate with its traditions and standing in the Gulf. In this undertaking the authorities were able to build upon Bahrain's existing assets: its situation half-way between Western Europe and the Far East – some two to four hours of time zone away from each, airline links with major centres and excellent telecommunications, a natural source of funds on its doorstep in an area of keen trade and growth, and the total absence of exchange control.

In 1975 the authorities were faced with an increasing number of applications by foreign banks to open branches in Bahrain as a result of the tremendous attraction of the Gulf to the international banking community. A further encouragement was the increasing problem in the Lebanon which traditionally had provided the Middle East with a financial centre. The local banking market in Bahrain was relatively small and an influx of foreign banks operating in this market could have caused very serious over-banking and possible instability in the market. The authorities therefore introduced licences to operate offshore banking units (OBUs) similar to the ACUs in Singapore. Banks could establish an office in Bahrain, fully staffed, but could not take deposits from local residents nor lend to local residents without sanction from the local monetary authority. The main purpose of such offices would be to provide international services within the Gulf, bringing the services available in other major financial centres to Bahrain within the working day and in the time zone of the Gulf itself.

There are fifty-two OBUs operating in Bahrain, representing the world's major banks. The effect of this influx has been to improve the foreign exchange and deposit markets through the increased competition with local Gulf banks. This improvement has been particularly marked for riyals and dinars, with spreads for both straight foreign exchange transactions and deposits tightening considerably. Moreover, although riyal spreads are still far wider than other currencies and rates are volatile, a forward market for Gulf currencies has developed, centred mainly in Bahrain, and today the forward market for Saudi riyals is at least as good as that in some of the European currencies. In June 1976 outstanding forward contracts with Bahrain banks were equivalent to $300m – by December 1978 this figure had risen to over $3.7bn, and was continuing to rise steadily.

The OBUs also came to offer euro-banking in the main Gulf currencies, such as the dirham, the riyal and the Kuwaiti dinar. They can operate in these markets without the restrictions placed on the national banks of those currencies in their own home markets. This, however, can take place only under the tolerance of the authorities of the currencies concerned, particularly when their own major banks are involved in placing funds in Bahrain and then borrowing them back. Indeed the

Kuwaiti authorities took steps in early 1979 to limit such dealings. But the lack of exchange control around the Gulf means that the development of an offshore market in Gulf currencies can develop relatively easily. Business has grown rapidly, as shown in Table 11.7; at $23bn the market's size is similar to that of Singapore. If the existing freedom from exchange controls continues, business should continue to grow relatively quickly.

TABLE 11.7: Bahrain OBU Assets
(*$ billion*)

1975	1976	1977	1978
1.7	6.2	15.7	23.2

Source: Bahrain Monetary Agency.
Note: Figures are 'end year'.

The local dinar market is extremely small, and offers little scope for foreign investment. However, there has been an increasing amount of longer-term Bahraini dinar financing. Four issues have been completed. Maturities have been relatively short – five to seven years – and coupon rates about $8\frac{3}{4}$ per cent. There is no true secondary market for these issues. One of the major problems in developing a viable capital market for eurobonds denominated in dinars is that Bahrain is not a natural creator or generator of capital. Thus the only prospect for the substantial use of the Bahraini dinar in these markets would be for it to be used as a unit of account with non-residents placing dinar funds to be borrowed by other non-residents – in effect mirroring the use of the deutschemark in the eurobond market. However, it is unlikely that the Bahraini dinar would be able to acquire such a standing in international markets as to be able to act in that capacity and compete with the other currencies which are available for that purpose. Most Bahraini dinar bonds are likely to be placed with local commercial banks and OBUs who fund these medium- to long-term commitments with short-term deposits. This can be extremely attractive when short-term interest rates are low, but is not a substantial base for the long-term development of the market. What is required for this are relatively safe and secure homes where these bonds can be placed on a substantial scale and on a permanent basis.

KUWAIT

The most complete financial centre in the Gulf is Kuwait, despite its policy of refusing to admit foreign banks. Kuwait was one of the first countries to realise the problem of having, in oil, an important and valuable but depleting asset in relation to a relatively small population. In the earlier years the value of the oil revenue would be well above any likely consumption needs of the population, but there was only a relatively short period over which this state of affairs would last, so in the longer term Kuwait would need other sources of income to meet its requirements. The Kuwaiti authorities have established over many years four very substantial and experienced organisations for managing their investments; the Kuwait Foreign Trading Contracting and Investing Company, the Kuwait International Investment Company, the Kuwait Investment Company and the Kuwait Investment Office. In addition to organisations which receive public funds for investment, the accumulation of private wealth has led to the establishment of other investment banking companies and investment holding organisations. Thus Kuwait is now very experienced in the accumulation of oil wealth and its investment in the major financial markets of the world. The scale of the extra income to Kuwait following the OPEC price rises was in no sense a source of major disequilibrium in the world economy, and was much less than in some other cases, because the Kuwaitis had been experienced in investing funds long before this new accretion of wealth occurred. They have behaved over the years since 1975 in a more experienced fashion than the *nouveau riche* OPEC countries.

A major development stemming from the existence of these large-scale investment companies was the development of the Kuwaiti dinar bond market. It is now seven years old and consists of a total float of forty-seven issues, with a nominal value of the equivalent of approximately $1.25bn, including six private placements for the World Bank. The market has developed steadily from a new issue volume of KD15m in 1974 to KD52.5m in 1975 and KD80m in 1976. In 1977 the Kuwaiti market suffered a severe liquidity crisis, and volume dropped to KD52m, most of which was raised in the second half of the year when the situation had improved. It is estimated that total volume for 1978 was well over KD100m. As with other Gulf markets the KD sector has suffered from a lack of quality borrowers, although this shows signs of changing. Finland has come to the market for three issues, and early in 1979 the City of Oslo announced a KD10m issue. The main attractions of the KD market are long maturities and low coupons. The differentials in interest rates between the KD and the US dollar markets are such that high grade borrowers can tap the KD market at rates in excess of $1\frac{1}{4}$ per cent below dollar rates. The Finnish Export Credit Bank, guaranteed by the Republic of Finland, an AAA rated borrower, has borrowed five-year KDs at $7\frac{1}{4}$ per cent. This borrower would have had to pay approximately $8\frac{3}{4}$–9 per cent for a similar dollar financing. This sizeable differential could well be more than sufficient to cushion the borrowers against any revaluation of the KD against the dollar. Assuming dollar rates remain at high levels, more higher grade borrowers may be attracted to the KD market. A good secondary market exists in Kuwait; prices are quoted on a $\frac{1}{2}$ per cent spread for amounts of KD100,000 or more, which compares favourably with the US dollar sector of the euromarkets.

A further market which has developed in Kuwait, and also to a lesser extent elsewhere in new financial centres, is that for promissory notes, not unlike the similar notes used in Germany. These are bearer securities of up to four years or so, often issued by first-class participants, at high interest rates for good quality risks. There are tested set legal procedures for obtaining payment. One reason for the use of this instrument is that borrowers would be unwilling to offer the financial information required to obtain more formal long-term financing. The loans are non-interest bearing and therefore carried on a discount yield basis. The local laws and business customs, particularly the interdict on interest, make this form of finance likely to develop throughout the Gulf, and possibly to the greatest extent in Saudi Arabia.

The Kuwaiti banking system is tightly controlled, and all banks and financial institutions must be totally Kuwaiti owned, with the government having a stake in various financial institutions, and 100 per cent ownership of the savings and credit banks. This clannishness could be an important feature in ensuring effective action to overcome any crisis of confidence – such as that in early 1977 in the stock market – and possible destablising interventions in the marketplace from the non-resident sector have been kept well under control.

The local money markets have progressed to a fairly advanced stage, with an active deposit market and the rapid development of the CD market. In April 1977 the Arab Company for Trading Securities (ACTS) was formed primarily to develop a secondary market in Kuwait for fixed income securities denominated in KD, including bank CDs. In August 1977 the Gulf Bank KSC announced it would issue, via the Kuwait International Investment Company, tranche KD certificates of deposit in maturities of up to two years. This offering took place in

October, and since that time other participants have followed suit. The marketability of dinar CDs has been found to be good, and there is thus an opening for international organisations to play an active part in this market if they so wish.

Significant developments have taken place in the Gulf area to establish positive relations between the local countries and the international financial markets, in the form of a more active 'trading' centre (Bahrain), developing sophisticated placing markets and money markets (Kuwait), and also instituting the means whereby the local monetary and investment authorities can place funds much more actively on the world-wide international markets, both short and long term (Saudi Arabia, United Arab Emirates, and again Kuwait). Mistakes have been made over this period in handling the domestic money markets and in some investment decisions, and institutional reforms and changes have had to be made. But a learning process is inevitable at a time when the financial flows into this part of the world increased so rapidly following the sharp increase in the price of oil in 1973, and the initial euphoria and heady excitement had to give way to a more sober appreciation of what could and could not be achieved in financial markets, and for that matter in real resource and trading markets, both abroad and at home. By and large this learning process has been achieved with no major disasters for the economies of the area, except for some minor sheikhdoms in the emirates, and substantial progress has been made in establishing and developing further viable financial markets. Of these the two most important are undoubtedly Kuwait and Bahrain, but the placing power in Saudi Arabia and the United Arab Emirates is a major factor for operators in international financial markets elsewhere.

OFFSHORE FINANCIAL CENTRES

One area of development of international financial centres are what one might call the exotics, such as Nauru in the New Hebrides. These are fundamentally booking centres – in this case linked to the main metropolitan centres in Australia and New Zealand – and are used for booking financial transactions to escape the legal, fiscal and reserve requirements of banks in those particular countries. Their existence illustrates the general point that booking centres may be established anywhere in the world where the scale of business in terms of sources and uses of funds justifies it, and provided an adequately representative and stable legal environment is found in which they can be set up. In most cases they have to be able to provide a certain amount of local talent in the form of legal expertise and management, but the local employment may bear little relationship to the scale of the actual business booked there. Other such centres exist all over the world.

THE BAHAMAS AND THE CAYMAN ISLANDS

An area where offshore banking has developed to a much more substantial extent is the West Atlantic and Caribbean, notably the Bahamas (Nassau) and the Cayman Islands. For booking transactions these centres feed mainly off North America, and in particular New York. Transactions there escape the legal, fiscal and regulatory requirements of New York itself. Moreover, they are attractive to other depositors in the American time zone, such as Latin America, who may wish their affairs to escape the legal surveillance of the American authorities.

The Bahamas and the Cayman Islands are much more substantial as offshore financial centres than most, in that they have established the legal framework for many other areas of financial business, such as insurance, chartering, holding companies and invoicing. The size and nature of these countries together with their long-established position as centres of financial convenience and low taxation mean that there is significant expertise management and legal knowledge. These centres are thus to some extent half-way between a pure booking centre and a major regional centre such as Singapore or Hong Kong. Very little in the way of major financial deals are actually arranged in these centres, but the growth of the business in these areas has been substantial in recent years, and foreign currency liabilities of US bank branches exceed $80bn. A more detailed breakdown of the size of the financial business in these centres is given in Table 2.11 (p. 34).

The development of the offshore banking centres in the Caribbean stems largely from the efforts of major US banks to extend their international operations to compensate for stagnating profits in the domestic market. The attractions of the Bahamas and the Cayman Islands are the absence of taxes on income, profits and earnings, low operating costs and a well-developed infrastructure capable of handling a large volume of business.

The emergence of the Bahamas as a centre for international financial activity owes much to its proximity to the US and its success as a tourist centre for US visitors. Many were tempted by the supply of land for sale at relatively low prices, and combined with the lack of taxation this made it an ideal place for retirement. From the early 1950s real estate development and allied activities grew rapidly, building an infrastructure which was useful to companies attracted by the tax haven possibilities of the Bahamas. The process was taken a stage further by the growth in the late sixties and early seventies of numerous limited service or 'shell' branches of US banks which opened up branches to facilitate eurodollar activities out of reach of US regulations. Most of the major financial institutions of the world are represented in the Bahamas in one form or another. There are now some 300 banking and trust institutions there and, more recently, a large 'captive' insurance company business has also developed, extending the range of financial operations carried out in the Bahamas. The authorities believe that the sophisticated financial network will enable the Bahamas to compete successfully with Bermuda for this type of business.

Banks and trust companies in the Bahamas are governed by the Banks and Trust Companies Regulations Act (1965) amended in 1969 and supplemented by the provisions of the Insurance Act (1969). Licences under the act, fees for which have recently been increased, may be unconditional or subject to certain conditions and they may be suspended or revoked. Issue of a licence is subject to individual negotiations and may be a restricted offshore licence or a full banking licence.

In the Cayman Islands the development of a financial centre can be traced back to 1962 when independence from Jamaica was secured. The islands became responsible for all domestic affairs and this proved advantageous when it was decided to introduce legislation for international business purposes. Since then the islands' government has encouraged offshore activities and has continued to make the Cayman Islands attractive to international business. This policy bore fruit during the late 1960s when with communications with the rest of the world improving significantly the Cayman Islands developed into a major offshore banking centre. Growth since then has been considerable, with some 200 bank and trust companies represented by the mid-1970s.

Banks and trust companies are controlled by the Banks and Trust Companies Regulations Law of 1966 and are licensed for a fee which varies according to the range of business conducted. The general calibre of banks and trust companies is high as a result of the careful investigation by the authorities of all new institutions.

PANAMA

Within the American time zone a new financial centre, Panama, has emerged in recent years. Panama intends to be a major recipient of funds from Latin America in particular, to be a major source of foreign exchange dealing outside American jurisdiction, and to become a genuine offshore and regional banking centre. Over eighty-five banks are represented, but development has been relatively slow (see Table 11.8) and deposit growth has not been as rapid as might have been hoped.

TABLE 11.8: Panama's Offshore Banking Business (*$ billion*)

1972	1973	1974	1975	1976	1977	1978 (*June*)
1.1	2.6	5.3	7.1	8.4	10.6	10.9

Source: National Banking Commission of Panama.

Panama has the advantages of excellent communications and transport links with the rest of the world and steps have been taken to establish a very active foreign exchange market. But the location itself is not the most physically attractive in which to work, and there must in any case be doubt as to the extent to which a new financial centre is needed to compete with the already established centres in the Caribbean. The main problems facing Panama are competition from these centres, and the doubt whether there is a sufficiently large market, which only it can satisfy, to justify the complete development of this financial centre over the years. But given its position on a major trade link, as a natural entrepôt country with limited resources, it is not unreasonable that Panama should aim to become a financial centre. Potentially she can offer other financial services, such as holding companies established on a low tax basis, to complement booking financial transactions.

REFERENCES

P. Clark, 'The making of the Asian dollar market', *Crown Agents Quarterly Review* (Autumn 1977).
W. A. Hahn, 'Investment opportunities in Arab currencies', Investment

and Property Studies Ltd. Conference, 19–20 June 1978.

'Bahrain', *Middle East Economic Digest*, supplement (March 1978).

'Banking in the Middle East: A survey', *The Banker* (March 1978).

'Banking and finance', *Middle East Economic Digest*, special report (March 1979).

'Banking '78', *Far Eastern Economic Review*, special survey (April 1978).

'Banking '79', *Far Eastern Economic Review*, special survey (April 1979).

12 Eastern Europe, China and the Third World

EASTERN EUROPE AND CHINA

The Eastern European bloc operates in the international financial markets like any other group of predominantly capital importing countries, although these are more advanced economies than those considered later in this chapter. Because Comecon's trading area is isolated by the non-convertability of its currencies from Western markets there can be no question of the countries' own currencies being used as a unit of account in international transactions. One problem involved in lending to these countries is that detailed statistics about their economic situation, internal and external, are largely for political reasons not available. Some progress is being made towards improving the flow of information, in that countries experiencing significant difficulties with their debt position are publishing further data as a precondition for additional finance, Poland being a recent example. The economic growth and hard currency balance of payments performance of these countries is shown in Table 12.1.

As they are dependent on Western export markets as a source of hard currency and as trade partners in acquiring the technology required to implement development plans, the Comecon countries were affected by the recession in the West following the OPEC price rises. Thus the balance of trade with the West deteriorated in 1974, 1975 and 1976 and the rate of economic growth slowed down. Borrowing from the Western markets took place at an increasing rate in later years in line with the deteriorating trade position and the aggregate debt at the end of 1978 was estimated to be $56 billion.

It is difficult to argue whether this outstanding debt represents a high or low ratio of debt to total resources. Comparisons have been made of the debt service ratios for the various East European countries, and comparisons have to be largely between them rather than in relation to other groups of countries because of the large volume of barter trade.

TABLE 12.1: Economic Growth and Trade of Eastern European Countries

	Change in net material product (%)						
	1972	*1973*	*1974*	*1975*	*1976*	*1977*	*1978*
Bulgaria	7.7	8.1	7.6	8.8	7.0	6.3	6.0
Czechoslovakia	5.5	4.8	5.9	6.4	4.0	4.5	4.0
GDR	5.6	5.6	6.4	4.9	3.7	5.2	4.0
Hungary	5.1	7.5	7.0	5.5	3.0	7.8	4.0
Poland	10.6	10.8	10.4	6.9	7.1	5.5	2.8
Romania	10.0	10.7	12.4	10.3	10.5	8.6	7.6
USSR	3.8	9.0	5.0	4.8	5.0	3.5	4.2
	Trade balance with West ($ million)						
Bulgaria	−5	−21	−524	−815	−422	−389	−570
Czechoslovkia	−9	−221	−400	−571	−758	−736	−870
GDR	−340	−750	−891	−1073	−1456	−1140	−1510
Hungary	−102	−89	−602	−639	−474	−729	−1230
Poland	−313	−1316	−2293	−2921	−3235	−2522	−1900
Romania	−166	−196	−435	−386	−4	−390	−600
USSR	−1288	−1748	−996	−6335	−5516	−3081	−4000

Sources: For net material product, CMEA Countries' *Statistical Year Book*; for trade balance with West, US Dept of Commerce.

But debt service ratios are certainly relatively high for some of these countries, and those in that category have had to approach their Western creditor banks from a weak bargaining position. Since a break-through by Hungary in 1972, Comecon countries have also managed to use the eurobond market. The East European countries have used the bond market around the world on regular occasions but long-term investors have been somewhat unwilling to over-commit themselves in this field, and the bond issues have been relatively few in relation to syndicated lending. Much lending from the West has been in support of Western exports, and it is for this reason that the German banks are very heavily involved in such credits. The breakdown of debt from Western banks in major countries to the Eastern bloc is shown in Table 12.3.

Assessment of lending to countries in the Eastern bloc is naturally somewhat difficult for Western banks, because of the ideological differences which separate East and West. The atmosphere regarding repayment of credits depends heavily on the continuation of reasonable détente between East and West, but future lending is also affected by whether countries reach levels of debt in relation to total

TABLE 12.2: Eastern European Bond Issues and Eurocurrency Bank Credits, 1972–8 (*$ million*)

	1972	1973	1974	1975	1976	1977	1978	Total 1972–8
Bulgaria	65	115	160	125	240	245	240	1190
Czechoslovakia	—	—	—	60	200	150	150	560
GDR	85	15	12	280	260	692	782	2126
Hungary	120	90	190	350	175	524	515	1964
Poland	20	370	508	475	546	94	404	2417
Romania	—	—	—	106	—	125	725	956
USSR	—	—	—	750	282	—	400	1432
CMEA Banks	140	50	100	480	600	1100	500	2970
Total	430	640	970	2626	2303	2930	3716	13615
of which bonds								
Hungary	50	—	40	100	25	175	—	390
Poland					47	75	30	152
Romania				100				100
Total	50		40	200	72	250	30	642

Source: World Bank, *Borrowing in International Capital Markets* (March 1979).

TABLE 12.3: Position of Western banks *vis-à-vis* Eastern European Countries (*$ million, end Dec. 1978*)

	Liabilities	*Assets*	*Net*
Bulgaria	492	3174	2682
Czechoslovakia	629	1985	1356
GDR	1195	6168	4973
Hungary	901	6450	5549
Poland	822	11732	10910
Rumania	223	2544	2321
USSR	5858	12821	6963
Total	10120	44874	34754

Source: Bank for International Settlements, *Press Release on International Banking Developments* (June 1979).

resources or export earnings which are regarded as excessive in terms of the credibility of eventual repayment. The need for Eastern bloc countries to export in order to pay for past and future imports is clear, but problems of protectionism in Western markets which have already surfaced in the cases of petrochemicals and textiles make it harder for these sales to be made. The availability of credit from the West could also be influenced sharply by changes in monetary policy in various countries; for instance if the Americans in particular tighten policy considerably, the availability of loanable funds in the euromarkets could diminish. This poses severe problems for the future because the availability of foreign credit is a crucial component of the development process of these countries, which in turn has political and economic implications. Trade with the West has an important political dimension for Eastern European countries in that it gives them some flexibility and room for manoeuvre within the Comecon framework. It seems most unlikely, however, that the banks would go so far as to refuse to extend credit at all to the Eastern bloc and the most likely outcome is that growth of credit will continue at a relatively steady rate in line with the overall growth of their economies, assuming no major deterioration in their balances of payments.

A major development in the relations between Western and Communist countries is the emergence of China, under its new leadership, as a major market for Western technology. The possibility of offering massive credits to China to help that country's future economic development has been received enthusiastically by Western banks. As China's debt is presently (1979) very low, the initial phase will present no difficulty. Western markets should provide sufficient finance to meet the requirements comfortably. But a time will come when the question of the ultimate repayment of these funds assumes increasing importance, and the maintenance of stable and acceptable ratios will be necessary for the continuation of credit on a significant scale. By the mid-1980s this will almost certainly become an important constraint upon the pace and manner in which China is able to develop and modernise its potentially enormous, but presently backward, economy.

DEVELOPING COUNTRIES

Relatively few developing countries are active participants on a major scale in the international financial markets, but some of the countries in this group are among the largest borrowers in the euromarkets. Developing countries are usually divided into categories by annual 'per capita' income. On the World Bank classification they fall into five groups: lower income, middle income, upper income, OPEC and developing countries amongst the centrally planned economies. Of these, the low income countries are dependent almost entirely on official aid flows for their financing; commercial links are on a relatively small scale and on a short-term basis, apart from the investment of their reserves. Although developing, some countries are nevertheless major capital suppliers to the world market. This applies on a continuing basis to countries such as Saudi Arabia and Kuwait, which are unable to absorb all their oil revenue, but it also included some other OPEC countries in the period immediately after 1974. Not only have some of these countries increased sharply their international reserves, they have also invested through capital exports on the world long-term financial markets.

TABLE 12.4: Non-oil Developing Countries: Economic Growth and Balance of Payments, 1972–8

	1972	1973	1974	1975	1976	1977	1978
Change in GNP (%)	6.1	7.3	5.3	4.1	4.8	4.9	5.3 (est.)
Current account ($bn)	−6	−7	−24.5	−38.5	−26	−24	−34

Source: IMF annual report (1978).

On the other hand there was a very sharp deterioration after 1972 in the overall economic and balance of payments performances of non-oil developing countries (see Table 12.4). This deterioration stems firstly from the sharp inflation which increased the real cost of food imports, and then the more drastic effect from the oil price rises of 1973/74 and 1979. Because they are developing countries they are naturally capital importers, and much indeed of their required capital inflow is supplied through international agencies such as the World Bank and the various regional development banks, through supplier credit in support of exports from industrialised countries, and through official aid programmes. Though increasing rapidly, the amount of money financed through the international syndicated loan and bond markets is a relatively small proportion of the total.

Some six developing countries – Mexico, Brazil, Argentina, Indonesia, Philippines and South Korea – account for a very large proportion of total LDC debt, and the overall health of the banking system and bank lending to developing countries depends essentially on the performance of just these few countries of which Mexico and Brazil are

TABLE 12.5: External Debt of Non-oil Developing Countries
(*$ billion disbursed debt outstanding*)

	1974	1975	1976	1977
Public debt				
Multilateral organisations	14.6	17.9	21.6	27.0
Governments	41.0	47.1	54.0	62.0
Total official sources	55.6	65.0	75.6	89.0
Financial markets	25.4	34.9	47.9	60.8
Suppliers and other	9.7	10.1	11.2	14.7
Total private sources	35.1	44.9	59.1	75.5
Total public debt	90.7	110.0	134.7	164.5
Private debt	29.3	35.2	41.2	46.8
Total external debt	120.0	145.2	175.9	211.3

Source: World Bank, *World Debt Tables*.

the most prominent. Total debt owing to banks from developing countries has increased enormously and the magnitude of the figures is such as to arouse concern in public statements. Nevertheless, according to the calculations of the IMF and the IBRD, if one allows for inflation and the change in scale of the world economy, the total level of debt from developing countries to the banking system is no more than ten or fifteen years ago, when no one was particularly concerned about the problem. In the World Bank's view continued major participation by international banks in lending to developing countries is an intrinsic part of the development process, a point made explicitly by Mr McNamara in his report to the 1978 World Bank annual meeting. In this he set out figures – calculated on the basis of certain other fairly cautious assumptions – which give some indication of the scale of financial market lending which would be required if developing countries were to achieve reasonable economic growth targets (see Table 12.6).

These forecast flows of capital through the banking system seem to many financial observers to be high in contrast with levels prescribed by prudent banking practice. Nevertheless, whether or not such figures are achieved commercial bank lending will be an intrinsic part of the development process for some time to come. This is also the view of many developing countries. At the UNCTAD IV meeting in 1975 in Nairobi a major theme was the need for a new world economic order and in particular for the renegotiation of debt owed by the third world to

TABLE 12.6: Capital Flows to Developing Countries, 1975–85 (*$ billion*)

	1975	1976	1977	1980	1985
Current account deficit[a]	46.1	42.5	51.2	61.9	132.5
Financed by					
Public sources					
(including grants)	17.1	15.7	19.2	32.2	50.9
Private sources	29.0	26.8	32.0	29.7	81.6
	46.1	42.5	51.2	61.9	132.5

Source: World Bank, address to the Board of Governors by the President of the World Bank (1978).
Note: [a] Includes interest payments.

industrialised countries. On this issue, however, the developing countries were crucially split. The poorest countries which had little commercial debt and were dependent upon aid supported this proposal; indeed this led later to the cancellation or easing of some aid debt to certain industrialised countries, notably Sweden, Canada, the Netherlands, Switzerland and the UK. But the developing countries which had used the commercial markets considered it much more important to retain access to them, and hence their freedom of action, rather than to have to undergo the surveillance of their policies that would be required if they were to seek renegotiation of debt or other concessionary terms. It was the view of the more advanced developing countries, such as Mexico and Brazil, that continued access to these markets was necessary and should not be jeopardised.

In the late 1970s sluggish loan demand in the industrialised countries has allowed the rapid expansion of credit to finance balance of payments needs, especially of the more advanced developing countries. The possibility that some of this debt may never be repaid cannot be ignored. Countries which have accumulated excessive debt include Zaire, Peru and North Korea, while others, such as Turkey and Egypt, are in financial difficulty. There are many reasons why a proportion of this lending may require extensive re-scheduling, the granting of moratoria, or ultimately prove irrecoverable. First, there may be some wholly unforeseen change of events of a nature so adverse as hardly to be expected when the loan was first agreed. The fall in the price of copper by three-quarters in real terms between the granting of major loans to Zaire and the period of most onerous servicing in the late 1970s would perhaps come into that category. Governments may pursue totally unsound policies and put themselves in a position whereby they have no choice but to come to terms with their creditors, because the necessary money needed to keep the economy going and repay the existing debt is not forthcoming. In this regard the banks can certainly be criticised for over-lending in certain cases and showing lack of discrimination. When the IMF does become involved with such countries, it expects the commercial banking system to operate a phased policy of re-scheduling debt and offering new debt in order to ensure both that the banking system pays the price for its past over-lending and that it does not undertake further lending on such a scale as to jeopardise the stabilisation programme. A third cause for difficulty could be revolution in a case where the new regime decided to break with the financial contracts maintained by the previous government. A fourth reason may be political unrest which leads to an otherwise sound situation turning sour and the economy being unable to fulfil what appeared to be reasonable financial plans. An important element in determining one's attitude towards commercial bank credit to the third world is whether the development process is thought to be fundamentally hopeful or fundamentally despairing. If the former, then it is reasonable for developing countries to assume external debt as a means of financing the necessary capital imports. If the latter, then the accumulation of debt becomes simply one more problem in a never ending list of insoluble problems. The view of the World Bank as evidenced in their published data is that the development process has been in many cases highly successful: steady progress has been shown, but in some cases, largely because of excessive population growth, growth in income 'per capita' has been retarded quite seriously. Singapore, normally classed as a developing country, is a prominent example of the first category, having overtaken some southern European countries in terms of 'per capita' income levels. Growth in other South-east Asian countries has also been phenomenal, based on success in exporting to the industrialised world. These countries provide examples of the underlying health and scope of the development process and suggest that one should not be too fearful of the accumulation of debt in the general development context. But debt levels in some cases are such that should anything go wrong with the country's economic and political progress it would be very difficult indeed to surmount the financial problems that would be created.

The considerable increase in total syndicated lending to developing countries has been accompanied by increases in the scale of individual loans, a lengthening of maturities, and narrowing margins. There have been some loans of up to $1bn, notably to Venezuela and Nigeria, and

TABLE 12.7: Syndicated Bank Credit Market Conditions

	1972	1973	1974	1975	1976	1977	1978
Average size ($m)	38.6	67.5	60.0	50.0	72.0	76.0	104.0
Average maturity (years)	6.7	8.6	8.2	5.5	5.8	6.5	8.5
Spread over LIBOR (%)	1.18	0.94	1.12	1.40	1.25	1.13	0.90

Source: Mainly OECD.

the maturities have been well beyond what was normally expected hitherto in the banking world. Table 12.7 gives the average figures for maturity, size, and margin of loans in recent years.

For many years developing countries were virtually barred from the eurobond and foreign bond markets because they were not thought to be sufficiently credit-worthy. But this barrier has been breached and there have been many loans for developing countries in various international bond markets (see Tables 1.8 and 1.9 pp. 8 and 9). In some cases these loans have been in the short-term expensive for the country concerned in view of the heavy exchange risk (in particular as regards yen borrowing), but provided these hard currency loans were only a small proportion of the total the cost could be borne. Moreover, the process of opening up new markets is important in the longer term in establishing the credit-worthiness and credibility of these countries. The number of developing countries which have entered the bond market is still relatively small, but includes some of the most successful higher income countries.

A significant feature has been the enormous improvement in the financial sophistication of the authorities in the developing countries regarding the management of both liabilities and assets. Ensuring that conditions remain favourable for their credit ratings and that access to financial markets is in no way jeopardised has become a major concern. Reserve management is also important; the accumulation of substantial liquidity in the form of reserves gives a country leeway in dealing with any short-term problems. Table 12.8 indicates the movement in the international reserves of developing countries.

Reserves of this group of countries improved sharply during 1977 and 1978 despite some of the worst forebodings expressed after the OPEC crisis. Moreover, in some cases much of the borrowing in these two years was used to build up reserve assets and thus give countries room for

TABLE 12.8: Reserves of Non-oil Developing Countries, 1972–8 (*$ million*)

	1972	1973	1974	1975	1976	1977	1978
Non-oil LDCs	21598	29627	32465	31257	42969	55009	67051
Total world reserves	159333	183653	220572	227615	258388	319184	351781

Source: IMF, *International Financial Statistics* (June 1979).

manoeuvre by increasing the ratio of reserves to annual imports. Managing the currency composition of reserve assets and liabilities has also become more important because of the losses and gains that have been made by bad or good linkages with exchange rate movements. Countries are beginning to diversify their financial assets around the world. Although the dollar is still the predominant reserve asset, the effect of its fall on developing countries may be less serious than it seems, for many of them also have massive debts denominated in dollars and thus have probably had net gains from the fall in the dollar's value.

A further significant phenomenon affecting conditions in the markets has been the policies pursued by borrowing countries. It was obviously the aim of the commercial banks to lend as far as possible relatively short to give themselves flexibility in their portfolio. Correspondingly it has been the aim of the developing countries, advised in some cases by the World Bank and the IMF, both to keep their borrowing under control and to make it as long as possible and at as low as possible or fixed rates. Thus, as countries' economic strength and balance of payments have improved, they have driven harder bargains with the lending banks. In many cases central banks have established tight systems of control over the borrowing by nationals in the international markets, and have enforced minimum borrowing terms. This is particularly true of South Korea and Brazil. Once the main crisis of financing was over, after the oil price rises, both countries increased the minimum period for which they would borrow from the banking markets, thus exerting a strong influence on the kind of business that the banks were able to obtain. Such action by developing countries influences the overall lengthening of maturities in the market, and also reduces the scale of part of the banks' most traditional short-term business.

In general the World Bank is not seriously concerned about the overall debt of developing countries, and regards it as a natural part of the development process. In the banking world itself, however, suitable guidelines have to be established for evaluating individual country lending propositions and for this reason the developing countries are assessed on various criteria which give some indication of their credit-worthiness. These indicators often include ratios of outstanding total debt to GNP, debt service (interest and repayment) in relation to exports of goods and services, the level of reserves in relation to imports, the overall growth and income level of the country, political factors, and an assessment of balance of payments performance. Perhaps the key element in assessing a country is that such ratios should not be deteriorating and preferably should be improving. The collection of indicators used varies from bank to bank, but measures that take these factors into account, even if in different ways, tend to give somewhat similar results in ranking the countries concerned. The main objective of all banks, of course, is to obtain an adequate spread of their business, diversify their portfolios, and not assume too many risks of unacceptable quality. A similar pattern of lending may thus be detected throughout the banking system. The difficulty of foreseeing the future inevitably means that any such lending is to some extent risky, even if a bank manages to avoid becoming involved in situations where reason-able foresight might have indicated that the country's economic policy was not on a sound path. But as far as any one bank is concerned, no matter what lending they do on their own account, the standing of that loan may be upset totally by future actions of the government, or by future excessive lending by other banks to that country. One bank cannot prevent other banks from destroying the credit-worthiness of its own loans.

Apart from the developing countries that for various reasons have chosen to become financial centres – and of those only in a few cases – the currencies of most developing countries are not used as units of account in international transactions. In many countries inflation rates alone would preclude that; in others the weak balance of payments and the degree of control over the exchange market make the currency unsuitable. Indeed for most of these countries the development of financial markets, except purely in such a way as to serve other development aims, is of low priority. Priorities are concerned with the 'real' economy.

CONCLUSION

In conclusion, the international financial markets play a key role in the economic strategy of the countries discussed in this chapter, providing them with capital and flexibility. These countries' actions have increased the breadth and size of the markets, creating a wider spread of risk between creditors and debtors. The markets are so vital to the future progress of these countries that maintenance of good relations with them is a major priority. Their use will continue unless prevented by major political events which undermine the credit-worthiness of the borrowing countries.

13 Conclusion

The material presented in the earlier chapters has set out some of the main factual features of the economic and financial history of the period, the structures and developments, in particular, international financial markets, and the policy changes implemented by major countries in response to changing circumstances. Writing a book is nothing if not a learning process and most authors probably end up drawing conclusions which are not necessarily the ones they would have been able to come to at the beginning of their study. This has been no less the case in this instance. One of the main purposes in preparing the book in this manner – incorporating a survey of detailed information about financial markets and countries' policies – was to shed light upon the 'texture' of changes in these financial markets. Many commentators have considered the global flows of funds between creditor and deficit countries, and it is a relatively commonplace observation that the international financial markets and the international banking system have acted as an effective channel for the flows of funds necessary to counter the serious balance of payments disequilibria of the 1970s. The converse of this unqualified approbation is to accept the contribution of the substantial flow of funds through the international banking system, but to regard this as fundamentally adverse in the sense of both incorporating excessively risky lending on too large a scale and of contributing to world-wide inflation and currency instability. Neither of these points of view should be dismissed completely out of hand, for no one would claim that every aspect of monetary development in recent years has been perfect. But after having examined in more detail the texture of changes in the international financial markets our underlying conclusion differs from both points of view.

THE ROLE OF INTERNATIONAL MARKETS

But before coming to that point some words about the role and function of the international financial markets are called for. These markets act as the 'inter-face' (to use a jargon word), or link, between countries, and thus allow countries to pursue their own policies, interacting with each other through a largely informal system of arms-length contracts in the trading and financial markets, but subject to co-ordination to the extent that this is covered by treaties and organisational agreements among them, such as through the IMF, the GATT and the OECD. These treaties and organisational arrangements circumscribe countries behaviour in the interests of ensuring good neighbourliness, but leave countries with considerable flexibility and freedom for individual action (at the national, corporate and individual levels) over a wide area of economic activity. Let us be frank about the alternative. This would be that all international economic relations be established on the basis of specific treaties, determining total trade and financial flows. If markets were not to act as the inter-face between countries the Western world would have to be run on a 'Comecon' system where specific and comprehensive bargains have to be struck over total trade and finance at the national level. Not only would this system be extremely inefficient economically, it would clearly be both impracticable and indeed intolerable as a system for Western governments. Thus whatever the imperfections of international financial markets as the link between countries, one must start by comparing them with this unattractive alternative.

A second point is that international economic relations can only be as harmonious and successful as the underlying policies of governments allow them to be. Over the long post-war boom, which was remarkably successful and relatively smooth in terms of international relations, the economic and financial targets of most of the major countries – the US, Japan and those in Western Europe – were either reasonably consistent with each other, or the countries which fared badly under this system were prepared to see their interests suffer to some extent. But once countries' economic targets became seriously incompatible with each other, there was no system of international economic arrangements which could avoid tension and change. If all the countries in the world wish to have balance of payments surpluses, then some must inevitably be disappointed. If all were determined to have balance of payments surpluses, then those which failed would be bitterly disappointed, and might respond with policies detrimental to the interests of, and their relations with, other countries. The degree of compatibility among national economic targets sets a limit to the degree of stability and harmony which can prevail in international economic and monetary relations.

STRUCTURAL CHANGES IN THE WORLD ECONOMY

In this context no one can deny that the period we are studying has been one of severe structural change in the real world economy. The massive increase in the real price of energy imposed structural problems on the industrialised countries and the rest of the world. The growing world-wide disequilibrium in the supply and demand for a wide range of goods – such as the capital intensive products of petrochemicals and plastics – and the over-capacity in shipbuilding and shipping led to severely increased competition in those markets. Moreover, there were much increased exports from developing countries amid growing threats of protectionism. As countries have attempted to preserve their interests in this turbulent and competitive period, incompatibilities among national policies have been unavoidable; and with them there has inevitably been change and friction in international financial markets.

One school of thought which was influential immediately after the OPEC price rise was what one might term the 'international Keynesians' who recommended that the industrialised countries should agree among themselves to keep their economies at a high level of activity in order to maintain demand and employment, and to accept between themselves a balance of payments deficit large enough to offset the OPEC surplus. Such a policy was pursued in effect by the US, the UK, Canada, Australia and certain other countries, and perhaps this was done at least as much for domestic political considerations as for a desire to solve the world's problems. But some other countries gave far higher priority to dealing with their own short-term balance of payments problems or with the inflationary potential at that time. Japan and Western Germany come clearly into this category. While one may accept some of the rationale for the Keynesian recommendations, there seems no need to apportion credit or blame between countries for the development of the world economy since 1973. One can argue that the Keynesian recommendations are based upon a political naivety, an assumption that all countries in the world should accept that the existing balance of power between countries is satisfactory and stable, and that it is in some way 'fair' for all countries to be expected to deviate equally from what they would otherwise have done, in order to fit in with the Keynesian prescription. A more realistic assessment would be that the relative power and standing of countries in the world is part of a permanently changing process in which there is considerable competitive struggle. Countries in Western Europe sheltering under what is regarded as a relatively determined American nuclear umbrella undoubtedly have a different attitude towards the tensions and fears of the world political scene than a country like Japan which is further away from the holder of its nuclear umbrella, and is adjacent to two of the largest and most powerful countries of the world. There is therefore no reason why countries should feel compelled – beyond a certain measure of co-operation – to sacrifice what they see as their vital interests for the sake of adopting other theories or helping other countries. But on the other hand the actions taken by the US and the other countries that pursued relatively expansionary Keynesian policies certainly had the effect of maintaining the level of world demand above what otherwise it would have been, whatever the ultimate effect upon particular currencies. If one were to analyse international economic and financial policies with any objectivity, one must pay a certain respect to the policies pursued by national governments all round the world in what they regard as their own interests. No reasonable analysis of the international markets can be made if one group of countries is regarded as necessarily right and another group as inevitably unhelpful and destructive.

It is the role of international financial markets to act as a means of transmitting economic forces as well as of recording the balance sheet of the debts and assets built up over that period. Because of the incompatibility of national targets some countries were bound to be disappointed in their performances and in the world's assessment of them. Weaker countries suffered falling exchange rates and hard borrowing terms, and may have been inclined to blame these factors on the markets themselves rather than on their own shortcomings. Some have argued that over this period the financial markets were unstable, and that they exacerbated economic and financial problems. This argument is inadequate. The essential point is that world affairs are inherently unstable and are always moving away from an existing equilibrium. While it may well be the case that a certain degree of stability may be seen in, say, the power relations between groups of countries for a limited period, or stability may be seen in economic markets for a limited period, the essential economic process is one of development and change, as new economic forces, new products, new powers and new markets develop.

Looking back over the past century, what stability has there been in world economic affairs? The system has continually been moving from one temporary plateau or ledge to another one, and this process has always been accompanied by considerable uncertainty. Since 1971 the world economy has been moving away from the 'plateau' established in the immediate post-war arrangements – essentially through GATT and the Bretton Woods treaties which established the IMF and the IBRD. That this post-war era came to an end is a matter now of fact, accompanied perhaps by regret. What the new plateau will be, or whether the world will quickly reach what may be regarded as a level of temporary equilibrium, is something which we cannot know. But it seems essentially an error of analysis to criticise recent events as instability about a hypothetical equilibrium. The way in which one should analyse developments in recent years is in terms of whether they appear to be realistic, helpful and long-lasting adaptations to new economic forces and the new structure of the world economy, or whether the changes in economic policies and in financial markets are fundamentally irrelevant, frivolous, and likely to be the source of yet further problems.

THE NEW PLURALISTIC STRUCTURE

The conclusion to which we have come in analysing the material which makes up this book is that in an enormous number of ways the detailed changes in financial markets and the detailed changes in countries' policies as they faced new economic forces and circumstances, represent almost entirely a solid, soundly based, thoughtful, development towards the new international monetary structure which will follow Bretton Woods. This new structure appears to be what one might term a pluralistic monetary structure based on new monetary poles or reserve currencies. The economic and political environment must appear now to most countries as exceptionally uncertain and each has to decide the policies most suited to its own interests. As has been argued above, one should respect each country's conclusion in this connection. No one can predict with certainty the development of the overall world economy, but reasonable harmonisation of policies is taking place through the major world economic organisations, such as the OECD and the IMF. And a critical analysis of this system should concentrate on the question whether the policies being adopted by countries tend to further this process in a relatively harmonious way, or are fundamentally destructive and backward looking. It is our conclusion that the great majority of changes were adaptive and helpful. But this is not to deny that mistakes have been made and some countries would no doubt do things differently if they had the chance.

CHARACTERISTICS OF AN INTERNATIONAL CURRENCY

Let us now look at some of the major changes that have taken place. The traditional characteristics of a reserve or major trading currency are that it is relatively non-inflationary and the parent country runs a current account surplus and is also willing to facilitate its capacity to export capital by allowing the markets to develop to enable that to happen. It seems fairly clear that over this recent period the US has ceased to be able or to wish to fulfil these responsibilities in regard to the dollar. American inflation has worsened substantially, as has the current account. If one also takes into account capital exports, the balance of payments performance has been even more adverse. Monetary expansion has been substantial and, if calculated on a 'domestic credit expansion' basis such as the IMF applies to debtor countries, would be even more unfavourable than US money supply data suggest.

On domestic policy one has more reason for doubt now than, say, fifteen or twenty years ago as to the relative priority given to anti-inflation policies in contrast with policies aimed at maintaining effective demand and employment. The school of thought that a strong anti-inflation policy is the best way of creating real wealth and of maintaining employment and output in the long term is one whose influence seems to have diminished significantly, to the advantage of the more Keynesian school of thought which has had such influence in the UK. Because of the relatively small trading component in the US economy the Americans have also not been unwilling to see the dollar depreciate in world markets.

On the other hand, West Germany, Japan and Switzerland have acquired the main characteristics of countries whose currencies have reserve and trading currency qualities. Each runs a current account surplus. All adopt strong anti-inflationary policies, and all have low inflation. In the case of Switzerland and Germany this reflects a long-standing commitment to price stability but both had to take determined action in the mid-1970s to reduce inflation after the high levels of 1973 and 1974. In Japan's case the commitment to low inflation is more recent; for much of the post-war period Japan has had relatively high domestic inflation (if not in the prices of exports), and indeed in 1974 it reached the exceptionally high level of 24.5 per cent. There has thus been a major change in Japan's attitude towards inflation. In recent years these three countries have created conditions for capital exports to take place to offset their current surpluses. In this connection they have allowed non-residents to purchase their foreign bond issues, so that in effect their currencies are being used internationally as units of account to a greater extent than before. Another feature shared by these countries is their exceptionally high level of industrial output and efficiency, and their acceptance of the inevitable structural changes resulting from the high levels to which their currencies have appreciated. They are able and willing to accept structural change and to proceed from a state in which they are exporters of a very wide range of manufactured goods to one in which they will have to rely more heavily upon service income and specialise in the manufactures in which they may have greatest comparative advantage.

The world-wide intellectual 'revolution', that has given greater importance to the monetarist school of thought, has in certain ways helped this process. If countries that regularly record a substantial current account surplus wish to control their money supply within relatively narrow limits, they need to export funds in the form of capital outflows. Thus monetarist thinking has encouraged – or forced – the Germans, Japanese, and Swiss to develop the capital markets that would enable capital exports to take place.

Because the Americans were no longer able or willing to fulfil the basic conditions of running a major world reserve currency, and the Germans, Japanese and Swiss have not only been willing to do so but have made several policy decisions consistent with that end, it seems hardly surprising that there has been a fundamental shift in the relative standing of the dollar in relation to these other currencies. The sharp depreciation of the dollar should not therefore be regarded as evidence of instability in the system of exchange rates, but rather to a large extent a reflection of this fundamental shift in the quality of the various currencies and in the policies pursued by the governments concerned.

JURISDICTION AND SUPERVISION

In this context of adaptation it is relevant to consider other detailed changes which have taken place in the markets. On the question of jurisdiction and supervision significant improvements have been made. Many countries, such as West Germany, have tightened bank controls, especially on foreign exchange. The risks of another Herstatt crisis have been substantially reduced. At a more global level, central banks have agreed that the central bank in the country in which a bank is headquartered is responsible for supervising that bank's global operations. Parent banks have also been asked to accept responsibility for subsidiaries, including stakes in consortium banks. Thus the formal structure of agreed central banking responsibilities has been delineated.

One must not ignore moreover that central banks have always had substantial authority over actions by their banks and in their own currencies, either at home or abroad. The idea that the euromarkets consist of activity taking place in a geographical zone outside any legal supervision has always been grotesque. Indeed, depicting the euromarkets in terms of geographical factors ('euro') has led to much confusion in this and other contexts. It would be more realistic to regard the markets in each currency in terms of two-tiers. In the first the banks and other participants come under the full legal controls of traditional domestic policy in terms of capital ratios, reserve requirements, etc. In the second tier (the euromarket) the legal jurisdiction and the restraints in terms of reserve requirements and capital ratios are different and in most cases less stringent. Thus the banks and other market operators have the choice of apportioning their business between the two tiers. Central banks certainly have the ability under many of their existing powers to control the development of the second tier. For example, it took a long time for a second tier yen market (that is to say a euro-yen market) to develop because the Bank of Japan took steps through its activities in the foreign exchange market, the forward exchange market and its guidance over the Japanese banks to ensure that it did not happen.

The range of powers available to central banks varies from country to country, as does their view of the most appropriate policies. But in nearly all cases the central banks have a significant influence over the relationship between the first and second tiers of financial activity in their currencies and hence over the conditions in which the second tier operates. The overall capital ratios applied by central banks include euro as well as domestic and other international business.

In some cases the second tier comes effectively under the close legal jurisdiction of the central bank concerned. Thus euro-deutschemark bonds and foreign deutschemark bonds are handled within exactly the same framework of the German Capital Issues Committee and the same co-operation and co-ordination between the major German banks. There is no 'second tier' market in Swiss franc bonds; all international Swiss bonds are through foreign bonds which come under the full legal jurisdiction of the Swiss authorities. Similarly, capital exports in yen take place almost entirely in foreign yen bonds (that is to say – in our terminology – in first tier bonds) which come under the full legal jurisdiction of the Japanese authorities. Although there have been a very few euro-yen bonds (that is 'second tier' bonds), the Bank of Japan has very substantial authority over their placing and their issuing because of its traditional powers and influence over the domestic and international activities of the Japanese banks.

TWO-TIER MARKETS

One should thus try to forget the geographical concept of the euromarkets and think more in terms of two-tier financial markets for both banking business and capital flows. It may well be that under certain circumstances and in certain currencies the second tier activity is relatively lax and this could have adverse monetary consequences. But that is as likely to be the consequence of the theories and policies dominant in the relevant central bank, as of any lack of proper authority. Because of the changes which have taken place in central bank attitudes towards supervision and their new arrangements, the international financial markets have come under comprehensive legal and practical supervision by the monetary authorities in the main industrialised countries.

As far as the markets themselves are concerned it is important to consider in greater detail who is using them and how they have developed. One of the key developments has been the very rapid expansion of the international bond markets in relation to bank lending. This feature involves a welcome lengthening of international debt which gives greater certainty to the borrower. There have been many innovations in technical features of bond issues, including floating rate notes and also convertible debentures. New borrowers have emerged into the commercial markets, bank and bond, and many borrowers have progressed 'up the scale' in the sense of moving to the more stringent markets over time. Many developing countries are now able to use the bond markets. In the banking markets many developing countries have also been able to demand terms and conditions which are more favourable from their point of view, notably in lengthening the maturity of the debt, as well as narrowing the margin. A major diffusion of risk has taken place as borrowers have diversified their sources of finance. The EIB and the IBRD have borrowed from virtually every capital market in the world. Many sovereign borrowers, including Australia and many European countries, have been able to use the Yankee bond market in New York. Borrowers from the public sector in other industrialised countries have been able to tap the New York commercial paper market. Some developing countries – notably South Korea – have progressed substantially and now rank as exceptionally credit-worthy.

A hard currency circuit has developed with countries and companies in the harder currency countries, such as Scandinavia, much of Continental Europe, the Middle East and Japan, and the major world-wide organisations being able and willing to borrow and lend in the hard currencies themselves. Many other borrowers have been less willing, and in some cases less able, to borrow these hard currencies because they had no corresponding mixture of assets and so have tended to stay with the 'soft currency' circuit, largely borrowing dollars. The detailed flows of lending and borrowing in these international markets have thus shown a substantial increase in scale, the arrival of new sources for borrowing and lending, significant diffusion of risk, the development of new markets and new sources and the availability of finance on more favourable terms to borrowers as they have obtained credibility in the markets.

A further development is the improvement in the financial expertise in many central banks, particularly in developing countries. The sophisti-cation of their asset and liability management has improved greatly. Given the ability of the market to provide facilities for minimising risks as far as possible, for example by supplying liquid reserves as a defence against short-term adverse changes, the maintenance of their credibility in the world financial markets has become a major economic objective for a large number of developing countries. Their development plans and their performance indicate that this is beneficial to their overall development progress.

MINOR CURRENCIES

A feature of international finance has been the continued use of minor currencies as units of account in international markets and their use in providing relatively small-scale capital exports from certain countries. At various times euro-sterling bonds, euro-French franc bonds, and foreign and euro-guilder bonds have been seen, and several other currencies such as the Canadian dollar and some of the Scandinavian currencies have been used as the unit of account in denominating international banking debt. These developments have not been crucial to the major functioning of the markets, in terms of the scale of funds which have at times flowed between countries and between creditors and debtors, but they have provided welcome flexibility and variety in this financing. Moreover, they have permitted at certain times countries and market participants who are less able to operate in some of the major currencies to play an active part in these markets. It seems difficult to argue that the use of these currencies is in any way harmful; as far as the countries and participants concerned wish to use these minor markets when they are particularly convenient that should be welcomed. The risks to the stability of the whole system are minuscule, and it is by such innovation and variety that further change takes place.

At the same time some new bank and bond market places have developed, such as those in Bahrain, Singapore, Hong Kong, and some Caribbean centres. In as much as they are purely 'booking' places where transactions are registered but managed elsewhere the supervision of these markets should rest with the central banks who control the parent banks of the market participants. Some small centres may be of lower standing than others, but providing supervision is adequate, the risk they pose to the system as a whole is again slight. In many cases such centres also provide other financial services in addition to their use as booking centres. Bahrain, Singapore and Hong Kong fulfil market making functions because of their geographical location in relation to sources of funds where management may meet and do regional business in areas where there are potential borrowers. Kuwait has become within its own scale of operation almost a reserve currency centre in its own right, although its refusal to allow foreign banks to be established limits its scale of operation.

The infrastructure of the markets has also improved. This is partly because of the great improvement in telecommunications, which allows head offices to supervise branches and subsidiaries more actively and more closely, and also because of the institutional developments such as the Euroclear and Cedel systems for holding and exchanging eurobonds which have broadened the structure of that market.

THE NEW MULTI-POLAR SYSTEM

The changes described above are by and large helpful in adapting the monetary system to a new structure following the breakdown of Bretton Woods. This new system has a number of currencies of more equal rank than in the past. Each of these currencies is operated on a two-tier system, with the first (domestic) tier under particularly tight monetary and legal control and the second tier under different legal restraints and supervision – but not necessarily wrong or lax for that reason. In some cases governments may refuse to allow a second tier operation to take place, in which case the currency is fundamentally a wholly domestic currency (for example the currencies of most developing countries).

In other cases governments differ about the relative freedom to be allowed in the second tier use of their own currency; some countries adopt different monetary policy targets from others. Within this framework market participants have the opportunity of choosing the currencies and the vehicles in which to transfer funds and to create monetary assets and liabilities between themselves. The stability of the overall system depends on the responsibility of the policies pursued by the main countries, the sophistication in their understanding of this system, that decisions taken in response to new developments tend to solve problems rather than make them worse, and that no major countries pursue policies destructive of this system as a whole. There is in reality no way whatever of reverting to a totally dollar-denominated Bretton Woods-type system; making the best of the system on the lines just mentioned seems to be the best that can be hoped for.

The changes which have taken place have been constructive in moving towards a workable successor to the Bretton Woods system. There have been mistakes, problems and false starts. Some countries have allowed their currencies to be used in certain euromarkets and then had to withdraw. It could well be argued that the massive creation of dollars in the euromarkets, which stemmed from the lax system of control over American monetary policy and over the American banks as a whole, might have been allowed to become too large for the good of the system. No doubt many countries have regrets over the course of their economic policy in the second half of the 1970s. But hindsight is always perfect. These disappointments represent frictions and failures in what has been on the whole a relatively constructive process, not decisive factors undermining the value of the developments that have taken place.

One of the main problems is to obtain acceptance of the view that we are in a multi-polar system and that movement of exchange rates among the main groups is inevitable at times. The underlying framework of thought in this new framework is different from that in Bretton Woods and one needs to abandon modes of thought that require fixity in areas where fixity is no longer possible. The areas of economic policy in which tolerance among countries is expected, and those on which co-operation is required, have changed. For countries to pursue economic policies that lead towards the maintenance of a relatively high level of world demand is desirable. But in many countries the handicaps to greater welfare and faster growth lie at least as much in adverse social and political domestic developments as in constraints imposed by the external environment. It would be undesirable if, with the aim of improving their financial position, countries deflated their own domestic demand, or imposed unemployment on other countries to an extent which could either damage other countries' specific interests or reduce the potential output of the system as a whole.

The new system will face major difficulties if any of the most important market participants get into difficulties which could threaten other elements in the system. This raises a particular question over some of the most important national borrowers, including major developing countries. Moreover, the need for effective co-ordination and super-vision over the foreign exchange markets as a whole and over the supply and demand for funds in the bank lending markets remains as important as ever. But by and large the importance of these problems is well understood by the world's major economic organisations and by those in the public and private sectors of the international banking markets. Fears for the stability of the banking system as a whole have receded following earlier scares, but the banking system is not able to deal with the problems it will face without an appropriate degree of co-ordination and co-operation in national policy-making and in the overall super-vision of the new system.

Postscript

The theme of this book is an examination of the way in which countries have responded to changing economic circumstances by changing their own international financial policies, and how such developments have affected the structure of the international markets. Such decisions reflect the countries' own situations, their international obligations, and the way in which they have been affected by changing economic conditions.

Changes in governments' international financial policies have in turn influenced the structure of the international financial markets, and there have been cumulative effects on financial flows, economic conditions and governments' decisions.

The differences between national situations, countries' perceptions of their interests, and the impact of economic forces have been so great, that countries have been bound to show substantial diversity in their approach to international financial matters. It is not feasible to force any single global policy onto this system; even if countries were able to agree such policies, which is unlikely, the diversity of interests, perceptions and economic conditions would generate such tensions that any consensus would almost certainly break down in a relatively short period. That the gold price and gold market have largely broken loose from central bank control has made the world financial system more pluralistic and more fragmented, encouraging countries to act on a more individualistic basis.

We are, thus, moving ever more into a situation where international financial events take place on the basis of 'sub-optimising', which means that the total effect is the combined result of a series of decisions taken by many independent or relatively independent economic agents acting as they think best for their own interests. These economic agents, countries, national institutions or companies, have on the whole behaved extremely responsibly. This process has led to very substantial creativity in the development of new market structures and financial flows. It has also accomodated the adaptation, development and growth of many market participants. Many economic agents have created new markets or obtained access to new or different markets. The system has shown considerable flexibility and adaptability in some of the most volatile economic conditions of recent decades.

Many positive specific benefits have resulted from this process. It has led to a reasonably stable relationship between governments and the international markets, sustaining the international financial system. The viability of the system is based, among other factors, on a massive diffusion of risk around the world, the perceived benefits to participants from staying in the system and therefore from behaving responsibly in financial matters, and the consequent willingness to take action to maintain credit-worthiness and freedom of action. It would be illuminating to challenge critics of this system to specify particular instances of ways in which this 'sub-optimising' process has created problems, or indeed has fallen significantly short of the best that could be expected from the world economy in recent years. Individual actions of governments are conditioned by their perceived desire to retain an orderly world economic framework. In the monetary field, governments are constrained by the formal conventions and informal contacts in negotiations such as through the IMF and OECD. As regards trade, despite strong protectionist pressures, countries do not wish to live without the formal framework of the GATT. The main danger, as seen by critics of this 'sub-optimising' process, is that countries might cumulatively create a much greater recession than any of them wish. After the first OPEC oil price rises action was taken to protect and co-ordinate the growth of worldwide effective demand (such as through the 'convoy' and 'locomotive' theories), but governments are now unwilling to make any such joint commitments, and regard the fight against inflation as being their most important objective. In any case, there is a significant counter-weight to this particular risk of lack of demand, namely the strong electoral pressure in the industrial countries, which in turn create world economic conditions, that employment and prosperity be maintained for the domestic population. This internal political pressure towards the maintenance of reasonable effective demand is a strong guarantee that the process of 'sub-optimising' will not lead to excessively sharp downward cumulative economic activity in the world at large.

Given the pressures on and changes in the world economy in the middle and late 1970s, the financial markets have played a necessary role of taking some of the tension and stress out of the situation. There may be disappointment about certain aspects of an individual country's economic performance over that period, or the condition of the world economy as a whole, but it is inconceivable that anything like as satisfactory an outcome could have been achieved had the international financial situation depended solely on specific treaty agreements between countries.

The previous chapters of this book have covered the situation as at August 1979. What changes have been seen between then and July 1980, and how do they fit in with the theme of this book? At the general level, this period has coincided with even sharper changes in the world economic scene, putting further stress upon the adaptability of countries, other economic agents, and the system as a whole. The last year has seen the second major oil price rise which changed substantially the economic growth, inflation and balance of payments prospects of most countries. The sharp increase in the price of gold had a similar dramatic effect on the value of many countries' reserves. Many countries changed their international financial policies in reaction to this situation and the new direction of capital flows played a major part in the adaptive process. The effect of these changes has been to broaden and diversify the international capital and banking markets by bringing in new economic agents as borrowers or lenders, increasing the total number of participants in certain markets, and diffusing the credit risk among more markets.

The assets available to investors have also become more diversified. The general process of governments acting to change their financial policies and encourage different capital flows has had a kind of ratchet effect of increasing the scale, depth and availability of world financial markets. This works through the process that each time governments change their financial policy, the existing operations in the markets remain in being, but new markets, market participants or flows are generated, thus adding to the organic structure of the pre-existing system. As governments have become even more closely involved in a wide variety of international financial markets through this evolutionary process, they cannot ignore international financial considerations in determining their future policy. The financial integration of the world economy is thus furthered. This has the effect of forcing governments increasingly to consider common interests in formulating their policy, and diffuses risks and responsibilities through the system.

The required recycling from the world financial markets has increased sharply towards the end of 1979 and in 1980, given the increase in the OPEC surplus from some $ billion in 1978 to about $65 billion in 1979, and an expected $115 billion in 1980. No doubt, in due course, the OPEC surplus will be invested in a wide range of markets, but for the time being it has increased the available liquidity. The corresponding balance of payments deficits, spread widely throughout the industrialised world, have increased the corresponding need for borrowing. The international bond markets have experienced volatile conditions, associated with American interest rate movements, and the greater part of this flow is likely to take place through the banking system. A wider range of borrowing agents, including countries, have come into the markets on an increasing scale. These include OECD countries, of which Spain is a conspicuous example, and also some developing countries, notably South Korea.

The aim of this postscript is to mention a few of the main developments in the period since August 1979, and to assess briefly how the main theme of the book stands up to this later experience. The postscript is not intended either to update all the information contained in the earlier chapters or to provide a comprehensive statistical and historical record of the past year. This latter would be impracticable for a variety of reasons, and could not be achieved within a reasonable printing and publishing schedule. Within this framework, it is relevant to note that there have been some major constructive developments in recent months.

The economic conditions of 1979 and 1980 have pushed many OECD countries into balance of payments deficit, including, notably, Germany and Japan. Switzerland is likely still to be in current account surplus, but this surplus is diminishing rapidly and a deficit might yet be recorded in that country. In the light of these changed economic circumstances, these three countries have each taken the necessary policy decisions towards liberalising capital imports into their country and towards accepting, if perhaps not encouraging, the greater use of their currencies as international reserve assets. These are major developments and enhance the role of the deutschemark, yen and Swiss franc correspondingly.

The role of sterling in the world financial markets has also been enhanced. Given the relative confidence concerning Britain's balance of payments in the light of the North Sea oil output and following the advent of a Conservative government committed to an orthodox monetary policy and liberal economic principles, a significant capital inflow into the British bond markets has been seen. Moreover, by abolishing exchange control on 23 October 1979, the government paved the way for the resumption of long-term capital exports from the UK. Even if Britain does not develop into a major net capital exporter, if sterling comes to be seen as a relatively stable currency with prospective low inflation, non-residents may be willing to use it as a unit of account, with non-resident money flowing into the UK to be invested through the capital markets to provide funds for foreign borrowers, rather in the way in which the deutschemark and Swiss franc are used.

A further enhancement of the role of the markets, if in a somewhat negative sense, has stemmed from the failure to date of the initiative that the IMF should create a substitution account which would provide countries with the opportunity to convert other currencies into deposits at the IMF denominated in SDRs. This proposal raises extremely complicated issues, and there are a wide range of potential benefits and obstacles associated with it. But it is noteworthy that some of the developing countries which have been the most active users of the international financial markets, notably Brazil and Mexico, are strongly opposed to the creation of such an account. Their argument is that if the international financial community makes it easier for countries to deposit funds with the IMF, there will correspondingly be a lower supply in the markets themselves. Moreover, such funds as become available through the IMF are likely to be lent also with international economic surveillance, i.e. with strings. The main borrowing countries are extremely concerned both to have a substantial supply of funds in the international financial markets and that they should be able to obtain finance without surveillance. Thus the international financial markets are regarded by the most prominent developing countries as playing a crucial role in their development process, and these countries are prepared to take effective action in international negotiations to preserve the flow of funds to the markets and the freedom of their operation.

There have, however, also been significant capital flows directly between governments. Thus, partly in the interests of currency stabilisation, the Americans have borrowed substantial sums, by Carter bonds, from Germany and Switzerland, and there have also been direct loans from Saudi Arabia to Germany. We may in the future see more credits direct from government to government, especially if industrialised countries, the OPEC countries and the developing countries manage to form a consensus as regards the way in which the current tensions in the world economy should be resolved through a common programme of burden sharing and apportionment of finance. We do not regard these government loans as in any way in competition with the market system, and indeed the sums flowing in such channels are significantly less than the flows through the financial markets. The governments themselves do not regard these direct loans as in conflict with market operations. Indeed, one of the purposes of this government to government finance has been in many cases to help to create conditions in which the markets may operate more effectively, by removing the causes of unstable financial flows.

A major potential disturbance to the functioning of the markets, in particular the banking markets, has been the confrontation between the United States and Iran, in the form of action to frustrate international financial contracts, following the invasion of the American embassy in Teheran. We do not wish to make any comment on the underlying factors in this issue, but in this context simply to note that one of the essential functions of the international financial markets has been to provide a mutual and non-political interface through which governments, companies and other economic agents may deal with each other in a practical manner as regards economics and finance. If political action and the frustration of contracts were to become prevalent, then the confidence which is the underpinning of the market structures would cease to exist. The markets have continued functioning effectively in most areas, even after this confrontation, yet bankers and financiers are naturally more concerned at the political risk in international business. There is no harm in that, and it is noteworthy that international credits have been less in 1980 to countries in areas of significant political tension.

The world central banking community has been active in attempting to lay the groundwork for more effective prudential supervision of the international markets. The principle has been accepted by central banks working through the Bank for International Settlements that the central bank of the country in which a banking group is domiciled should be responsible for supervising that bank's worldwide operations. Information is being gathered by central banks in particular as regards maturity transformation and country exposure. Some consolidation of balance sheets is to be achieved, and banks will be tested by their parent central banks more severely than in the past as regards capital adequacy. The Bank of England is likely to tighten its prudential supervision over the liquidity, capital and foreign currency exposure of international banks in London and British banks worldwide. The monetary measures introduced in the United States on 6 October 1979 and 14 March 1980 have influenced the flows of dollar funds through the American banks and between the US itself and the euromarkets. Central banks have, in effect, decided collectively that it is not practicable to impose monetary control measures on the euromarkets, such as the reserve requirements used frequently in domestic economies, but that prudential supervision is desirable and should be increased. Banks as a whole have no objection to this concept in principle, and indeed are generally in favour of the objectives of the central banks. The only doubts in bankers' minds would be whether the prudential requirements were unnecessarily tight to achieve the stated objectives, and whether in being too tight they might reduce the market's flexibility and thwart its ability to supply the financial services which the world economy needs.

In conclusion, over the past year many countries have significantly changed their international financial policies. These changes have in turn affected both the direction and scale of capital flows and the structures of the markets themselves. Credit and capital movements are being seen increasingly by countries as an integral part of their own adjustment process, and the ability of countries either to use their international assets or to borrow from the markets is regarded increasingly as an important component of a country's room for manoeuvre in formulating its domestic and international policies. The international financial markets now provide an enormously wide range of services to countries, companies, international organisations and other economic agents, and most of these agents take considerable pains to ensure that their creditworthiness and their access to these markets is maintained. Looking to the future, the international economic situation faces the challenge of the second major round of OPEC surpluses, and the outlook for growth, inflation and countries' balance of payments is in many cases most uncertain. The international financial markets are well placed to play a major part in helping deal with these issues and problems, and if recent experience is any guide they will increasingly be called upon to do so.

July 1980   D.F.L.
                                                                             P.T.G.G.

Index